The Myth
Modernism
Twentieth Ce
Literatur

By the same author

The Early H. G. Wells

Heroes' Twilight

The Situation of the Novel

Anthony Powell

T. S. Eliot

The Turn of a Century

Gerard Manley Hopkins

Reading the Thirties

*

Years: Sixteen Poems

*

The Roman Persuasion: A Novel

The Myth of Modernism and Twentieth Century Literature

Bernard Bergonzi

Professor of English,
University of Warwick

THE HARVESTER PRESS

First published in Great Britain in 1986 by
THE HARVESTER PRESS LIMITED
Publisher: John Spiers
16 Ship Street, Brighton, Sussex

British Library Cataloguing in Publication Data

Bergonzi, Bernard
The myth of modernism and twentieth century literature.
1. Modernism (Literature) 2. English literature — 20th century — History and criticism
I. Title
820.9'00912 PR478.M6

ISBN 0-7108-1002-4

Typeset in 11/12 point Garamond by
Ormskirk Typesetting Services, Ormskirk, Lancashire.

Printed and bound in Great Britain by
Anchor Brendon Ltd, Tiptree, Essex

THE HARVESTER PRESS PUBLISHING GROUP
The Harvester Press Publishing Group comprises Harvester Press Limited (chiefly publishing literature, fiction, philosophy, psychology, and science and trade books), Harvester Press Microform Publications Limited (publishing in microform unpublished archives, scarce printed sources, and indexes to these collections) and Wheatsheaf Books Limited (a wholly independent company chiefly publishing in economics, international politics, sociology and related social sciences), whose books are distributed by The Harvester Press Limited and its agencies throughout the world.

I.M: G. 1938-1984

Make It New
Ezra Pound

Aftermath: Second or later mowing; the crop of grass which springs up after the mowing in early summer.
Oxford English Dictionary

Contents

Introduction

Once certain words could be used interchangeably, such as 'modern', 'new', 'twentieth century' and 'contemporary'. Thus, in the 1930s there appeared *The Faber Book of Modern Verse* and the little magazines *New Verse, Twentieth Century Verse* and *Contemporary Poetry and Prose*, with overlapping contents. Since then the words have developed in different directions. 'Twentieth century' once indicated the new, the exciting, the unfamiliar, the promising and the slightly threatening: things still preserved in the anachronistically futuristic title display which opens Twentieth Century Fox films. The 'twentieth century' was first seen in this way at the end of the nineteenth century; by now it is nearly over and it denotes not a future but a past. Its rich associations, now more threatening than promising, are being transferred to the looming twenty-first century, or, more portentously, the 'third millennium'. Twentieth century now refers to no more than a period, which is how I use it in the title of the present book, indicating that its subjects extend from the Bloomsbury Group to the Marxist-structuralists. 'Modern' and 'contemporary' began to move apart in the early 1960s, with the publication of Stephen Spender's quietly seminal book, *The Struggle of the Modern*. Spender used 'modern' to refer to the great wave of innovation and transformation which affected all the arts in Europe and America in the years immediately before the First World War and which seemed at the time to embody the essence of twentieth century newness. Its representatives were Picasso and Stravinsky and Marinetti and Apollinaire as well as Eliot and Pound and Joyce and Wyndham Lewis. The modern was replete with paradox: it repudiated the present and the recent past in order to establish contact with a more authentic remote past; yet in its interweavings and superimpositions of past and present it seemed to make both terms problematical, as Eliot implied in 'Tradition and the Individual Talent' and *The Waste Land*. The modern artist was alienated from the everyday social world, and yet he had a vision of a new, unified and transformed order of things. Art assumed a new importance, as the aestheticism of the late nineteenth century was metamorphosed into the more radical and ambitious programme of the modernists. So, too, did subjectivity, with parallels to the development of psycho-analysis. Outer objects became symbols and correlatives for inner states of feeling. At the same time, the transforming vision of the modern had its political implications: a revolutionary art might lead to a revolutionary culture and a new social order. But the political implications might be either right-wing or left-wing. Mayakovsky and Brecht brought modernism and Communism together. If the Russian Futurism of Mayakovsky took the Marxist path (and only for a time, until it was suppressed by Stalinist social realism), the Italian Futurism of Marinetti merged easily into Mussolini's Fascism. The 'fascist' proclivities and leanings of the major anglophone modernists have been extensively discussed with reference to Yeats, Eliot, Pound, Lawrence and Lewis. Frederic Jameson, though a Marxist, admiringly discusses Lewis in his book *Fables of Aggression* as 'the modernist as fascist', a left-wing revolutionary *manqué*, who saw through the shams of modern society though he adopted the wrong prescription for dealing with them. I am personally sceptical about assuming any necessary connection between modernist literary art and right-wing sentiments; if the writers named above showed them, others did not, such as Joyce, Virginia Woolf, Ford and Beckett. Attitudes to the Spanish Civil War were something of a touchstone.

Against the 'modern' Spender set the 'contemporary', exemplified by Wells, Shaw and Bennett. The 'contemporary' writer was not alienated from the society he lived in; he might well be a reformer and zealous to improve it, but he began with an act of acceptance of the here-and-now, in contrast to the rejections of the modernists. He upheld the traditional qualities of rationality and will, as opposed to the open responsiveness to the flux of experience which was one aspect of the modernist aesthetic; and he had no doubts about what Lawrence called 'the old stable ego', whereas the modernists saw the self as fragmented and potentially in dissolution. And if the contemporaries had a workmanlike respect for the craft of writing they did not regard art with the transcendental seriousness of the moderns. Spender was writing at a time when the high artistic aims of modernism had been superseded in England by the formal conservatism and unambitious common-sense realism of the young poets and novelists of the Movement, who were very much 'contemporaries' in his sense. Since Spender wrote, the empirical distinction between the modern and the contemporary has become blurred, largely because of the diffusion of modernism not as vision but as technique. Young writers are now clever enough to deploy a whole range of modernist devices, just as the once puzzling or disturbing distortions and juxtapositions of cubism and surrealism have become part of the basic idioms of commercial design. The differences in style and structure between the novels of the Amises, *père et fils*, illustrate this point. Furthermore, English writing has come a long way from the insularity of Movement days and is subject as a matter of course to a variety of influences which if not precisely 'modern' are certainly not 'contemporary' either, such as the 'magic realism' of Borges, Garcia Marquez and Calvino.

'Modern' is now established as a historical category, with paradoxical results. In ordinary parlance the word still means new or recent or up-to-date, whereas for critics a 'modern' text might be seventy years old, and the 'modern' is inevitably followed by the 'post-modern'. A further paradox is suggested by the title of the large compilation of literary and philosophical documents going back to the eighteenth century, edited by Ellmann and Fiedelson, called *The Modern Tradition*. This book was published in 1965 and was certainly planned and in preparation when Spender's came out in 1963. It would be a mistake to regard him as the only instigator of what was a broad trend, but *The Struggle of the Modern* gave it a clear and accessible formulation. The collective phenomena which Spender described as modern were for a time known as 'the modern movement', which was the title of a book by Cyril Connolly, but that phrase seemed lame and long-winded, and before long was replaced by 'modernism', which is now in common usage. There was already a well-established sense of 'modernism', referring to the reforming movement in Catholic theology which was condemned by the Pope before the First World War but which has since largely triumphed in the wake of the Second Vatican Council. Confusion between the theological and literary senses need not often arise, and the latter is altogether too convenient not to use. Nevertheless, it has its dangers. The emergence of modernism as a literary category coincided with the explosion in the academic study of modern literature and the erection of the major modernists into canonical figures. 'Yeats scholarship' has been followed by Eliot scholarship, Lawrence scholarship, Beckett scholarship. . . . The rage or outrage which their works once provoked are either forgotten or relegated to interesting footnotes to literary history. Twenty years ago, in *Beyond Culture,* Lionel Trilling wrote with puzzled concern about the bland way in which the great challenging modern texts of extreme experience were effortlessly assimilated by the academy. The process has gone a lot further since then. In 1918 Eliot wrote of *Ulysses* and *Tarr:* 'Both are terrifying. That is the test of a work of art. When a work of art no longer terrifies us we may know that we were mistaken, or that our senses are dulled: we ought still to find *Othello* and *Lear* frightful.' Most Shakespeare scholars, and their students, it seems reasonable to assume, do no such thing. Eliot himself, some of whose greatest poetry springs from fear and terror, is no longer allowed to be very disturbing, having been safely enclosed with commentaries, readers' guides and casebooks (one of which I must plead guilty to having edited myself). It was this situation which Fredric Jameson addressed himself to in *Fables of Aggression,* where he sees Wyndham Lewis as less tamed and ordered by academic exegesis than the other modernists; reading him, he says, we 'sense that freshness and virulence of modernizing stylization less and less accessible in the faded texts of his contemporaries.' And yet what is Jameson's own book, so original and challenging in itself, but one more attempt at academic placing of a major modernist author, written by an eminent and influential critic of a remarkably subtle and scholastic cast of mind? F. R. Leavis's relation to Lawrence, a generation earlier, was broadly similar.

The dominance of a limited canon of unquestionably great authors is to be resisted, since it implies that non-canonical authors are not worth spending time on. It is best resisted, though, not by arguing against the idea of a canon, or even against the idea of literature itself, as in some recent Marxist discourses, but by discovering, reading, discussing and making available other texts which may be excellent and interesting without necessarily bearing the numbing accolade of 'great'. In this context feminist criticism, despite its sometimes jejune theoretical foundations, has been unexpectedly positive and stimulating, by drawing attention to a lot of intestesting but neglected or forgotten books which happen to be by women. See, for instance, the extensive programme of paperback reprints embarked on by the Virago publishing house.

Of the words I set down in the opening sentence of this introduction, 'new' has endured best, perhaps because it is least specific. To call a book 'new' is to say something important about it, without saying whether its spirit is modern or post-modern, contemporary or plain old-fashioned. Works of literature which remain worth reading are always somehow new, or have something new to say, which does not mean that they are 'timeless' in some simplistic sense. Their historicity has to be understood and respected, but their literary importance is more than historical and has to address a reader living *now*, not *then*, Gadamer's formulation of the need for a fusion of the 'horizons' of the text and of the reader is helpful. When Ezra Pound called a volume of his essays *Make It New* he was alluding to this point, I believe, though 'new' itself has not entirely escaped historicizing, as when we have to refer to the old New Criticism (and perhaps the old *nouveau roman)*. Modernism is inevitably becoming historical, even though its greatest texts still seem 'modern' in the everyday rather than the critical sense: *Women in Love* or *The Waste Land* for instance. Nevertheless, we cannot forget that we are late twentieth-century readers of early twentieth-century literature, and the distance is bound to grow greater as we move into a new century.

In fact, the modernist achievements and innovations are currently under attack or revision. *The Waste Land* is a special and remarkable case. When it was first published it was widely regarded as a hoax, and it has never been totally accepted or decisively rejected, so that every few years there are fresh challenges and fresh defences; it seems that for the foreseeable future this poem will provide an arena for critical argument, which may indicate its continuing but unstable vitality. Many of the assumptions of modernist criticism are now in question, such as the notion of the literary text as a separate monad or icon, possessing its own peculiar unity and harmony: by deconstructionists who believe that texts ultimately embody *aporia* and contradiction rather than unity and harmony, and by Marxists who believe that unity and harmony are ideologically objectionable, since to pursue them in literature might encourage one to pursue them in life, with a resultant slackening of the class struggle; and by Harold Bloom and his followers, who reject the iconic text in favour of a Freudian restatement of the importance (or the anxiety) of influence. Bloom has also overturned the map of English poetry outlined by Pound and Eliot and systematized by Leavis; he has restored the Romantics, and Shelley in particular, to a prominence from which they once seemed to have been permanently dislodged.

If forced to take sides I would align myself with some revisionist version of the New Criticism rather than its opponents. It is in any case inevitable in pedagogic situations, having arisen in Cambridge in the 1920s from an extraordinary coming together of Eliot's creative and critical example and the demands of undergraduate teaching in the expanding English School. The present situation is undoubtedly far more complicated than it was in the heyday of modernism and its immediate critical consequences in the work of *Scrutiny* and the American New Critics. Modernism, or rather the ahistorical myth of modernism, was seen as a total revolution, a once-for-all transformation. Nobody would, or could, write novels like Arnold Bennett or poetry like Tennyson or plays like Shaw or criticism like Edmund Gosse, ever again. The myth is still very strong, as much among creative writers as in the academy, and more so in America than in Britain. Yet modernism, though demythologized, is not reduced in importance when it is seen as a historical phenomenon.

When the major phase of modernism ended is a matter for speculation. By 1930, when Lawrence died, the seminal texts had been written, though major canonical works continued to appear in the 1930s and 40s: *Finnegans Wake, Four Quartets,* the *Pisan Cantos.* What happened afterwards, with reference to English writing, is what is implied by 'aftermath' in the epigraph, a word with pleasant associations of new and later growth in its original agricultural sense, though it has acquired subsequent implications of loss and destruction; both seem appropriate in placing later developments. Modernism has never completely triumphed in English literary culture; such major writers as

Hardy and Kipling were unaffected by it, and in the 1920s, despite Eliot's rapid rise to fame and influence, he was much less widely read than the Georgian poets. The later writing looked at in this book shows conflicting attitudes to modernism: a desire to continue or at least use it versus a desire to evade or ignore it. In the early 1960s, about the time Spender published *The Struggle of the Modern,* there was an interesting attempt by conservative critics to discover, or construct, a truly native, non-modernist line of development in English poetry, which by-passed Pound and Eliot, and ran through Hardy, Housman, Edward Thomas, Robert Graves, to John Betjeman and Philip Larkin. Donald Davie rejected this approach, but he took it seriously in *Thomas Hardy and British Poetry*. The later responses to modernism in England are neatly emblematized by Davie and Larkin, and discussed in one of these essays. Both were originally Movement poets, exact contemporaries, of similar background and education. Larkin became rightly regarded as the leading poet of his generation; his public pronouncements have been consistently anti-modernist, and he is capable of a provocative philistine insularity. Yet a moderately attentive reading of Larkin's poetry shows that he has not been unaffected by the modernist innovations in poetic language; his tone is not that of a Georgian or a naive *pasticheur* of Hardy. Davies has always been a standard-bearer for modernism, a life-long admirer of Pound, yet still feeling an undertow towards the qualities exemplified by Hardy.

The assumption that nothing worthwhile followed modernism in England is made from time to time by academic critics of sufficiently aloof and austere temperament, like Leavis or George Steiner. It is not, of course, one that I share, believing that supposedly minor works may give pleasure and instruction and that the good need not be the enemy of the best. The problem of coping with the modernist example and legacy, whether by emulating it or ignoring it or reinterpreting it, continues in late twentieth-century literature and criticism. I believe it forms a recurring theme in these essays.

These essays have been lightly revised in places, but I have not attempted any substantial rewriting or updating; their dates of publication (which in one or two cases are appreciably later than the date of composition) remain part of their meaning. They first

appeared in the following publications, to whom my thanks and acknowledgements are due:
Contemporary Literature, 'Davie, Larkin and the state of England'; *Critical Quarterly,* part of 'Poets of the 1940s' and 'Leavis and Eliot'; *Encounter,* 'Eliot's ghostly voices' and 'The decline and fall of the Catholic novel'; *Enemy News,* 'Wyndham Lewis: II'; *Form* (Bangladesh), 'A note on *Sons and Lovers'; New Review,* 'The Bloomsbury pastoral' and 'Mr Bennett and Ms Drabble'; *PN Review,* part of 'Poets of the 1940s' and 'The Terry Eagleton story; *The Tablet,* 'Wyndham Lewis: III'; *Times Higher Educational Supplement*, 'The 1930s'; *Times Literary Supplement*, 'Wyndham Lewis: I', 'Ezra Pound' and 'George Steiner: on culture and on Hitler'; *Donald Davie and the Responsibilities of Literature,* ed, George Dekker (New Carcanet Press), 'Pound and Donald Davie'.

1

The Bloomsbury pastoral

A minor character in Virginia Woolf's first novel, *The Voyage Out*, published in 1915, reflects, 'of course they would want a room, a nice room, in Bloomsbury preferably, where they could meet once a week. . . . ' The sentiment was picked up more recently by a popular song about the joy of a 'Room in Bloomsbury'. The idea of Bloomsbury, however tenuous and indefinable, has been alive for seventy years now. When Sir Leslie Stephen died in 1904, his sons and daughters, Thoby, Adrian, Vanessa and Virginia, abandoned the gloomy and oppressive family home in Hyde Park Gate and set up in Gordon Square, at that time an unfashionable and inexpensive locality. There the young Stephens were joined by Thoby's Cambridge friends and an idea, a legend, a way of life, was born. Later, other parts of Bloomsbury were colonized so that from an obscure postal district it became a magical region where, as the phrase had it, 'all the couples are triangles and everyone lives in squares.' In time the idea of Bloomsbury seemed to lose its potency, denoting a rather faded kind of intellectual superiority, a self-consciously emancipated attitude to personal relations, and a dated experimentalism in the arts. But the myth persisted. Twenty years ago J. K. Johnstone's *The Bloomsbury Group* made a strong case for the coherence and seriousness of Bloomsbury ideas and attitudes. Since then we have had a long row of books on the subject, mostly memoirs, letters or biographies; including Leonard Woolf's autobiography in several volumes, which was solidly informative if rambling and ill-written; Michael Holroyd's 1,100 pages on Lytton Strachey, a form of scholarly overkill that contrasted curiously with Strachey's own severely selective essays in biography; and, above all, Quentin Bell's admirably succinct and evocative life of his aunt, Virginia Woolf. And much, much more, by or about central or peripheral figures:

Clive Bell, Roger Fry, Rupert Brooke, Dora Carrington, Mark Gertler, Lady Ottoline Morrell, right down to a Boy at the Hogarth Press.

On the face of it there is still more to come and the market seems to be holding up well. After a wait of eleven years the second volume of Ottoline Morrell's memoirs has now appeared (*Ottoline at Garsington: Memoirs of Lady Ottoline Morrell 1915-1918,* edited by Robert Gathorne-Hardy). The long delay was necessary, it seems, because too many people referred to adversely in the book were still alive and it took time for mortality to do its work. With ironic appropriateness the editor himself died once he had seen the book through the press. In his introduction Robert Gathorne-Hardy vehemently defends Ottoline Morrell's memory against Michael Holroyd's belittling account of her in his life of Lytton Strachey. Meantime Holroyd himself, whilst retaining a controlling interest in Strachey Enterprises, has turned to another dominant figure of the period, Augustus John. Too vigorous and colourful to be a Bloomsbury person, his presence was certainly felt in that quarter. To quote from *The Voyage Out* again: ' "There's a clever man in London called John who paints ever so much better than the old masters," Mrs Flushing continued. "His pictures excite me—nothin' that's old excites me." ' Augustus John's portrait of Ottoline Morrell is the frontispiece to this volume of her memoirs; it is forceful and striking rather than particularly flattering, but Ottoline insisted on hanging it in her drawing-room at Garsington. 'Whatever she may have lacked', John remarked after her death, 'it wasn't courage.' In 1908 when John was doing a succession of watercolours and drawings of Ottoline, she fell for him heavily and flung at him not only her baroquely conspicuous person but a succession of expensive presents. John coped manfully but he was relieved when the affair dwindled into friendship. All of which is described in the first volume of Holroyd's new biography of John (*Augustus John: Volume I: The Years of Innocence*). This book shows the same relentless accumulation of detail as the life of Strachey but Holroyd's ventures into art criticism are both briefer and more convincing than the long and usually turgid essays in literary criticism in the Strachey book. Holroyd has also collaborated in bringing out a nice book of John's pictures (*The Art of Augustus John* by Malcolm Easton and Michael Holroyd) which usefully complements the biography.

Returning to the squares and magic circles of Bloomsbury, I am dismayed but hardly surprised to observe that the proliferation of memories is now beginning to generate a secondary growth. Like, for instance, *The Loving Friends: A Portrait of Bloomsbury* by David Gadd, a book apparently written as a guide to the Bloomsbury myth for busy readers. It is a work without originality or insight; a properly programmed computer, if fed with all the recent books about Bloomsbury and told to produce a readable, undemanding summary in 200 pages, might have done equally well; might even, indeed, have achieved a marginally less flat and platitudinous prose style than Mr Gadd's. He is a sentimentalist, who is over-ready to take the personnel of Bloomsbury at their own valuation, and finds them entirely fascinating as people, regardless of their work or achievement: 'Human beings are less available than their works and always more complex and exciting. There is infinitely more in Lytton Strachey than in *Eminent Victorians,* and Roger Fry's aesthetics are dull compared with Roger Fry.' As an introduction to Bloomsbury, Mr Gadd's book is far less useful than Quentin Bell's short study, *Bloomsbury*, which came out in 1968 and is a genuine essay in the history of ideas, which tries to understand the Bloomsbury group in terms of their beliefs and works.

Another and more curious piece of cultishness is Peter Luke's play, *Bloomsbury*, which briefly held the stage of a West End theatre. My guess is that it is now destined for oblivion and I wouldn't wish to call it back, except to remark that it has a certain symptomatic interest and is pervaded by a comparable, if quite opposite, quality to Mr Gadd's sentimentalism. Mr Luke manifests a vigorous iconoclasm, projecting the Bloomsburyites as figures of fun and no more. His play has some lively dialogue and extracts laughs from predictable situations, like Lytton Strachey pleading for exemption from military service during the First World War. Despite the title, none of the action takes place in Bloomsbury, and although Mr Luke has used the same sources as Mr Gadd he has rearranged them to suit his theatrical purposes. Thus, an episode at Garsington coincides with the outbreak of war in August 1914, even though Ottoline Morrell didn't move there until 1915. History is swallowed up by comic myth-making and the effect is trivially vulgar. Yet there is a certain cruel justice about it, for Mr Luke's iconoclasm is a crude version of the spirit that seemed so marvellously liberating in a book like *Eminent Victorians*. It is easy enough now to see the Bloomsburyites as self-evidently absurd, much as they once saw the Victorians. Yet for a group which included Maynard Keynes and Virginia Woolf, leaving aside the lesser talents, this is clearly an inadequate response, no less so than sentimentality and the retailing of gossip.

However one looks at it, there is plenty of mystification about Bloomsbury: who was in the group, and when it started, are questions that have caused fine-drawn scholastic discussions. If 1904, when the Stephens set up in Gordon Square, looks an obvious starting date, others have suggested 1910, when Desmond MacCarthy's wife first referred to the 'Bloomsberries', or 1912, when Leonard Woolf returned from Ceylon and married Virginia Stephen. Quentin Bell turns firmly back to Cambridge at the turn of the century, claiming that Bloomsbury was begotten at Trinity College in the autumn term of 1899, when Leonard Woolf, Lytton Strachey, Saxon Sydney-Turner, Thoby Stephen and Clive Bell all met as undergraduates, with Desmond MacCarthy, Maynard Keynes and Roger Fry as subsequent additions to the group. Clive Bell has even doubted if Bloomsbury ever existed in any coherent way. This is a game that any number can play without hoping for a conclusion. The point is that this smallish group of ex-Cambridge intellectuals and their wives attracted a mythical aura from the very beginning, even before 1914. By 1917, wrote Quentin Bell in his *Virginia Woolf*, 'the old pre-war Bloomsbury was already beginning to acquire a sort of mythical existence'; at that date the Oxfordshire extension of Bloomsbury was going strong under Ottoline Morrell's bizarre tutelage at Garsington. She was never really part of Bloomsbury, though she lived there before the war in Bedford Square. The Bloomsburyites used to visit Garsington regularly, above all Lytton Strachey, who spent much of the war living there, but they preserved their independence by mocking and abusing her in correspondence. D. H. Lawrence was an occasional visitor, and Aldous Huxley a regular one, and both described Ottoline and Garsington in fictional portraits which caused her bitter resentment and severed, at least for a time, her friendship with their authors. She appears as Hermione Roddice in *Women in Love* and Priscilla Wimbush in *Crome Yellow.* (Robert Gathorne-Hardy, whilst admitting that much of *Crome Yellow* reflects life at Garsington, denies that Priscilla is a portrait of Ottoline. But the ascription seems generally accepted.) Ottoline appears in her memoirs as an injured party, who bestowed plentiful hospitality and was neglected or abused for her pains. She was, as she put it, regarded as the 'kind manageress of a hotel'. But hers is a one-sided and self-justifying account. There was evidently an aggressive and emotionally predatory aspect to her which upset many of her acquaintances, though she could also inspire fierce loyalties and devotion, like Robert Gathorne-Hardy's; he was convinced that most people got her wrong. She was at best a sad, absurd, confused, generous woman, with extravagant ambitions, who never really understood many of the people she gathered round her. That she was no fool, even though under-educated, and was capable of critical insight is shown in her posthumous memoir of Lawrence included in this volume. A common ambivalence about Ottoline is reflected in Dora Carrington's letters. After visiting Clive and Vanessa Bell in 1915 she wrote: 'What traitors all these people are . . . I think it's beastly of them to enjoy Ottoline's kindnesses and then laugh at her.' It was indeed a characteristically Bloomsbury response. But the following year, Carrington wrote from Garsington, 'I lie exhausted after swimming in that cess-pool of slime.' She herself was unsympathetically portrayed as Mary Bracegirdle in *Crome Yellow*, which she called 'a book which makes one feel very, very ill.'

Bloomsbury's relations with Ottoline and Garsington were close but ambiguous, and its true rural extension was not in Oxfordshire but in East Sussex, where from the twenties Leonard and Virginia Woolf lived at Rodmell, with Clive and Vanessa Bell and Duncan Grant in a snug triangle not far away at Charleston, where Grant, now approaching 90, still lives. Lytton Strachey moved to Ham Spray in Berkshire, where he set up with Carrington in a strange but quite domestic menage. Carrington loved Strachey and devoted her life to looking after him, whilst conducting a succession of affairs with other men. After Strachey's death from undiagnosed cancer of the intestine in 1932 she committed suicide, in a tragic end to a slightly farcical career.

Carrington's story represents what one might call the humane end of the Bloomsbury spectrum, and not surprisingly it is prominent in David Gadd's book and Peter Luke's play. Yet there was far more to Bloomsbury than this kind of engaging human interest, despite Mr Gadd's conviction that people *per se* are always more interesting than ideas or works of art. The diametrically opposite approach is taken in J. K. Johnstone's *The Bloomsbury Group* which presents Virginia Woolf, Lytton Strachey and E. M. Forster as systematically expounding G. E. Moore's beliefs about the pursuit of beauty and the importance of personal relationships, and Roger Fry's ideas about the nature of art. Johnstone's book had a pioneering importance, but was mistaken in attributing to Bloomsbury a theoretical rigour that it never really possessed. It was misleading, too, in making Forster a central member of the group. According to the diagram on page 15 of Quentin Bell's *Bloomsbury* Forster was a distinctly peripheral figure, at least in 1913, the central people being the Woolfs, the Bells, Roger Fry, Duncan Grant, Keynes, Strachey, and the enigmatic Saxon Sydney-Turner, who burnt out early after a dazzling undergraduate career. His early promise was not fulfilled and he was notorious for his long, almost unbroken silences and his addiction to setting and solving puzzles, though he remains a weird recurring presence in the annals of Bloomsbury. The pull of gossip and biography remains strong, but one must somehow escape it if one is to try to understand the phenomenon or idea of Bloomsbury, and to speculate about its continuing appeal. If there was no central body of coherent doctrine, there was a way of living, and a set of recognizable attitudes and implied beliefs. They can be described in a way that makes them seem very positive. Bloomsbury believed in absolute honesty in thought and speech, in the supreme importance of personal relations, preferring not to distinguish between love and friendship. Life was to be taken seriously but not solemnly; reason was the most reliable guide to human conduct, and a high importance was attached to conversation. Victorian conventions were resolutely attacked, and a rather idealized version of eighteenth-century wit and sensibility was held up for admiration.

This was Bloomsbury's official version of its beliefs and life-style, or, as we say in our harsher fashion, its ideology. But despite these generally admirable convictions the realities of Bloomsbury life were often less attractive if more interesting. Despite a deep conviction of the theoretical importance of love, friendship and personal relations in general, the Bloomsburyites were not considerate in their dealings with each other. Though quick to close ranks against outsiders, they were bitchy and malicious in a way that makes David Gadd's assumption about a circle of 'loving friends' naive and untenable. The following passage from Quentin Bell's *Virginia Woolf* has a representative flavour: 'Clive always accused Virginia of being a mischief-maker and he believed, perhaps rightly, that the unkind remarks which he and Desmond MacCarthy had made about Katherine Mansfield at Hogarth House were repeated by his hostess. This of course led to some trouble; but there was worse to come.' They had difficulty in speaking well of each other and the passing on of malicious gossip was a commonplace occurrence. This is a familiar human failing, of course, but it does not fit well with the high-minded ethical idealism of G. E. Moore. And if they were like this in their dealings with each other they were still less loving in their attitude to humanity at large. The trick of shaking hands without smiling, the in-group jokes, Strachey's profound, intimidating silences, the precisely calculated rudeness, were ways of keeping the broader, coarser world in its place. Bloomsbury was hedged round with a formidable exclusiveness that had a complicated cultural lineage. On the Stephen side there was the tradition of the evangelical Clapham Sect, in which Leslie Stephen was nurtured. Indeed, Noel Annan has described Bloomsbury as a secularized version of Clapham Sect exclusiveness. This inheritance was reinforced by the Cambridge background of the Bloomsbury males, particularly those who had been elected to the Apostles, otherwise the Cambridge Conversazione Society, that intensely select and long-lived little body, of which Tennyson and Hallam had once been members, and which was still active 70 years later. As Roy Harrod wrote in his life of Keynes, 'there was certainly a feeling that Apostles were different from ordinary mortals', a sentiment that was readily assumed by Bloomsbury at large.

What, in the end, did they have to be so exclusive about? Some important work, certainly: Keynes on economics, Fry on art; Virginia Woolf's novels; Lytton Strachey's biographies; Duncan Grant's paintings. All the same, several members of Bloomsbury produced nothing, or nothing of any great value, however highly they were regarded in the circle; like the incurably indolent Desmond MacCarthy, who was always expected to write a great novel, which somehow never got written. Bloomsbury was not in fact a powerful creative source, whatever the talents of its individual members. If in the years between, say, 1908 and 1915 one had wanted to find the real centres of artistic innovation and energy in London, one would not have looked in Gordon Square or Fitzroy Square (where Virginia and Adrian Stephen moved after Vanessa's marriage) but several miles to the west, in Ford Madox Ford's house on Campden Hill or Ezra Pound's small flat off Kensington High Street. Between them these two men, one half-German, the other expatriate American, either discovered or actively encouraged most of the major modern writers: Lawrence, Yeats, Wyndham Lewis, Joyce, Eliot, none of whom had come from a distinguished English family like the Stephens or the Stracheys, nor been an Apostle at Cambridge. Bloomsbury's contacts with the essentially cosmopolitan or *déclassé* modern movement were limited and uneasy, though some of their entrepreneurial activities were valuable, like Roger Fry's sponsoring of the first Post-Impressionist exhibition in 1910, and the work of the Woolfs as publishers, with the Hogarth Press. Virginia Woolf is the one Bloomsbury figure who now looks like a major modern writer, and it is interesting to see how her reputation has grown in recent years. Twenty years ago she was readily dismissed as one more unreadable relic of the daft experimentalism of the twenties, soon to be forgotten. Now, however, she seems a real, even pervasive, presence, and the focus of two separate kinds of contemporary interest: in feminism and the dilemmas and opportunities of the woman writer; and the theory and practice of the *nouveau roman*, of which Virginia Woolf can be seen as some kind of forerunner. But her attitude to modernism was reserved and cautious, despite the Woolfs' friendship with Eliot, and her feelings about Joyce, far from being a generous recognition of *il miglior fabbro*, were a complicated mixture of jealousy, admiration and snobbish distaste.

Other Bloomsbury figures now look less substantial. If Lytton Strachey still seems interesting it is because of the oddities of his life and personal style as described in such detail by Michael Holroyd and other recent annalists of Bloomsbury, rather than because his work as critic and biographer has really endured. The iconoclast is often bound by obsure but profound ties to the object of his derision, and Strachey, who made his name with the delicious ironies of *Eminent Victorians*, now looks like a recognizable kind of Victorian eccentric, of whom the Strachey family had already produced some choice specimens. Lytton gave, as it were, a special twist to the role by adopting the manners and proclivities of a *fin de siècle* sodomite. Our own view of the Victorians is inevitably different from that of *Eminent Victorians,* and I doubt if the book is well written enough to endure purely as literature. In some ways the productions of Bloomsbury are more remote than those of the Victorians they so despised. Clive Bell's *Civilization*, for instance, which was supposed to crystallize Bloomsbury ideals, the pursuit of fine states of mind and true values, now seems an extraordinarily superficial and intellectually shoddy performance. As Virginia Woolf put it, in her waspish fashion, 'in the end it turns out civilisation is a lunch party at No. 50 Gordon Square'. It was a complacent world, secure in a sense of its own rightness and superiority. Large and uncomfortable questions were ignored: religion was self-evidently absurd, and politics, except for those members who had a commitment to public affairs, like Keynes and Leonard Woolf, a manifest bore. Only the Woolfs seemed touched by tragedy and heroism, in Virginia Woolf's intermittent madness and Leonard's marvellously selfless and devoted efforts to help and protect her. The symbolic end of Bloomsbury's individualism and self-sufficiency perhaps occurred when Julian Bell, the son of Clive and Vanessa, was killed in the Spanish Civil War.

If one makes the effort to stand back from the fascinating accumulation of gossip and empirical detail about life at Gordon Square or Garsington or Charleston, and tries to get a total view of Bloomsbury, it looks very like the end of something. The point has already been made that the spirit of Bloomsbury represented a trivializing of the potent philosophical and ethical ideas that were in the air in Cambridge at the turn of the century. But in a longer perspective still, Bloomsbury represents the running-down of the immensely complicated Victorian family system described by Noel Annan in his *Leslie Stephen*. Interrelated families like the Stephens, the Stracheys, the Grants, the Thackerays, had been at the heart of the Victorian administrative and professional classes, but by the end of the nineteenth century they were beginning to lose their assured places in the scheme of things. It was threatened in one way by the extension of educational opportunities and the emergence of young men like Charles Tansley, who is such a jarring presence in *To the Lighthouse*. And in another way, in the very practice of literature, so long a reserved pursuit of the English middle-class, the new and revolutionary work was being done by unfamiliar kinds of people: James and Pound and Eliot, who were Americans; Lewis, who was half-American; Conrad, a Pole; Ford (or Hueffer), half-German; Yeats and Joyce, Irishmen and one of them a lower-class, Catholic Irishman at that; and Lawrence, who was very English, but a miner's son and no gentleman. When the young Stephens left Sir Leslie's house to set up in Bloomsbury, to lead their own lives to pursue total freedom of thought and speech—if in rather juvenile forms; 'the word bugger was never far from our lips', wrote Virginia Woolf—and, less confidently, of behaviour, it looked like a radical severance with the Victorian past. It was a displacement, certainly, and a change of ideas and styles of living. But it also represented a move to a new and defensible position, where, reinforced by memories of Clapham Sect and Apostolic exclusiveness, and hints of Cambridge philosophy, the latest generation of Stephens and Stracheys and their spouses and friends could continue to preserve what they regarded as valuable: love, friendship, talk, good states of mind. Their way of life depended on much that was familar and unquestioned, like assured private incomes, servants, and inexpensive housing. Ideas, too, could be familiarized and easily handled, however challenging and provocative they may at first have appeared; the deeper modes of subversiveness already germinated on the Continent by Marx and Kierkegaard and Nietzsche had not yet threatened the calm of Bloomsbury.

In essence, then Bloomsbury is remote both as a period and a set of ideas and attitudes. And yet, paradoxically, it is inescapably present, with so much being written about it, and such a seemingly eager public demand for the small change of its daily existence. It is partly, of course, that we are in love with the Edwardian years, in a spirit of desperate nostalgia which tries to recapture the glittering never-never land on the further side of the catastrophe of 1914. It is a spirit which looks for images and emblems and not for accurate interpretations of historical change. I feel it strongly myself: a photograph taken in 1910 of the hauntingly beautiful Vanessa Bell in a wide straw hat (it is reproduced in *Journey to the Frontier* by Peter Stansky and William Abrahams) has an absolute sense of the period that is beyond analysis and argument. But apart from the mute poignant fascination of such images I believe that much of the current cult of Bloomsbury stems from the covert appeal of opposites. Reliving in imagination the kind of life favoured by Bloomsbury offers a momentary escape from the pressures of social-democratic orthodoxy. We are egalitarian and cannot abide the thought of elites; they were exclusive and thought it a very natural thing to be. We believe, or are told to believe, that the family is absurd, if not harmful; they, for all the conscious individualism of their ideology, took family ties and traditions very seriously. They were dogmatic and superior; we are tentative and humble. They liked displaying their cleverness, but we are embarrassed by that kind of thing. They had leisure; we have no time to do anything properly. They had just discovered permissiveness, or acted as if they had; we have to live with its consequences. Bloomsbury, in short, offers all the attractions of a modern pastoral, however unhelpful, even damaging, such exercises in nostalgia are in our present difficulties. Remote, bright, stylish, it still invites a backward glance as we trudge on into the deepening gloom of our *fin de millénaire.*

1974

2

Mr Bennett and Ms Drabble

Margaret Drabble tells a good story in her life of Arnold Bennett. It is also an interesting modern instance of a kind of book perhaps more common in the last century than now, where a novelist of emerging reputation writes about an older, illustrious and usually dead master. If there is an element of discipleship in such books there is also an assertion of independence, in which the younger writer defines his or her attitude to the subject: James on Hawthorne, for instance, or Gissing on Dickens. Margaret Drabble establishes her admiration for Bennett in the introduction, a rather uneasy piece with too many personal pronouns in it, which analyses the quality of her admiration in excessive detail and suggests that the book may be less about Arnold Bennett than about the special relationship existing across fifty years between Arnold Bennett and Margaret Drabble. She is, she says, interested in his background, childhood and origins because they recall her own, and a few pages later suggests that she may even be distantly related to her subject: 'it is widely believed in the family that there is a close family connection with Arnold Bennett.' She confidently compares her own emotions on revisiting Sheffield to check on childhood memories whilst writing a novel with the sentiments expressed by Bennett when he similarly revisited Burslem. We observe her actually writing parts of the book in the North Stafford Hotel 'which Bennett knew well' and follow her in vividly described little expeditions in the back streets of the Potteries. All of which might be charitably—and fashionably—described as a phenomenological immersion in her material, but is a little too self-centred in the telling.

As the story develops such immodesty largely disappears and Bennett moves into the centre of the picture. He would probably have approved of Margaret Drabble's biography as a solid, workmanlike job, carefully researched and told with the narrative skills of an experienced novelist. If it isn't a 'big' definitive biography, festooned with scholarly apparatus, it will do until one comes along. She has a particularly useful opening chapter on the social economic background of the Potteries, describing the place of Methodism in the lives of the people and defining the difference between Primitive and Wesleyan Methodism, a nuance of some importance in Bennett's fiction about the Five Towns. Margaret Drabble makes full if unobtrusive acknowledgement of her sources, which include a very wide range of printed material, some of it fugitive and out-of-the-way, though it isn't clear if she has consulted the manuscript material in Keele University Library. But it is the story-teller who dominates, and the outline of the story is simple and appealing: Bennett as the naive provincial boy who made good. Though his childhood in Burslem—now a part of the city of Stoke-on-Trent—wasn't spectacularly poor, it was pinched and limited; Bennett's mother had a hard time bringing up a large family, while the ambitious father worked first as a potter and then as a draper and pawnbroker, before finally qualifying, in his thirties, as a solicitor. Enoch Bennett influenced Arnold in many ways, above all as a living embodiment of the Protestant ethic committed to hard work and self-discipline; negatively, his influence is probably apparent in Arnold Bennett's later taste for high living and conspicuous enjoyment, a predictable reaction against the family's Methodist rigour.

Bennett worked as a young clerk in a solicitor's office for several years after he came to London. He was skilled at shorthand and was clearly good at his job; but he had no particular vocation for the law, and found a helpful circle of literary and artistic friends who directed him to more congenial interests. Eventually he moved into the small-scale journalism that was both easily available and lucrative in the eighteen-nineties, and then on to the writing of fiction. Thereafter, from about 1900 onwards, his career developed in an almost unbroken curve of successful achievement. Though Edwardian writers were accustomed to much higher rates of productivity than most of our contemporaries would think desirable or even possible, Bennett was notorious for the volume of his output. All his life he was fascinated, even obsessed, by the number or words he wrote from one year to the next. There were, of course, his 'serious' novels, written in a full sense of literary commitment, like *The Old Wives' Tale, Clayhanger* and *Riceyman Steps*. But there were also the dazzling comic novels like *The Card* and the potboilers deliberately written for commercial success, of which *The Grand Babylon Hotel* was the first and most celebrated. There were many other novels of mediocre quality, now mostly forgotten; there were, too, plays and collections of literary and general essays, as well as Bennett's steadily kept-up *Journals*. Margaret Drabble does her best to do justice to this enormous *oeuvre*. Although she is more interested in writing biography than in criticism, she tried to be discriminating, whilse confessing to a personal taste for Bennett's writing even when he is at his most slapdash and superficial.

Bennett had exceptional energy and a remarkable capacity for work; he made writing into a daily habit that could be carried on under any circumstances; what he wrote was of secondary importance to the fact of writing at all. The combination of talent and energy made him successful, and success made him rich. Not rich, certainly, by the standards of the entrepreneur or the industrial magnate, but rich for a man of letters; what Scott and Balzac had dreamed of but lost in financial disaster Bennett actually achieved. As Drabble says, he made an exceptional amount of money for someone who relied on his earning-power rather than inherited wealth or investments. And what he earned he spent, in the showy Edwardian way, which did not make him popular with his less affluent or less successful rivals. Hence the common notion of him as a materialist and careerist, summed up in Ezra Pound's portrait of him as 'Mr Nixon', offering good advice about the best way of getting on in the literary racket:

> In the cream gilded cabin of his steam yacht
> Mr Nixon advised me kindly, to advance with fewer
> Dangers of delay.

It is, as Drabble shows, a distorted and inadequate representation. Bennett was by no means a mere money-maker. He was very serious about writing and a lover of art and music, including art that, for its time, was scandalously avant-garde. As a man he was good-hearted and tolerant, lacking the malice that is second nature to so many writers. Despite his self-confidence and cockiness he was at heart a shy man, troubled all his life by a stammer, and not much at ease with women, except perhaps French whores, whom he inclined to sentimentalize. He did not marry until he was forty and then not very successfully. Throughout his life he was 'difficult' about small matters, keeping up the compulsive daily rituals of one who was a bachelor for many years. He was, in short, an unpredictable and many-faceted person, which is how Margaret Drabble presents him, whilst insisting that he was a very nice man whom she wishes she had known. (She gives a pleasant extract from a memoir of Bennett written after his death by Somerset Maugham: 'I remember that once, beating his knee with his clenched fist to force the words from his writhing lips, he said: "I am a nice man." He was.'). Bennett emerges from this book as a more convincing character than the male figures in Drabble's novels.

Yet despite the success of her portrait of Bennett as a man and writer, Drabble's account raises issues that she doesn't go into, perhaps because of her close sympathy, even partial identification, with Bennett. Taking a long view, one can see Bennett not only as a writer but as a remarkable cultural phenomenon, who came to maturity in the critically transitional Edwardian years. The sheer volume of his output seems suspect to us, and so does the cool professionalism with which Bennett embarked on any literary task he had to undertake. These, indeed, are the attributes of a wholly commercial writer and not of a literary artist, which Bennett always insisted that he was. There is an obvious contrast with Bennett's friend and contemporary, H. G. Wells, who was also highly prolific but who by early middle age had abandoned any pretensions to be an artist, and became avowedly interested in fiction as a form of journalism and a vehicle for the discussion of ideas. Bennett, unlike Wells, was not insular in his literary tastes and had served what looks like the customary modernist apprenticeship with the nineteenth-century French masters. But if there is a Flaubertian quality in the best of Bennett's fictional realism, there is no sign of a Flaubertian martyrdom in his life. We naturally tend to believe that the dedication of the writer must involve active suffering and possible material deprivation. Conrad's agonizing difficulty in writing anything at all seems far more authentic than Bennett's calm, triumphant clocking up of wordage, which is all too reminiscent of Trollope. To say that is not to say anything very damning about Bennett, of course. We have by now come to accept Trollope as a major novelist by concentrating on those of his books that interest us and not bothering with the rest, unless we are addicts. One can do the same thing with Bennett, whose finest novels still need little defence, but who is disconcertingly recent to be seen in that tolerant perspective. Joyce's ideal of 'cunning, exile and silence' appears proper for the dedicated artist, whereas Bennett's imaginative fascination with and material taste for the steam yacht and the de luxe train and the grand hotel seem scandalous and anachronistic (Balzac, though, might have found them very natural).

Margaret Drabble does, in fact, engage in some interesting critical reflections about this aspect of Bennett's imagination in her final chapter, apropos of *Imperial Palace*. At the same time she firmly rejects the common idea that Bennett was no more than a crude materialist. He was never merely crude, but he was probably some kind of a materialist, if one can use that word with a degree of philosophical neutrality. Indeed, Bennett might be seen as expressing, first, the peculiarly assertive materialism that was, paradoxically, part of the spirit of the Edwardian age, and, secondly, the implicit materialism of the nineteenth-century realistic novel, at least as practised in France and England, in which man is either dominated by objects or himself trying to dominate them, and where human will or sentiment is asserted in contrast or challenge to the impassivity and massiveness of things. In the modernist novel, as we know, things are subordinated to, or swallowed up by, consciousness: Virginia Woolf's 'luminous halo.' This was a frontier that Bennet approached but did not cross.

Similarly, Bennett's attitude to language was scrupulous but pre-modernist. When writing is a habit it is a neutral activity, a pure vehicle, whereas for Lawrence it is a potential invocation of the Holy Ghost and for Eliot an intolerable wrestle with words and meanings. For Forster, indeed, after the production of one certain masterpiece, it becomes something one ceases to engage in, at least of fiction. Forster's silence rather than Bennett's constant production seems to us the more heroic, even saintly way for a dedicated writer. Bennett, indeed, is like a man with a gearbox in his mind, changing smoothly from 'serious' to 'light' to 'potboiling' fiction and back again, according to the demands of the moment. As Drabble shows, while writing *The Old Wives' Tale*, his greatest novel, and a work which he had long prepared for and regarded with the utmost seriousness, Bennett broke off to write two short, light novels, a play and many articles and stories. And when he had finished *The Old Wives' Tale* he went straight on to write *The Card*, which is a very delightful book, but which treats the same settings and objects, even some of the same minor characters, in a farcical rather than an elegiac spirit. Again, one thinks of Balzac rather than of Bennett's slightly younger contemporaries. What is hard for us to accept, being habituated to the quasi-religious categories of modernism, is that for Bennett it was quite natural to write on different levels and to believe that each level had its own validity. Only a writer much more at home in his culture than we think appropriate could do such a thing.

One of Bennett's best novels, *Clayhanger*, came out in 1910, in which year, as Virginia Woolf has assured us, 'human character changed'. We customarily assume that Bennett, for all his merits, had the historical misfortune to live and work on the wrong side of that great temporal divide; even though the neatness of the division is complicated by the knowledge that Bennett was a champion of the Post-Impressionist painters whose exhibition in London in that year is seen by Virginia Woolf as a major symptom of the change of consciousness. Virginia Woolf has, in fact, been Bennett's major critical adversary ever since her remarkably influential essay, 'Mr Bennett and Mrs Brown' was published in 1924. She placed Bennett alongside Wells and Galsworthy as Edwardians who had had their day, as compared with those younger writers whom she rather misleadingly called 'Georgian' but whom we would call modernist: Joyce, Lawrence, Eliot, Forster. Much of Mrs. Woolf's argument was not false, but it was not wholly true either, and the resultant half-truth has been an obstructive element in literary history for the past fifty years. If asked, 'Who's afraid of Virginia Woolf?' one has to answer, 'practically everybody' (including, it must be admitted, the present writer, on previous occasions). As Margaret Drabble shows, Bennett responded to Virginia Woolf's attack with great calm, even indifference; his friend Eliot invited him to reply in *The Criterion* but in the end Bennett didn't bother. And after

Bennett's death Mrs Woolf expressed regret about him in her diary: 'Arnold Bennett died last night, which leaves me sadder than I should have supposed. A lovable, genuine man. . . .' Still, her public attack could not be undone. For Virginia Woolf, Bennett was too unspiritual, too much concerned with bricks and mortar and furniture and objects in general, and too little with the uniqueness of personality and the fine movements of consciousness. As Drabble points out, Bennett had come to learn quite a lot about bricks and mortar when he worked as a rent-collector for his father's firm, and she truly observes, 'people were not disembodied spirits, and the houses that they built were as much a part of them as their bodies.' In this respect Bennett can be regarded as defensibly traditional rather than modernist, though Lawrence, too, thought that houses were important. Where Virginia Woolf's essay is most dangerous is in the assumption that Bennett can be easily classed with Wells and Galsworthy. Admittedly there are resemblances, though Galsworthy was a more limited novelist, and Wells, though a writer of enormous gifts, was interested in so many more things than writing novels. One can agree that *The Old Wives' Tale*—to make the case for Bennett at its strongest—has things in common with *The Man of Property* or *Tono-Bungay*. But given Bennett's significantly transitional position, it is also true that it has less obvious things in common with *The Rainbow* or *Parade's End*. Or, to put it differently, the comparison is well worth making and the differences between Bennett's major novel and these canonical works of the modern movement are not all to Bennett's disadvantage.

I am not arguing that a careful comparison between *The Old Wives' Tale* and *The Rainbow* would in the end show that Bennett's novel was better than Lawrence's. But it might help to liberate us from Mrs Woolf's powerful suggestion that Edwardian books are necessarily inferior. Historically *The Old Wives' Tale* and *The Rainbow* cover the passing of a similar period of time—from the middle of the nineteenth century to the opening years of the twentieth—and are mostly set in provincial England. Both have elements of the family chronicle, though Bennett concentrates throughout on his two central characters, Constance and Sophia Baines, from adolescence in the eighteen-sixties to late middle age and death in the nineteen-hundreds. The placid and conventional Constance stays in Bursley (in real life, Burslem) throughout, while the spirited Sophia makes a disastrous marriage and spends much of her life in Paris, living through the Siege and the Commune before ultimately returning to Bursley to spend her final years with her sister. Some aspects of Bennett's art seem to me to stand up very well when compared with Lawrence's. Consider, for instance, the rightly admired account in *The Rainbow* of the startling clash of wills between Tom Brangwyn and his little step-daughter Anna, whilst Lydia is in bed upstairs giving birth to another child; the episode is resolved in the marvellously visionary account of Will carrying the little girl out to look at the cattle in the barn. If this is poetry, Bennett's account of a naughty child is prose, but no less effective. I am referring to the misadventure of Constance's little boy Cyril. At the age of four he is the assured and condescending host at a children's party until another child is given the last slice of a cake that Cyril has long had his eye on. In the resultant explosion of greed and rage Cyril behaves abominably, and Bennett renders the episode superbly, seeing it through Cyril's outraged consciousness. Both novelists had no experience of parenthood when they wrote, but Bennett has come closer to the unsentimental day-to-day reality of childhood; Lawrence is, in comparison, struck by the inherent mysteriousness of the child, and his description of little Anna in the barn is not only visionary but literary and even scriptural in its associations. The point is not that Bennett is better but simply that he is, in his own way, just as effective.

Where Bennett comes close to the great themes of modernist literature is in his fascination with time. He shares the twentieth-century anxiety about history, and *The Old Wives' Tale* is un-Victorian in its acute historical sense, whether shown in the carefully researched accounts of life in Paris during the Siege, or in less dramatic ways such as Bennett's observant noticing of changes in small-scale technology—bicycles and motor-cars and trams—or his considerable knowledge of developments in the retail drapery trade between the 1860s and the 1900s. Walter Allen has described *The Old Wives' Tale* as 'the most impressive record we have in English of life in time, of birth, change and decay'. More than any novel I know, *The Old Wives' Tale* conveys a sense of life as process, in small ways as well as large. In a very literal sense it is 'life-like'. Nothing ever stays the same, time offers no stability, and even the most familiar things are always subtly changing. The appearance of friends alters, for better or for worse, from one year to the next, children outgrow their clothes, buildings are restored or pulled down. We are accustomed in modern literature to the idea of time as flux and randomness; Bennett, I believe, sees it in rather different terms, as process, something that is inexorable but also orderly. Indeed, Bennett's preoccupation with time is challengingly different from that of specifically modernist writers. They tend to see time as something that must be escaped, into a higher or deeper significance, time in itself having no point or meaning:

> Ridiculous the waste sad time
> Stretching before and after.

So one escapes into epiphanies and symbolic visions, timeless moments, flashes of transcendence. But in *The Old Wives' Tale* Bennett shows that time must be lived in and through and that there is no escaping from it. Time is not in itself either meaningless or meaningful, but it can be given meaning by human endeavour. Bennett preserves quite a fine poise in *The Old Wives' Tale*. If he does not try to escape from time in transcendence or to subvert the quotidian with myth, as the great works of the modern movement do, he does not see life in time as no more than defeat and humiliation, with an alien order of objects and circumstances inevitably triumphing, as Zolaesque naturalism does. In a sense, perhaps, Bennett is a materialist, but in another sense there is a Christian element in his art (despite his personal reaction against all forms of religious belief, following his Wesleyan upbringing): at least, I see in *The Old Wives' Tale* an enactment of the Christian conviction that significance occurs in each successive moment of life, and not in rare and selected moments of unusual insight, which may be reserved for mystics and not for ordinary men. It might be just as plausible to argue for a residually Protestant sensibility in the unbelieving Bennett as it is to argue for a Catholic one in the equally unbelieving Joyce. *The Old Wives' Tale* is an elegy rather than a lament, and its spirit is decently stoical and endeavouring. The final sentance is indicative of its mood; after Sophia's death and funeral her ancient and ailing poodle, Fossette, a survivor of

Sophia's life in Paris, is disturbed and off her food. Finally, though, she thinks again about the possibility of eating. 'She glanced at the soup-plate, and, on the chance that it might after all contain something worth inspection, she awkwardly balanced on her old legs and went to it again.'

If Benett's art, unlike the masterpieces of modernism, accepts the burden of life in time, it does provide us, the readers, with a chance of reversing its inexorability. That is to say, by rereading *The Old Wives' Tale* we can once more rediscover Sophia and Constance in their poignantly hopeful girlhood in the opening chapter, before following them on their long and sometimes bitter journeys through life. And if the story moves inevitably towards death, Bennett's admirable sense of humour offers a traditional human defiance of death. It seems appropriate that Bennett. always ready to move from one level of his mind to another, and fascinated with the variousness of things, should have gone on to write *The Card* as soon as he had finished *The Old Wives' Tale*. The elegiac masterpiece, generally sombre despite its exuberant and comic elements, was followed by a light-hearted farce. Denry Machin, known as 'The Card', the cheerful, ingenious and not over-scrupulous adventurer from the Five Towns, was projected by Bennett as a deliberate twin of himself, being born on the same day of the same year: 27 May 1867. They were both energetic and resourceful men, and it could be said of Bennett as it was said of The Card, 'He had scored supremely and, for him, to score was life itself.' And one had to keep on scoring, for life never stood still.

1974

3

A note on *Sons and Lovers*

Like many novels in the realistic tradition, *Sons and Lovers* begins with childhood, family and community. The community it describes is working-class, but *Sons and Lovers* cannot be called an 'industrial novel'. Though it is about life in a mining district, the mine is not nearly so oppressively present as it is in Zola's *Germinal,* for instance. Lawrence shows us a society that is as much rural as industrial, where the mines have not yet swallowed up the Nottinghamshire countryside, and where nature is still close to the lives of the miners and their families. The blocks of miners' houses called the Bottoms all have nicely kept front gardens, as well as small back gardens; and the Morels, who live in a slightly superior house at the end of a row, have a strip of garden along one side as well. *Sons and Lovers* is in several senses a novel of border country, showing us the frequently crossed boundary between the mines and the countryside, and between rural and industrial ways of living and feeling. In its later sections it traces Paul Morel's movements across a metaphorical border from family and community to a twentieth-century mode of individualism and lonely selfhood.

Lawrence is most a traditional realist in the early parts of the novel that show daily life in the Morel household. Walter Morel is presented in a sympathetic even affectionate way. He gets up at five each morning and prepares his own breakfast:

> He went downstairs in his shirt and then struggled into the pit-trousers, which were left on the hearth to warm all night. There was always a fire, because Mrs Morel raked. And the first sound in the house was the bang, bang of the poker against the raker, as Morel smashed the remainder of the coal to make the kettle, which was filled and left on the hob, finally boil. His cup and knife and fork, all he wanted except just the food, was laid ready on the table on a newspaper. Then he got his breakfast, made the tea,

> packed the bottom of the doors with rugs to shut out the draught, piled a big fire, and sat down to an hour of joy. He toasted his bacon on a fork and caught the drops of fat on his bread; then he put the rasher on his thick slice of bread, and cut off chunks with a clasp-knife, poured his tea into his saucer, and was happy. With his family about, meals were never so pleasant. He loathed a fork; it is a modern introduction which has still scarcely reached common people. What Morel preferred was a clasp-knife. Then, in solitude, he ate and drank, often sitting, in cold weather, on a little stool with his back to the warm chimney-piece, his food on the fender, his cup on the hearth. And then he read the last night's newspaper—what of it he could—spelling it over laboriously. He preferred to keep the blinds down and the candle lit even when it was daylight; it was the habit of the mine.

We readily identify with Morel in his cosy solitude, as he eats his bacon like a countryman, with a clasp-knife (even though a knife and fork have been laid for him by Mrs Morel in her incessant campaign to make her husband respectable). The feeling of snug enclosure is a little exaggerated, suggesting an idealizing or pastoralizing element in the description. But Morel's 'hour of joy' is soon over and at six he has to leave the warm kitchen to walk to the mine. As fictional description this passage is in the mainstream of English realism, as it dwells in a loving way on familiar actions and things, appealing to a sense of shared experience and human community. The contents of the Morels' kitchen are vividly present to us as elements in a way of life, and not just as items in an inert naturalistic notation. If there is an idealizing note about the description this does not undermine its authenticity; such idealism is frequently present in the major English realists who, unlike the French, are generally inclined literally to 'make the best of things'. If the whole of *Sons and Lovers* were written in this way we would have no difficulty in regarding it, like many other works of early twentieth-century fiction, as an essentially nineteenth-century novel, particularly if Lawrence had preserved his original title, *Paul Morel.*

But Lawrence, like Hardy, one of his early influences, was a poet in fiction as well as a realist. These terms are not necessarilly exclusive, but the poetic register of Lawrence's prose is noticeably different from the realistic. Consider another well-known passage from the early part of *Sons and Lovers*, in which Mrs Morel, pregnant with Paul, has been locked out of the house by a drunken Morel after a quarrel. In realistic terms, what Mrs Morel does is to stand for a few moments in the back garden in the bright moonlight, helplessly staring at the great glistening rhubarb leaves near the door; then she walks up and down the side garden between currant bushes and a thorn hedge, and finally goes into the front garden where she stands among the lilies, looking over the front gate at the moonlit countryside until she almost faints. Yet this bald summary conveys nothing of the impact of the passage, which has a poetic intensity that is peculiarly Lawrentian:

> The tall white lilies were reeling in the moonlight, and the air was charged with their perfume, as with a presence. Mrs Morel gasped slightly in fear. She touched the big, pallid flowers on their petals, then shivered. They seemed to be stretching in the moonlight. She put her hand into one white bin: the gold scarcely showed on her fingers by moonlight. She bent down to look at the binful of yellow pollen: but it only appeared dusky. Then she drank a deep draught of the scent. It almost made her dizzy.

Eventually Walter Morel wakes up from a drunken stupor and lets his wife back into the house. Just before she goes to bed she looks in the mirror and 'smiled faintly to see her face all smeared with the yellow dust of lilies'.

Flowers of all kinds abound in *Sons and Lovers,* and such passages, with their pervasive nature mysticism, remind us that if the realistic Lawrence writes in the tradition of nineteenth-century fiction, the poetic Lawrence writes as a late heir of English Romanticism. In the first part of the novel, whether Lawrence is writing poetically or realistically, in describing the early married life of the Morels (the title of chapter 1) or Paul's childhood, his view is disinterested and contemplative. He is presenting life, not making a case. Even in describing the sadly ill-matched couple, Lawrence tries, at first, to be fair to both Mr and Mrs Morel. Their violent quarrels, I believe, provoke a response of compassionate sadness rather than outraged partisanship. There is, for instance, the distressing occasion when Walter Morel in a fit of temper throws a drawer at his wife, which cuts her brow open. The instantly contrite Walter tries to minister to her, but she dismisses him in anger. She is holding the baby Paul and as Walter watches in horror, drops of blood fall from the wound onto the baby's delicate head. It is a most sensitively rendered episode, where the realistic and the poetic are momentarily fused to produce a disturbing image that it is appropriate to acall 'symbolic', though Lawrence leaves the symbolism implicit and undeveloped.

As Paul grows up and becomes the central agent of the story, Lawrence can no longer be so disinterested. There is a story to be told and he has to pass beyond seeing into the life of things, or the steady contemplation of waht James called 'felt life'. *Sons and Lovers* becomes a *Bildungsroman* focused on Paul's personal development. The Morel parents are no longer treated even-handedly, with his passion and energy balancing her sensitivity and refinement. The growing Paul takes his mother's side against his father, and Walter Morel is diminished in stature until he is virtually written out of the novel. This is something different from undergoing a process of moral decline, in a way which might invite the reader's pity or concern. Put at its simplest, Walter has to go. There is little room for him in a story which becomes increasingly concerned with Paul's conflicts with the women in his life. One of the things that sharply distinguishes *Sons and Lovers,* in its later sections, from a novel of traditional English realism is the degree to which all the major relationships are or become adverse. From an early stage Mr and Mrs Morel have been frequently hostile to each other, though within the context of a marriage where something of value persists for a long time. Then, as Paul grows up, he finds himself in absolute opposition to his father. His relationship with his mother is, on the face of it, tender and loving, but he has to resist her emotional possessiveness. With the two women with whom he becomes sexually involved, Miriam and Clara, Paul becomes caught up in a conflict of wills and they, though once friends, inevitably become hostile to each other. Even in the Gissingesque sub-plot concerning Paul's brother William who goes to London to better himself and who gets engaged to a smart, empty-headed young lady from Streatham, we see William treating his fiancée with undisguised dislike. Taken one by one, none of these relationships seems necessarily implausible or exaggerated: but the collective psychology of *Sons and Lovers* reflects a degree of mutual hostility that is closer to French realism than to English.

We all know that *Sons and Lovers* is an autobiographical

novel; indeed, there are many external inducements to dwell on its personal dimensions, whether in the memoirs of Jessie Chambers, the original of Miriam, or the knowledge that Lawrence, in writing the final draft, deliberately emphasized the Oedipal aspects, in the light of his wife's early acquaintance with Freudian theory. Yet even without such contextual information, it is likely that a responsive reader new to the book would sense the pressure of personal experience. The autobiographical novel is the natural vehicle for a young writer trying to make fictional sense out of his life (Lawrence was twenty-five when he began work on *Sons and Lovers*). Roy Pascal has written pertinently about the differences between autobiography and autobiographical novel:

> The novel demands a narrative structure much more coherent and firm than the autobiography, a sequence of symbolical events, and a significant climax such as we have in *Sons and Lovers* and *A Portrait of the Artist* . . . . A young man cannot shape his autobiography without imposing rather arbitrary limits on his conception of himself. For him the autobiographical novel is much more appropriate, where he both interprets himself and invents situations to reveal what he feels is his potential reality.[1]

The autobiographical novel of a young man or woman is likely to be a work not only of self-interpretation but of self-justification. And such an active aim is not easy to reconcile with the disinterested pursuit of felt life, the enactment and contemplation of human tragedies and comedies. Even in great novels by mature writers the pressure of evidently autobiographical elements is likely to have an unsettling effect; Levin in *Anna Karenina* is a generally acknowledged example.

In his essay, 'Morality and the novel', Lawrence made what looks like a firm plea for disinterestedness: 'When the novelist puts his thumb in the scale, to pull down the balance to his own predeliction, that is immorality.' The implication is that the predeliction will be some imposed ideological or propagandist aim. But what if the predeliction is simply the author's need to justify himself? I believe that some such predeliction is at work in much of *Sons and Lovers*, despite its many fine effects of characterization and the realistic or lyrical rendering of experience. Lawrence, in short, becomes manipulative in the pursuit of self-interpretation. In chapter XI there is an intense passage of flower-description that reveals Paul's state of mind at a crucial phase of his life. He is not then on particularly good terms with his mother. ('There was between him and his mother a peculiar condition of people frankly finding fault with each other'); he has just begun sleeping with Miriam, after years of abstention, and is not finding the experience satisfying; and he is becoming increasingly attracted to Clara.

> The beauty of the night made him want to shout. A half-moon, dusky gold, was sinking behind the black sycamore at the end of the garden, making the sky dull purple with its glow. Nearer, a dim white fence of lilies went across the garden, and the air all round seemed to stir with scent, as if it were alive. He went across the bed of pinks, whose keen perfume came sharply across the rocking, heavy scent of the lilies, and stood alongside the white barrier of flowers. They flagged all loose, as if they were panting. The scent made him drunk. He went down to the field to watch the moon sink under.
>
> A corncrake in the hay-close called insistently. The moon slid quite quickly downwards, growing more flushed. Behind him the great flowers leaned as if they were calling. And then, like a shock he caught another perfume, something raw and coarse. Hunting round, he found the purple iris, touched their fleshy throats and their dark, grasping hands. At any rate, he had found something. They stood stiff in the darkness. Their scent was brutal. The moon was melting down upon the crest of the hill. It was gone; all was dark. The corncrake called still.

A lyrical piece of writing, certainly, and one that echoes Mrs Morel's similar experience in a garden by moonlight, long ago, before Paul was born, though it lacks the visionary quality. In that passage, we recall, Mrs Morel had breathed deeply of the lilies' scent and had ended up with their pollen on her face. Later one of the things Paul disliked about Miriam is her possessive attitude to flowers: 'When she bent and breathed a flower it was as if she and the flower were loving each other. Paul hated her for it.' The earlier episode associated Mrs Morel with lilies; and a reference that immediately follows the later passage associates Miriam with pinks. The emphatically sexual description of the irises invokes Clara, who is as physical as Miriam is spiritual. The flowers are used in this schematic way to illustrate what Paul feels about relations with these three women; the effect is surely much inferior to the earlier account of Mrs Morel in her garden. We have now a flatly emblematic account, where lilies, pinks, irises stand for, respectively, Mrs Morel, Miriam, Clara. This is followed by a strange little episode, when Paul holding a pink between his lips, goes indoors and tells his mother that he intends breaking off with Miriam, news that Mrs Morel had long hoped to hear. 'He put the flower in his mouth. Unthinking, he bared his teeth, closed them on the blossom slowly and had a mouthful of petals. These he spat into the fire, kissed his mother, and went to bed.' Paul chewing a flower is presumably a parodic reminder of Miriam's desire to absorb flowers into the depths of her being by inhaling them. (Already, in an earlier episode, on a country walk with Clara and Miriam, Paul has been seen eating cowslips.) Finally, with unsubtle symbolism Miriam is spat out of his mouth.

A page or so later the rejection of Miriam is literal and explicit. However tiresomely spiritual and high-minded Miriam is, she has always been shown as physically attractive, a well developed girl and very handsome. Indeed, when Paul first makes love to her he thinks, 'She had the most beautiful body he had ever imagined.' But he is already succumbing to the more mature attractions of Clara, among them her arms: 'When she lifted her hands, her sleeves fell back, and her beautiful strong arms shone out.' Three pages later it is precisely in this physical attribute that Miriam is found lacking: 'Those short sleeves, and Miriam's brown-skinned arms beneath them—such pitiful resigned arms—gave him so much pain that they helped to make him cruel.' The opposition is forced and over-emphatic. A young man falling out of love with a girl is very likely to change his mind about her attractiveness; but in *Sons and Lovers* we are too close to Paul's consciousness to be sure that what we are seeing is, in fact, meant to be inconsistency on his part.

Sons and Lovers is the kind of early twentieth-century *Bildungsroman,* like, in a more complex way, *The Rainbow* or *A Portrait of the Artist,* in which the central character seems to go through a developing process of emancipation, moving from fixity to freedom, from social or familial limitations to complete openness to experience. But I believe the underlying imaginative structure of the text moves in the opposite direction, from the freedom of contemplation to a certain ordering of experience in the interests of a self-justificatory aim or predeliction. This remark is not meant as a particular criticism of Lawrence, since I believe that what I am describing is common in autobiographical novels. There is a similar pattern in Joyce's *Portrait*. Douglas Hewitt, in his perceptive and suggestive book, *The Approach to Fiction,* has plausibly developed the idea that novels, even the most admired, are not seamless wholes or perfect organic unities, but are built up on a tension between what is immediately and locally appealing—characters, episodes, incidents—and the author's over-riding need to complete his fiction and achieve—or impose—some kind of total direction and unity. The tension often imposes a sense of strain, but most good novels are big enough to take it. Hewitt describes the well-known tendency of some novelists to use their fiction for speculations and theories about life and the world; again, Tolstoy is an example. The tendency, Hewitt acknowledges, can produce flaws, though he adds, 'But these are the flaws of strength and it seems that in fiction, unlike some other arts, only minor works are flawless.'[2] The tendency of autobiographical novels to impose distortions on the life they present might be described in similar terms. *Sons and Lovers* is likely to remain a classic of autobiographical fiction, though it is, I think, flawed by the tendency I have tried to describe. Readers can decide for themselves how important the flaws are.

1983

NOTES

1. Roy Pascal, *Design and Truth in Autobiography* (London, 1960), pp. 175-8.
2. Douglas Hewitt, *The Approach to Fiction* (London, 1972), p.181.

4

Wyndham Lewis: coming to terms with the Enemy

I

In the nineteen-twenties Wyndham Lewis presented himself to a philistine world as the Enemy. The enmity was duly returned. Twenty-three years after his death he is regarded with unenthusiastic respect as one of the 'men of 1914' and a pioneer English modernist in art and letters; theses are written about him and, as these books show, he is becoming the subject of academic studies. But people find it difficult to speak well of Lewis: he is thought of as a fascist, a racist, a sexist, a man whose opinions, delivered with brutal provocativeness, were repugnant to the liberal consensus. Nevertheless, extreme and uncompromising controversialists seem, by some law of intellectual life, to attract passionately devoted followers. Accordingly, there are Poundians and Leavisites; and a small but articulate band of Lewisites, working hard to get due recognition for the Enemy. Still, it would be idle to pretend that he is very widely read, even if his novels are easier to obtain than they once were.

Some major modernist texts, once thought difficult and subversive, have been quite easily assimilated and incorporated into the general practice of novel reading, and subsequently canonized by academic syllabuses. Young readers can now respond very comfortably to, or, as they put it, 'relate to', *A Portrait of the Artist* or *The Rainbow.* It is difficult to imagine them feeling the same way about the hard, aggressive, seemingly inhuman comedy of *Tarr,* which was written at the same time as those novels. Last year *Enemy News* the newsletter of the Wyndham Lewis Society, published a sad little item reporting that a lecturer in English at University College, Lampeter, had found that his students reacted with 'universal antipathy' to *The Revenge for Love,* a much more approachable novel than *Tarr.*

Jeffrey Meyers is not a Lewisite; indeed, his reservations about Lewis are wide and deep. But he has done the Enemy good service by writing his life and editing a volume of essays about him. The biography is solid and well documented, without being pointlessly massive or tediously long; there is probably more material to be drawn on, and aspects of Lewis's deliberately mystified life remain to be illuminated. But Mr Meyers provides the basic record of Lewis's personal story and his career as painter, novelist, critic and polemicist at large. He is particularly helpful in his account of Lewis's earliest years, showing what a tangled but potent set of influences he grew up with. His father was a wealthy, idle American dilettante, who had had his moment of glory fighting in the Civil War and apart from a little dabbling in business did nothing much for the rest of his life. Lewis's mother was a British girl of Scots-Irish stock, who married at the age of sixteen. Percy Wyndham Lewis was born in 1882 on his father's yacht, when it was moored at Amherst, Nova Scotia; he was christened in Montreal, and throughout his life kept Canadian nationality, which enabled him to serve as a war artist with the Canadian army during the First World War and to live freely in Canada during the Second.

Lewis spent the first six years of his life on the East Coast of the United States, in Maine and on Chesapeake Bay; there were no other children who survived. Then in 1888 the family moved to England. When Lewis was eleven his father ran off with a housemaid and never returned. Thereafter Lewis and his mother lived a peripatetic life of shabby-genteel poverty. There was always some money, received unreliably and in insufficient amounts from Lewis senior and the paternal family, and Lewis was given a conventional English middle-class education, culminating with two fairly unhappy years at Rugby. Between the ages of sixteen and nineteen he studied painting at the Slade and began a lifelong friendship with Augustus John. From 1901 to 1908 he was an art student on the Continent—based in Paris, where he lived the kind of life later rendered in *Tarr*—but also spending time in Brittany, Spain and Germany. During these years Lewis began writing as well as painting. He read Nietzsche and Dostoevsky and acquired an advanced European culture which gave him ideas and interests uncommon in young Englishmen of his generation. He also became an energetic and ruthless *coureur de femmes.*

He remained very close to his mother, who continued to support him as best she could and, without husband or other children, concentrated all her love on him. Lewis returned her devotion and wrote very frank letters to her from Paris, telling her about his current amours and intended seductions. For the present-day reader the flip phrases of social science hover waiting to be invoked: 'disturbed childhood . . . one-parent family . . . excessive dependence . . . inability to form mature relationships'. Undoubtedly much of Lewis's later behaviour originated in those early experiences, and Fredric Jameson remarks in a footnote to his book that Lewis 'cries out for a psychobiography of the quality of those of Sartre or Erikson'. Meyers does not attempt anything so ambitious, perhaps wisely, though near the beginning of his book he does quote Freud to the effect that 'a man who has been the indisputable favourite of his mother keeps for the life the feeling of a conqueror'. Meyers's judicious, even-handed narrative does not conceal the fact that Lewis grew up to be an unpleasant human being, without many redeeming features. This is a hard statement, but the evidence is there; he was bullying, arrogant, ferociously selfish, paranoid, evasive, hyper-sensitive. The other men of 1914 were difficult personalities, certainly, but they had attractive qualities: Pound was celebrated for his generosity to fellow-artists; Eliot, however personally buttoned-up, did much service for public and intellectual life as editor, publisher and committee member; Joyce was monomaniac in the pursuit of his art, but an affectionate family man. There is no point in being moralistic, but Lewis was evidently a man with many, many problems. 'They fuck you up, your mum and dad./They may not mean to, but they do.'

All the same, he had loyal friends, some of whom he kept to the end of his life. Women seem to have been attracted throughout, though he left a trail of discarded mistresses and unacknowledged bastards behind him. After the art students of Paris, Lewis went sexually up-market when he returned to England. One gets the impression from Meyers's account that many of the cleverest, most beautiful and well-born women in London were queuing up at Lewis's door to be treated, more or less, like dirt. One notes this, not without *ressentiment,* as a prevailing ontological problem in the relations between the sexes, and no doubt the kind of thing that gets discussed behind the closed doors of women's consciousness-raising groups. In 1918 Lewis met a young art student called Anne Hoskyns, with whom he lived—allowing for many affairs on the way—for the rest of his life, though they did not marry until 1930. Lewis always called her 'Froanna', derived from a German acquaintance's description of her as 'Frau Anna'. In his way he seems to have been devoted to her, though it was a very odd way, which involved keeping Froanna as invisible as possible. Friends and regular visitors to Lewis's studio had no idea that he was married, and even to those who became aware of Froanna's existence she was often no more than a pair of hands passing dishes through a serving hatch. Despite his earlier illegitimate progeny, Lewis refused to have any children by Froanna, presumably because he would have had to recognize them. But there is a strange tenderness in certain portraits of his wife painted in the late 1930s, and, in a different way, in his fictional representations of her as Margot in *The Revenge for Love* and Essie in *Self Condemned.*

Lewis may have been a conqueror where women were concerned, but his professional and social relations were liable to end disastrously; in particular, he had a compulsion to quarrel with people who might have helped him. One such early quarrel, which had lastingly bad results, was with Roger Fry, over decorations commissioned from the Omega Workshop in 1912. Meyers gives a detailed account of the quarrel and convinces me that Lewis was in the right; but as a result of it, Lewis earned the intense and undying opposition of the Bloomsbury group—who previously had been well disposed towards the young artist and writer—which certainly harmed his later reputation. His alienation from his contemporaries was extended by the satirical overkill of *The Apes of God,* and in the early 1930s he quarrelled with Charles Prentice, his editor at Chatto and Windus, who had been a keen admirer of Lewis's books and published many of them. Jeffrey Meyers sums up the decline in a melancholy paragraph:

> *The Apes of God* was the first of a long series of tactical errors and personal disasters that oppressed Lewis during the 1930s. His book in praise of Hitler (1931) damaged his literary career in the same way that the quarrel with Fry hurt his artistic progress. These ill-advised works were followed by his break with Chatto

> and Windus in 1932, the withdrawal of three of his books between 1932 and 1936, the serious illness that plagued him from 1932 to 1937, his association with Sir Oswald Mosley's British Union of Fascists, his two unpopular Rightwing political tracts in 1936-37, the rejection of his portrait of Eliot by the Royal Academy in 1938, and his ill-timed and ill-fated exile to North America in 1939. Lewis was indeed self-condemned; his greatest enemy was himself. . . . Lewis's political opinions intensified the neglect of his literary works and made him one of the loneliest figures in the intellectual history of the thirties.

Meyers's criticism of Lewis's books, whether fiction or polemic, is cautious and sensible but at the same time quietly dismissive of a good part of the *oeuvre.* He remarks, 'Too many of his imaginative books—like *The Childermass* and *The Apes of God*—had great promise but limited success. They start brilliantly and evoke an exciting visual quality, but gradually disintegrate, to go on too long, and finally seem over-written, tiresome and unreadable.' Meyers is unhappy with the anti-humanistic side of Lewis, expressed in the hammering polemics and paranoid pamphleteering, the emphasis on hardness and exteriority, the preference of the mechanical to the organic, and the reduction of human beings to animated puppets. After Lewis's long illness in the 1930s Meyers suggests that he became more humanistic, as is apparent in the great portraits of his wife, Pound and Eliot—though the quality of his painting declined sharply after his ill-judged departure for the United States and Canada—and in fiction with *The Revenge for Love.* For Meyers, Lewis's greatest novel is *Self Condemned,* a bitter, tragic and powerful distillation of the self-acknowledge that came to Lewis in his North American exile. Meyers interestingly compares it with *Women in Love* as a civilian response to wartime pressures, and to Trilling's *Middle of the Journey* and Mann's *Doctor Faustus* as a tragedy of intellectual defeat. At the end of *Self Condemned* Lewis explicitly disowns the ideology that had informed his earlier personal aesthetic: the commitment to exteriority, extolling the hard carapace over the soft organic mess within. His persona, René Harding, an evident projection of many of Lewis's own attitudes, is reduced to a 'glacial shell of a man', in a fate that is a living death. I share Meyers's high opinion of this novel; but one has to point out that it is a work of traditional, quasi-autobiographical fictional realism. As always with Lewis, the prose is sharp, colourful and original. But the book marks a retreat from the innovating modernism of Lewis's early writing, exemplified in *The Wild Body, Enemy of the Stars* and *Tarr.*

Jeffrey Meyers economically reprints his discussion of *Self Condemned* in the volume of essays on Lewis that he has edited. The title *Wyndham Lewis: a revaluation,* is slightly misleading since one cannot revalue what has not, in any systematic way, been valued. It is an uneven collection, with the Lewisites well represented. Meyers's introduction reflects his own uncertainties about Lewis, whom he refers to as 'perhaps the liveliest and most stimulating intellectual force in modern English literature'. If one is going to use superlatives one should have the courage to do without that pusillanimous 'perhaps'; and what, I wonder, would the author of *Time and Western Man* and *The Diabolical Principle and the Dithyrambic Spectator* have made of 'lively' and 'stimulating' as terms of high praise? The finest essay is certainly John Holloway's 'Machine and Puppet: a Comparative View', which engages, with sensitivity and insight, in a comparison between Lewis's pictorial art and his fictional prose. Such comparisons between one art and another are difficult to do at all, and almost impossible to do convincingly; nevertheless, John Holloway shows common ground between the different media, in respect of Lewis's concern with machines and puppets; what interested Lewis, he argues, were two contrary movements: 'That of humanity *into* machine, and that of the puppet who, wonderfully, reanimates into humanity'. Marshall McLuhan, who had befriended Lewis in Toronto, contributes a brief but suggestive note on Lewis's prose style. E. W. F. Tomlin, writing on Lewis's philosophical influences, is informative and judicious about his dealings with Bergson, Schopenhauer and Nietzsche, though he makes Lewis seem a much more conceptually coherent thinker than he ever appears to be on the page.

One of the most solid essays is by a French Lewisite, Bernard Lafourcade, on *The Wild Body,* discussing first, in a scholarly way, the various drafts and stages through which Lewis's early stories passed before they were made up into a volume; and then moving on to some quite acute critical reflections. Lafourcade asks, in passing, 'out of what timorous superciliousness the critics have refused to contemplate the appropriateness of applying Freudian analysis to a notoriously complex, secretive and aggressive author?' The fear of what Lewis himself might have said about such a procedure is one possible though inadequate answer. Wendy Stallard Flory does in fact offer a psychologically directed account of *Enemy of the Stars,* with interesting results, seeing the Hanp-Arghol division as reflecting opposed drives within Lewis himself. Alistair Davies provides an illuminating reading of *Tarr* as a largely Nietzschean novel, and concludes with a disturbing Nietzschean flourish of his own, which recalls Lewis at the height of his anti-humanistic phase: 'We must not attribute to *Tarr* that inner spiritual depth, that moment of tragic insight, the glimpse of resolution or immortality with which classical or Christian fiction ends. For these conclusions are those of a sentimental, banal, herd culture.' This has an almost fascist ring, though it also echoes, in a different key, the rigorous anti-humanism of current Marxist-structuralism, a connection made explicit in Fredric Jameson's book.

Some of the contributors seem to share Lewis's ideological stances, while nearly all the others are tolerant or neutral. Even Valerie Parker, writing on a sensitive topic—'Lewis, Art and Women'—restricts herself to level-headed exposition without overt judgement. The one exception is William M. Chace, who plays the devil's advocate in this company, writing about Lewis's politics in a polemically attacking way. If any kind of consensus emerges from this book it is that three novels are central, *Tarr, The Revenge for Love* and *Self Condemned*, and that everything else is still a matter for argument. Paul Edwards insists that *The Apes of God* is 'one of the major pessimistic achievements of literary modernism' and a neglected masterpiece, but that novel, for all the brilliance of its prose and the colossal energy directing it, is not, I think, likely to emerge very far from neglect; there is too little to transcend its obsessive concern with remote, unimportant quarrels. Comparisons with *The Dunciad* are wide of the mark, and, significantly, both Jeffrey Meyers and Fredric Jameson agree in finding it unreadable. The best of the essays in this collection suggest new ways of reading and assessing Lewis, though none of the contributors produces the aphoristic perceptions of some of Lewis's earlier critics; such as, for instance, Eliot, who reviewing *Tarr* in 1918 said, 'In the work of Mr Lewis we recognize the thought of the modern and the energy of the cave-man'; or Edgell Rickword, who wrote in 1931 appropos of *The Apes of God,* 'latterly his energy has been spent in a reckless way; one is reminded of a powerful man tormented by gnats. The apostolic fervour with which the campaign for their extermination develops threatens to become a breathless pursuit of the insignificant.' (Rickword's essay, reprinted in his *Essays and Opinions 1921-31,* is an outstanding critique of Lewis.)

Timothy Materer contributes an essay to *Wyndham Lewis: A Revaluation* on Lewis's dealings with three older writers or artists, Augustus John, W. B. Yeats, and T. Sturge Moore, all of whom he admired; Materer suggests that they to some extent played the role of the vanished father in the pattern of his life. In *Vortex: Pound, Eliot, and Lewis* Materer deploys a similar comparative approach on a larger scale. The book is not easy to classify; it brings together biography, literary and art criticism, and cultural history, and renders them down into a kind of soup which is palatable but not very sustaining. Vorticism as a movement was invented by Pound and Lewis in the early months of 1914, and publicized in *Blast;* Eliot had no connection with the movement in its origins, but published some of his early poetry in the second and last issue of *Blast* in 1915. For Lewis Vorticism was primarily a movement in painting, design and sculpture, in which Edward Wadsworth and Henri Gaudier-Brzeska were associated. It marked a particular phase in his life; which certainly did not survive the First World War. Pound saw it as his role to provide a literary dimension to Vorticism—as Lewis later confessed in *Time and Western Man,* he was not much impressed by these attempts—and tried to keep alive the idea of Vorticism; as late as 1936 Pound was proposing a revival of *Blast* to Lewis. Towards the end of his life, in the catalogue of the Tate Gallery exhibition in 1956, *Wyndham Lewis and Vorticism,* Lewis wrote with abrasive finality, 'Vorticism, in fact, was what I, personally, did and said at a certain period.'

This is the firm but not extensive foundation of fact on which Materer erects a shaky edifice of speculation and analogy. One can see what prompted the attempt: Pound, Eliot and Lewis were three masters of modernism, all more or less associated with *Blast;* it must surely follow that they had much in common and that the pattern of shared beliefs could profitably be explicated. It is true that the vortex is a potent emblem of modernist aspirations: a focus of intense energy that is self-contained, centripetal, non-linear, non-discursive. Historically there were good reasons for Pound and Lewis to adopt the vortex in 1914; by embodying circling, self-contained energy it enabled Lewis to define his movement in opposition to Futurism, which was fascinated by sheer speed and dynamic forward impetus. At the same time Lewis was certainly influenced by Futurist ideas and rhetoric—the aggressive layout of *Blast* was imitated from Apollinaire's manifesto, *L'Anti-Tradition Futuriste*—and may have been inspired by a series of paintings by the Futurist, Giacomo Balla, called *Vortice*. The relations between Vorticism and Futurism have been clarified in some interesting articles, written in English and Italian, in a recent special issue *Futurismo/Vorticismo,* of the periodical *Quaderno* (No. 9) published by the Facoltà di Lettere of the University of Palermo. As a literary image the vortex has some distinguished antecedents. Materer quotes from Blake's *Milton*, 'Everything has its / Own Vortex' while Pound wrote in a very early poem, 'Plotinus', 'As one that would draw through the node of things, / Back-sweeping to the vortex of the cone'. Materer refers to a book known to have influenced Pound, Allen Upward's *The New Word* (1908), which talks of thought flowing in funnels and waterspouts and vortices. There is other evidence, not quoted by Materer, which suggests that the idea was in the air in the early years of the century. John Davidson wrote in *The Testament of John Davidson* (1908), 'while one design / Engulfed as in a vortex all my thoughts' and H. G. Wells referred in *The New Machiavelli* (1911) to London as 'a vortex of gigantic forces'. As Materer remarks, vortical forms can be found throughout nature, from the galaxy to the DNA code, and Pound was correspondingly impressed.

The problem with these analogical resemblances is that if they work, they work only in a weak and generalizing way, and do little to account for the complex of similarities and differences that Lewis and Pound were involved in during their years of collaboration. Eliot, as Materer has to admit, had little to do with Vorticist ideas and aims, even though, years later, he wrote in *East Coker*, 'Whirled in a vortex which shall bring / The world to that destructive fire . . .' Hugh Kenner went over similar ground in

The Pound Era, a book which is itself like a vortex, unified by the central presence of Pound and proceeding by an associative method akin to that of the *Cantos*. Materer's book is like Kenner's, a collection of bits and pieces, and some of his observations and discoveries are valuable. Materer shows, for instance, that Lewis's *Enemy of the Stars* has a much stronger claim to be called Vorticist writing than anything by Pound. There is a discussion of Vorticist painting and sculpture, which is adequately illustrated with reproductions. Materer entertainingly describes the feuding between Lewis and Joyce; after Lewis's attacks in *Time and Western Man* Joyce took good-humoured revenge in *Finnegans Wake*, where Lewis is satirized as 'Professor Jones'. Joyce, Eliot and Pound were all commendably tolerant of the critical onslaughts launched upon them by their old friend. Among items of biographical interest are previously unpublished extracts from Sophie Brzeska's diary, showing Pound as he appeared to an unfriendly observer in pre-war London.

Materer's book is carefully documented and makes extensive use of unpublished letters and manuscripts in American libraries. But he shows some startling lapses from scholarly rigour, particularly when he refers to an alleged meeting between Lewis and Pound in New York at the start of the Second World War. This meeting is as fictitious as Schiller's encounter between Elizabeth Tudor and Mary Stuart; Pound did visit America in the early summer of 1939 but had been back in Italy for many weeks when Lewis arrived in New York; the dates can be easily verified from Lewis's letters and Noel Stock's biography of Pound. Materer also pushes the Pound-Lewis connection to unsubstantiated lengths when he claims that *Self Condemned* is about Pound's career as well as Lewis's. There is not much evidence for this assertion apart from a certain physical resemblance between Pound and Lewis's protagonist René Harding; But Harding also resembles Descartes, the philosopher of dualism, whose Christian name he bears, and for whom Lewis had good philosophical reasons for feeling an affinity. Materer suggests that Harding's London flat is based on Lewis's memories of Pound's flat in Kensington, back in 1914; why not of his own flat in Notting Hill, which he had hurriedly vacated in 1939, and which the biographical evidence shows it resembled? *Self Condemned* is so intensely self-absorbed a novel that there is little room in it for a Poundian subtext. Lewis did indeed write a short story about Pound called 'Doppelgänger' (published in *Encounter* in 1954), but its tone is very different from *Self Condemned.* Materer makes a much juster observation a little earlier in his book when he sees *Self Condemned, The Pisan Cantos* and *Little Gidding* as major works reflecting their respective authors' personal crises under the stress of war.

For all the interest of its material, *Vortex* does not hang together, and many of its connections are forced or too generalized. A similar criticism might be made of *The Pound Era,* but Materer lacks the manic conviction and energy of mind which enabled Hugh Kenner to pull together so many fragments in a unifying field of force. Fredric Jameson, in *Fables of Agression,* is concerned not with the similarities between Lewis and his contemporaries but with the differences. He believes that Lewis was a very different kind of modernist from Pound or Eliot or Joyce—and suggests that because Lewis has received so much less exegesis and academic institutionalizing he remains intact as an archaic survival from an earlier era, like a miraculously preserved prehistoric monster. As we read him, Jameson claims, we can 'once more sense that freshness and virulence of modernizing stylization less and less accessible in the faded texts of his contemporaries'. *Fables of Aggression* is by far the cleverest and most original of these studies of Lewis. Jameson is full of ideas, rather as Lewis himself was, though I am reminded of Edgell Rickword's cautionary remark about Lewis, 'to have a lot of ideas is no more to be a good thinker than to have a lot of soldiers is to be a good general'. As a critic Jameson employs that potent but unstable combination of Marxist-structuralism and psychoanalysis which is visibly destroying some good brains among younger British academics. He does it, though, with skill and panache; his argument is dense and at intervals loses intelligibility altogether, like a stream running underground for part of its course; but his style has a redeeming drive and energy, resembling Lewis's own.

Though a Marxist, Jameson is paradoxically ready to praise in Lewis those qualities that other readers find embarrassing or detestable: his aggressiveness, his elitism, his proto-fascism, his racism, his dislike of women and homosexuals and indeed of sexuality itself. Or perhaps one should not say that he praises the qualities themselvs, but Lewis's frank expression of them. In order to maintain these paradoxes Jameson invokes a complicated theoretical apparatus. The normally individualistic approach of psychoanalysis is boldly collectivized to bring it in line with Marxist-structuralism, which takes little account of the self as a separate entity. Jameson posits a 'libidinal apparatus', not connected with any particular individual's libido, but a collective entity formed by historical and political pressures, objectively existing in, so to speak, societal deep space.[1] (At this level of speculation critical theory turns into something like science fiction.) This apparatus is capable of giving a particular shape and direction to the individual fantasy life. So, early in his career, Lewis's 'political unconscious' was formed not primarily by inheritance or personal upbringing but by the political conditions of pre-1914 Europe. The result was *Tarr,* which Jameson places 'among the most characteristic monuments to the aristocratic-bohemian cosmopolitan multilingual European culture of that period, whose most substantial expression is *The Magic Mountain* of Thomas Mann'. The First World War destroyed that society and brought in a new libidinal apparatus, which turned Lewis in the direction of proto-fascism and satirical onslaughts on the established order.

Jameson reads Lewis as a great political writer, with an unsurpassed insight into the dehumanized culture of his time, and much preoccupied with how far a self is possible in the Age of Reification. He was a man of rich revolutionary potential, who could—and should—have been on the left, but whose petty bourgeois insecurity made him anti-Marxist and deflected him to proto-fascism. There is nothing inherently impossible in this analysis, even though Lewis lacked the humanitarianism that is usually a starting point for leftist commitment, however tough-minded or bloodyminded it becomes in practice. The label 'fascist' has been applied, often in a simple abusive sense, to Pound, Eliot, Yeats and Lawrence; there seems to be more ground for calling Lewis at least a 'pro-fascist' because of his aggressive and authoritarian temperament, his anti-liberal convictions, his sense of society as an inert mass or herd to be manipulated; and also because, unlike any of the other major anglophone modernists, he had fought in the First World War, the matrix of

Fascism, which so deeply affected Céline and Drieu, not to mention Hitler and Mussolini and Mosley. Lewis's self-image, in his prodigiously productive phase of the late 1920s and early 1930s was of a hard, cold, armoured figure, contemptuously standing aloof from the soft, swirling mess of democratic society, which is in love with time and flux and unhealthily dominated by Jews, primitivists, homosexuals and women. This image, of the archetypal Enemy, can easily be seen as an embodiment of fascist rhetoric and fascist iconography.

In a conventional reading of Lewis's career, like that of Jeffrey Meyers and the contributors to his book of essays, we have to put up with the nasty side of Lewis, in order to take the good art that went with it, and then move on, with some relief, to the later, humanistic phase of his writing and painting. But Jameson, reading Lewis through Althusserian spectacles, is not so soft or evasive:

> his artistic integrity is to be conceived, not as something distinct from his regrettable ideological lapses (as when we admire his art, *in spite of* his opinions), but rather in the very intransigence with which he makes himself the impersonal registering apparatus for forces which he means to record, beyond any whitewashing and liberal revisionism, in all their primal ugliness.

If one believes that the primary—indeed the only—purpose of art is to unmask, to reveal ideological conflicts and contradictions, and that this purpose has nothing at all to do with the artist's conscious aims, then such a view of Lewis will seem plausible. But if one believes that there is much more to art than that, then Jameson's approach creates more difficulties than it resolves.

There is a rather sinister relish about his analysis, as though across the decades and the deep ideological divide, he finds a commendable affinity between Lewis's anti-humanism and Althusser's. His book, for all its coolness and toughness, is affected by the atmosphere of recent Marxist-structuralist thought, so oddly reminiscent of the era of alchemy and astrology, where ideology permeates every aspect of life, nothing is ever what it appears to be, and hidden but irresistible forces dominate human behaviour. At the same time, Jameson confirms my suspicion that Marxist-structuralism is such a perverse mode of discourse that no one can keep it up for long, and that when its practitioners' attention lapses they slip, despite themselves, into conventional literary criticism. Thus, Jameson says of *Self Condemned:*

> In this novel, then, unconscious material rises dangerously close to the surface. With that uncomfortable honesty so characteristic of him, Lewis here always seems on the point of blurting out the truth, both to himself and to us; and *Self Condemned* is surely the closest he ever came to self-knowledge.

This is surely true; but it is strange to find such a judgement, rooted in Lewis's personal situation, being made by a critic whose method does not permit him to think in terms of selves and individuals; Jameson has no business to speak of 'self-knowledge', and believing, as he writes elsewhere in the book, that ethics is a bourgeois mystification, he should not use such old-fashioned ethical terms as 'honesty' and 'truth'. Stripping the mask from this critic, I perceive that beneath the sophisticated and learned deployment of Marxist, structuralist and psychoanalytic terms and concepts, there is one more marginalized intellectual of apocalyptic tendencies, lost in the Age of Reification; he actually uses phrases like 'at this late hour in Western culture'. Once again, it is closing time in the gardens of the West.

And yet, despite everything, *Fables of Aggression* contains some of the best criticism that anyone has ever written on Lewis. Put simply, it is evident that Jameson greatly admires Lewis, is excited and disturbed by his writing, and has erected an elaborate system of special pleading to justify what is in fact a personal and instinctive admiration. He is, of course, right to try to read Lewis in a historical and political context as well as in a personal and psychological one, though the concept of 'libidinal apparatus' is too abstract and cumbersome to take seriously. Fortunately it does not stop Jameson from getting close to Lewis's texts and reading them acutely. Long ago Eliot remarked that there is no method, except to be very intelligent; Jameson's book suggests an amendment to this dictim, to the effect that any method can serve provided that the critic is very intelligent, which Jameson certainly is. He makes excellent sense of the way Lewis's style works, and shows how Lewis pitches verbal cliché against gestural cliché, producing a freshness of perception from the clash. There is a particularly illuminating chapter showing how Lewis anticipated Beckett in manipulating what Beckett later called the 'pseudo-couple', an opposed but closely linked male pair, with many literary antecedents: Boucard and Pécuchet, Faust and Mephistopheles, Don Quixote and Sancho Panza. Lewis exemplifies them in Hanp and Arghol in *Enemy of the Stars* and Pullman and Satters in *The Childermass*. Jameson writes, in distinctly Lewisesque prose, of 'the very element of Lewis' novelistic world, this combative, exasperated, yet jaunty stance of monads in collision, a kind of bouyant truculence in which matched and abrasive consciousnesses slowly rub each other into smarting vitality'.

As these books show, Lewis is now being increasingly written about; whether he is being any more widely and appreciatively read remains uncertain. Particular puzzles and contradictions recur throughout them. Lewis's contempt for the exaltation of the ego and for Romantic self-expression went along with an essentially Romantic egoism and cult of the artist in his own writings. Indeed, one might argue that an assertive literary neo-classicism, of the kind that Lewis flaunted in the 1920s, is, in our century, a further version of Romanticism. Lewis disliked modern civilization because it reduced men to the status of puppets and machines, yet depicted them as such in his own painting and fiction. There seems to be a division between importance and value in Lewis, which is implied by several of his critics but not brought clearly into focus. That is to say, Lewis was without doubt a major modernist innovator; in painting and design with the abstraction and near-abstraction of the years 1912 to 1915; in prose with *The Wild Body, Enemy of the Stars,* and *Tarr*; and in cultural politics with *Blast* and Vorticism. These works and activities imply an anti-humanist attack on bourgeois order, which, as Jameson correctly points out, has affinities with the iconoclasm and radicalism of the proto-fascism which emerged from the First World War. But what most writers about Lewis—Jameson apart—seem to value, 'relate to', are those works of the late 1930s and after, where he returns to a humanistic mainstream; the serene paintings of his wife, Eliot and Pound; *The Revenge for Love* and the powerful but traditional realism of *Self Condemned*. A sufficiently flexible and pluralistic criticism can come to terms with these paradoxes. But Lewis remains what he always was, a very difficult man to deal with.

1980

II

Alan Munton's edition of Wyndham Lewis's *Collected Poems and Plays* is a useful, sensibly edited volume that reprints previously published material by Lewis that has long been unobtainable plus a couple of unpublished poems. It shows that Lewis the writer, though putting his principal energies into fiction and criticism and polemic, did attempt all the main literary forms during the course of his life. The first piece in the book is a poem called 'Grignolles', a product of the period in Brittany that gave rise to Lewis's early stories, originally published in a magazine in 1910. It has a curiosity value, and shows the kind of perception of people and places more fully expressed in Lewis's fiction, but as verse it is limp and unmemorable. Lewis's claim to serious attention as a poet, or at least as a verse-writer, rests on his long satirical poem, *One-Way Song,* first published in 1933. This work has been highly praised, not only by committed admirers of Lewis, like Eliot and Geffrey Grigson, but even by an ideological opponent like Stephen Spender, in a review written in 1933 and reprinted in his *The Thirties and After.* As an admirer of some of Lewis's books but certainly no Lewisite, I find *One Way Song* a hard work to assess or to come to terms with at all. The verse, carries one along smartly, with a certain noisy rattling energy, like a goods train going flat out, though Lewis, whether writing in heroic couplets or fourteeners, was often casual about metre, and remarkably so about rhyme. There are nice satirical touches scattered through the poem, like the vignette of his old friend Eliot:

> I seem to note a roman profile bland,
> I hear the drone from out of the cactus-land:
> That must be the poet of the Hollow Men:
> The lips seem bursting with a deep Amen.

But much of *One-Way Song* is deeply obscure. This may not sound like a very penetrating objection, since it has been said in

* CUSTOMER RECEIPT *

Newcastle
92 Westgate Road

Date: 18/09/2021 Time: 17:23:13

Reference: AMNE189522

SALE

CONTACTLESS
VISA payWave
************2933
AID: A0000000031010
PAN SEQ NO: 00

Approved
AUTH CODE:976850

TOTAL SALE

GBP £9.5

PLEASE DEBIT MY ACCOUNT

NO CVM REQUIRED

MID:***84273 TID:****9191

PLEASE RETAIN THIS COPY
THIS IS NOT A VAT RECEIPT

the past—still is said, on occasion—about such major modernist texts as *The Waste Land* or the *Cantos.* In those poems the difficulties are part of the method; in time one learns to recognize the unexpected transitions and juxtapositions, the musical rather than logical development, the use of image instead of statement, the occasional fragmentation of syntax, the reliance on quotation or allusion. In *One-Way Song,* though Lewis is not writing as a modernist; he employs a traditional verse form, normal syntax and a conversational or argumentative tone. On the face of it, Lewis was aiming at the directness of communication proper to satirical writings; in the concluding 'Envoi' he writes, 'I meant that you should get it, classical and clear', comparing his idiom to that of Dryden or Defoe. In fact, long stretches of the poem recall a man who seems to be engaged in direct, vigorous, hard-hitting discourse, but who nevertheless conveys little sense of what he really wants to say. Alan Munton, in his explanatory notes does his best to clear up difficulties, though he is himself sometimes reduced to guesswork. What his edition lacks, and what C. H. Sisson's brief introduction doesn't supply, is an adequate account of the context of *One-Way Song,* and of the elusive positives in Lewis's thought that underlay the sometimes muffled polemical swipes. I say 'muffled' advisedly; in his prose polemics, such as *Time and Western Man* or *The Diabolical Principle* or *Men Without Art* Lewis was not afraid to name names, and clearly to identify the persons or causes he objected to. In *One-Way Song* he seems anxious to cover his tracks, in a way that undercuts the satirical directness. Old hobby-horses are ridden hard, too. There is a fairly impenetrable attack on Einstein and Relativity, continuing a preoccupation from *Time and Western Man.* Mr Munton does his best to explicate this passage, quoting at length an article by two other Lewis scholars, but I wasn't all that enlightened.

Another cause of difficulty in *One-Way Song* is Lewis's use of personae, whose relation to his own voice and opinions is problematical. Even when he seems to be speaking *in propria persona,* Lewis's heavily ironical or sarcastic tone can lead to a self-defeating obliquity. There is an interesting instance in the section called 'The Song of the Militant Romance', a lively sequence of fourteeners, which Lewis describes in the 'Envoi' in this way:

> Song Two was a sketch of a critical cake-walk.
> The romantic standpoint (a good standpoint too).

In an earlier draft of the 'Envoi' quoted in the notes these lines read:

> Song Number Two was a sketch of a critical cakewalk—
> The romantic standpoint, its programme in prosody,
> Melpomene brought to bed.

Why, I wonder, did Lewis find it necessary to insert the prudent parenthetical observation, 'a good standpoint too'? It runs completely counter to the emphatically 'classical' stance of his prose polemics of the late twenties and early thirties. Did he really mean it? 'The Song of the Militant Romance' seems to me to be an exposure of the kind of modernist subjectivism and fragmentation of form that we know Lewis disliked, though spoken by a persona who approves of those things. Alan Munton in his notes on this section takes his clue from that odd phrase 'a good standpoint too' and argues that Lewis really approved of the persona's opinions:

> Originally entitled 'The *Duc de Joyeaux* Sings', a punning reference to Joyce, who is clearly represented in the drawings of the same title; the correct name is Duc de Joyeuse. Despite 'Romance' in the title, this section represents a Lewisian persona approving the non-classical outlook, and defending the aggression and disturbance to consecutive thought and to syntax required by true satire. Lewis did not reject all 'romantic' attitudes: see 'Envoi'.

I am not convinced by this. Joyce is certainly present in the section, and we know from *Time and Western Man* that Lewis was no great admirer of Joyce's later work. The section ends with the lines:

> I sabotage the sentence! With me is the naked word.
> I spike the verb—all parts of speech are pushed over
> on their backs.
> I am the master of all that is half-uttered and
> imperfectly heard.
> Return with me where I am crying out with the gorilla and
> the bird!

I have always assumed, taking the point from earlier commentators on Lewis, that Lewis is here satirically attacking the avant-garde journal, *transition,* which advocated a Revolution of the Word, and in particular Joyce's *Work in Progress,* as it then was, which featured prominently in *transition.*

These contradictions are, I think, characteristic of *One-Way Song,* where an apparent outspokenness co-exists with considerable obliquity and indirectness. It is not at all easy to get any sense of implied audience from the poem; and satirical verse needs to know whom it is written for and trying to persuade. Lewis's problem, as the self-proclaimed Enemy, may have been that he felt he didn't need an audience, or needed at best a very small one. So the poem suggests the curious and indeed rather sad spectacle of a man talking eloquently and vigorously, but talking to himself. *Paradise Lost* was once described as 'a monument to dead ideas', and after forty-six years *One-Way Song* might be described in the same way; or, more precisely, as a monument to dead arguments.

Lewis called *One-Way Song* satiric verse rather than poetry, though at the highest levels verse satire *is* poetry, as in Dryden or Pope or Johnson. Lewis came much closer to poetry in the other principal work in this volume, *Enemy of the Stars,* which appears in two versions; the first, published in *Blast* in 1914, and the second, considerably expanded, published as a separate book in 1932. *Enemy of the Stars* was supposed to be a play, but the earlier version made only the most perfunctory attempt at dramatic form and could never be acted, though something interesting might have been done with it by employing the techniques of the expressionist cinema. In fact, in the list of his early writings published in *Enemy News* No. 10, Lewis described the first *Enemy of the Stars* as a prose-poem, which is an appropriate way of thinking of it. It presents a genuinely modernist prose, vivid and sharply realized, which at the same time thwarts any easy movement from the signifier to the signified:

> His eyes woke first, shaken by rough moonbeams. A white crude volume of brutal light blazed over him. Immense bleak electric advertisement of God, it crushed with wild emptiness of stress.

> The ice field of the sky swept and crashed silently. Blowing wild organism into the hard splendid clouds, some will cast its glare, as well, over him.
>
> The canal ran in one direction, his blood, weakly, in the opposite.
>
> The stars shone madly in the archaic blank wilderness of the universe, machines of prey.
>
> Mastodons, placid in electric atmosphere, white rivers of power. They stood in eternal black sunlight.
>
> Tigers are beautiful imperfect brutes.
>
> Throats iron eternities, drinking heavy radiance, limbs towers of blatant light, the stars poised, immensely distant, with their metal sides, pantheistic machines.

No one else was writing prose quite like that in England in 1914, and it shows Lewis's profound early originality as a writer. Incidentally, the generous spacing of the text as printed in *Blast* makes it easier to read as poetry than in Mr Munton's edition. The symbolist, self-referential quality of the first *Enemy of the Stars* deflects questions as to what it is 'about', though Lewis's two characters, Arghol and Hanp, evidently reflect a version of the archetypal opposition between master and servant, Don Quixote and Sancho Panza in early modernist guise, and with a homicidal ending. The second version preserves the striking prose passages of the 1914 text, but has been expanded in the direction of greater realism and looks more like a play, with recognizable dialogue, though it would still be hard to put on the stage. The dialogue is argumentative rather than strictly dramatic, in the manner of what I regard as the tedious interchanges in *The Childermass*. By the early thirties Lewis had become polemical and discursive, and in the later version of *Enemy of the Stars* Arghol is made a spokesman for Lewis's ideas about art as the manifestation of the Not-Self, first put forward in an essay of 1925, 'The Physics of the Not-Self', published as an appendix to the 1932 text and reprinted in Mr Munton's edition. Here, as elsewhere in Lewis's work, a paradox obtrudes; he disliked romantic subjectivism and the cult of the self, but he was an intensely self-centred writer, with a broad streak of the romantic egoist about him, and he had distinctly *fin de siècle* notions about the nature of the artist.

It is a convenience to have these works by Lewis brought together in a single volume. They are minor, marginal texts, interesting and provocative in places, but not likely to change very much anyone's sense of the comparative strengths and weaknesses of Lewis as a literary artist.

1979

III

Self Condemned was first published in 1954, three years before Wyndham Lewis's death. He had been writing fiction all his life, in addition to painting, drawing, and turning out satirical or angry polemics on art and politics. By 1954 he had become blind, and his career as an artist was at an end. But his energy of mind was undiminished and he continued to write, completing the strange fantasia, *The Human Age*, which he had begun in the 1920s, and producing *Self Condemned.* A reader knowing nothing about Lewis would find it a compelling and powerful novel; but it gains considerably when one knows something of his earlier career, for the book dramatically repudiates many of his previous attitudes to art and life.

The central figure of *Self Condemned,* Professor René Harding, sees the world much as Lewis did in the 1930s and undergoes similar experiences in the Second World War. There is a substantial element of autobiography in the novel, transmuted into art, certainly, but still conveying a sense of personal pressure and involvement.

The novel opens in the summer of 1939 when Professor Harding, an historian of some eminence, has just resigned from his chair at London University. His resignation is prompted by a strong but obscure motive of principle; he no longer believes in either his subject or the way he has to teach it. The resignation, in fact, seems not much more than a plot device. Harding is cutting loose from the English academic and social establishment; and, being convinced that the coming war will destroy civilisation, he wants no part in the war or in the life of the country whose official stupidities, he believes, have brought it about.

Harding and his wife Hester sail for Canada on the day before Britain declares war on Germany, here following precisely the events of Lewis's own life. In the novel, Harding is half-French by birth, just as Lewis was half-American, and he takes a cold, detached view of English society and culture.

The middle section of the novel describes the appalling life that Harding lives in wartime Canada—though admittedly 'self condemned' to it. He and his wife spend most of their days in a large room in a seedy hotel in the dreary provincial city of Momaco. They are marooned by their material poverty—exchange control regulations prevent Harding getting any money from Britain—and by the harsh Canadian winters, which seem to be never ending. The hotel is staffed by criminals or drunkards, and many of the occupants are prostitutes and their clients; the account of these figures provides good occasions for Lewis's energetic comic prose.

The Hardings' incarceration corresponds quite closely to the experiences of Lewis and his wife in Toronto in the early 1940s. Yet the novel is more than mere fictionalized autobiography, for it has an actively metaphorical dimension. The hotel, with its constant comings and goings, its large transient population of wartime travellers, many of them soldiers, is presented as the microcosm of the world at war. Eventually, on a night of sub-zero temperatures, it catches fire. Harding and his wife escape and observe the latter stages of the fire from outside.

The firemen direct water at the fire and after much difficulty put it out; as they do so the water freezes all over the gutted building and encloses it in a shell of ice which will stay in place until the spring thaw. This, too, was based on something that Lewis himself experienced in Toronto, and the whole episode is magnificently described. The frozen shell of the hotel remains as a potent symbol for a kind of death-in-life.

René Harding lives in a world of thought, resenting the body and its demands. He is, in fact, a complete Cartesian dualist; he bears Descartes' Christian name and early in the novel his appearance is compared to that of the French philosopher. Such dualism was characteristic of Lewis's thought before the Second World War. And like Lewis, Harding despises the common herd of humanity, which he sees as inveterately stupid. He even despises the attractive, loving Hester for what he regards as her characteristically feminine dim-wittedness, though he acknowledges and resents his sexual need of her. In Lewis's fiction and polemics of the 1920s and 1930s these anti-democratic and mysogynistic attitudes would have been assumed to be self-evidently right. In *Self Condemned*, from the beginning, they are presented with a degree of irony directed at Harding; the reader is not expected to endorse them without question.

After the hotel fire Harding's fortunes improve; he becomes a quite well-paid newspaper columnist and then professor of history at the local university. He is prepared to continue his public career in Canada. This so disturbs his wife, who up to now has been totally subservient to all Harding's wishes, that she commits suicide; she loathes Canada and cannot bear to live there any longer. The exploration of Harding's state of mind after this disaster, in the final stages of the book, is masterly, and it is quite unlike anything in Lewis's earlier fiction. Harding takes on some of the stature of a ruined tragic hero, but his ultimate condition is more pathetic than heroic. On the last page the shattered Harding is about to move to a new and better post in an American university, but he is described as a 'glacial shell' of a man.

The echo of the frozen, gutted hotel is deliberate; but the word 'shell' resonates from the whole of Lewis's career (indeed the final chapter is called 'The Cemetery of Shells'). He had once preferred shells and carapaces to the bodies and messy guts of living beings; such renderings were familiar in his painting as well as in his writing. He favoured the hard outsides of things rather than their soft insides, metaphorically as well as literally. His once celebrated polemical book of 1927, *Time and Western Man,* develops a series of related oppositions: the eye is to be preferred to the ear, painting and sculpture to music, light to darkness, shells to vital organs. As Rowland Smith of Dalhousie University points out in the useful 'Afterword' to the new edition of *Self-Condemned,* in this novel Lewis for the first time came to explore interiority. The exterior world and his previous view of humanity as comic or absurd puppets were found to be insufficient; human beings also had interiors, psychologically and spiritually as well as physically.

Given Lewis's contempt for music it may be ironic to describe *Self Condemned* as having something of the structure and forward surge of the large-scale nineteenth-century symphony, but it falls naturally into symphonic movements: London, threatened by war, before the Hardings' departure; the long, dismal imprisonment in the hotel room; then the revival of René's fortunes after the fire and Hester's collapse into despair. It belongs, too, in nineteenth-century literary tradition. René Harding is not a novel-reader, but when he is crossing the Atlantic he starts to read *Middlemarch,* which a friend has urged on him. He tries it for a while but eventually throws the book overboard in disgust: 'This sodden satire, this lifeless realism, provoked him into saying, "Why am I reading this dull nonsense?" '

Lewis is directing a further irony at Harding here, for *Self Condemned,* though not particularly like *Middlemarch,* is also a work of mainstream fictional realism, concerned with the painful process of moral exploration and self-discovery. To this extent it is a relatively conservative work; the prose, though always clear and energetic, lacks the peculiar sharpness and originality of Lewis's early and provocatively avant-garde fiction, such as *Tarr* and *The Wild Body,* which was imbued with the spirit of the dualist and the puppet-master. But taken on its own terms *Self Condemned* is one of the outstanding achievements of post-war English fiction and it is good to have it available again.

1983

NOTE

1. Jameson subsequently pursued this concept at some length in *The Political Unconscious* (London, 1981).

5

Ezra Pound: from imagism to Fascism

In death, as in life, Ezra Pound is caught up in the events of contemporary history. In the wake of Watergate, Elliot Richardson, when Attorney General of the United States, made available under the Freedom of Information Act the FBI files relating to the arrest and indictment of Pound in 1945. This new material gives a particular value to C. David Heymann's book, *Ezra Pound: The Last Rower*, which otherwise follows closely, and frequently acknowledges, the earlier biographies by Charles Norman and Noel Stock.[1] He also completes the story of Pound's life; his final chapter describes his two meetings with Pound in Venice, not long before the poet's death in 1972. Pound's career up to 1939 is familiar enough, and Mr Heymann disposes of it rapidly and selectively in his first eighty pages, though in doing so he throws out some remarks that I find surprising. One of them is to the effect that *Homage to Sextus Propertius* and *Hugh Selwyn Mauberley* 'demonstrate to a greater extent than any of his other work the influence of Eliot'. It may be so, but the general critical assumption is that at that time the influence was running the other way. Another is his remark in passing that Rapallo, where Pound lived from 1925, was 'the seaside hamlet described in "Ode on a Grecian Urn" by Keats'.

In the spring of 1939 Pound returned to America for the first time in nearly thirty years. His mission as he saw it was to avert the coming war, or at least to keep America out of it, by exposing the machinations of bankers and munition-makers, and to urge monetary reform on his fellow countrymen. He did not want to make America Fascist, but he believed that Mussolini was animated by the same principles as Jefferson. He talked to congressmen and other political leaders, was heard sympathetically by those who, like Pound, hated Roosevelt, but found no real encouragement or understanding. His old literary friends like William Carlos Williams were dismayed by Pound's monomaniac tendencies and his defiant pro-fascism and anti-Semitism. After two months he went back to Italy in an embittered and baffled state of mind, with nothing accomplished and the war drawing ever closer. When he next came to the United States it would be under armed escort, to stand trial for treason. Later, mythologizing this visit of 1939, like so much of his past, Pound saw it as a descent into Hades. (Pound's self-image as Odysseus or the Seafarer explains the rather cryptic title of Mr Heymann's book, taken from Cocteau's description of Pound as 'un rameur sur le fleuve des morts'. But it is the Ulysses of Dante and Tennyson, rather than the Odysseus of Homer.)

Pound began his broadcasts from Rome Radio in 1941. Before America entered the war they could be regarded as no more than an indiscretion; afterwards they were legally acts of treason, even though Pound believed that the treason lay not in Rapallo but in the White House. One biographical question still in dispute is whether or not Pound tried to return to America after the declaration of war in December 1941. One version, for which there is some evidence, is that Pound tried to join the last diplomatic train taking American citizens from Rome to Lisbon, but was refused permission by a consular official. If so, he had no alternative but to stay in Italy. On the other hand, the State Department certainly wanted him back; in July 1941, his passport had been restricted for immediate return to the United States only. Mr Heymann quoted a State Department memorandum dated June 1942, which states that Pound 'refused to return home'. He records, too, that Pound is said to have made himself very obnoxious to the American consulate in Genoa by abusing the United States government on its premises and giving the Fascist salute when entering and leaving; as a result an irate American official might have refused Pound the necessary permission to return home. Another possibility noted by Mr Heymann is that the consulate would not renew the passport of Pound's daughter, Mary, which had expired, and that Pound and his wife would not leave without her. One wonders what would have happened to Pound if he had managed to get aboard that train and return home. As a prominent and vociferous supporter of the enemy he might well have been incarcerated or subject to some form of restraint, three years before the prison camp at Pisa and St Elizabeth's Hospital, Washington.

Mr Heymann's account of the remainder of Pound's wartime life in Italy, drawing on unpublished letters and documents in the FBI files and recent Italian research, makes absorbing but melancholy reading. In the face of the evidence it will no longer be possible to play down Pound's political beliefs by saying that he mistakenly thought Mussolini was a great man and the Italian Fascists were putting into effect his favoured monetary ideas, but that he was in no way a real Fascist. In fact, as Mr Heymann shows, Pound's commitment both to Fascism and the Axis cause was total. He admired Hitler as well as Mussolini; in 1940 he wrote 'Heil Hitler' as the salutation in a letter, and in 1941 he observed, 'Mussolini and Hitler follow through magnificent intuition the doctrines of Confucius'. This was in one of the ninety articles that he contributed to a Fascist newspaper called *Il Meridiano di Roma* between 1939 and 1943. And Mr Heymann remarks of the Rome Radio broadcasts that Pound's propagandist line 'was more often Nazi than Fascist'. Like the Nazis, Pound insisted that Roosevelt was a Jew, referring to him as 'Jewsfeldt' and 'stinkie Roosenstein'. In his broadcasts, as Mr Heymann puts it, 'he spoke of "Jewspapers and worse than Jewspapers", of "Franklin Finkelstein Roosevelt", of "kikes, sheenies, and the oily people". He noted that history had been "keenly analysed" in *Mein Kampf* and recommended for reading purposes the forged *Protocols of the Elders of Zion*." All this at a time when Hitler's Final Solution was moving into its major phase.

When Mussolini was overthrown in July 1943 and the war was clearly lost for Italy most Fascists jumped off the bandwagon; the institutions of Italian Fascism collapsed like a house of cards. But Pound remained loyal. In September he made his way north from Rome to visit his daughter in the Tyrol. He then returned to Rapallo via Lake Garda, where at the small town of Salò, Mussolini, after his rescue by the Germans, had set up a new Fascist Republic with a group of diehard followers. Pound made contact with the functionaries of this regime and became one of its most committed supporters, even though he was unable to meet Mussolini, whom he had so passionately admired ever since their one interview in 1933. The Salò Republic was no more than a German puppet, whose authority, such as it was, extended only over a limited part of northern Italy, which was increasingly disrupted by civil war between partisans and Fascists. Yet for Pound that last apocalyptic phase of Hitler's Europe was a period of hope and excitement. He took completely at face value the claims of the Salò Republic to be establishing a new and purified form of socialistic Fascism, and approved of the programme adopted by the Republican Fascist Party at Verona in November 1943. Pound continued to believe, despite everything, in an Axis victory. The Salò Republic became, and remained, one of the utopias, the Good Places, in his scheme of things. He referred to it thus in the *Pisan Cantos:*

> and the water flowing away from that side of the lake
> is silent as never at Sirmio under the arches
> Foresteria, Salò, Gardone to dream the Republic.

And in the *Pisan Cantos*, in *Rock-Drill* and *Thrones* there are brief recurring allusions to the Verona Programme.

In Rapallo, Pound picked up as far as he could the threads of his earlier wartime life. He contributed copiously to the new journals and newspapers of the Fascist Republic and in December 1943, broadcast from the German-controlled station at Milan, concluding with the words, 'every human being who is not a hopeless idiotic worm should realize that fascism is superior in every way to Russian Jewocracy and that capitalism stinks'. He did not broadcast in person again, but he regularly wrote scripts for Milan Radio until the end of the war. And he sent frequent letters of advice and admonition to the government at Salò, some of which are included in an appendix to Mr Heymann's book.

Mr Heymann provides a very adequate answer to the question I recently raised in the *TLS* about the nature and whereabouts of Cantos 72 and 73, still missing from the new edition. Pound wrote these two Cantos in 1944 and sent copies to Mussolini. Mr Heymann says of them:

> With the war as *mise en scene*, the two cantos salute a swarm of Ezra's Fascist friends: Manlio Dazzi, F. T. Marinetti, Gioacchino Nicoletti, Ubaldo degli Uberti. . . . Dante, or a version of Dante, speaks in Canto 72; and 73 is given over to Cavalcanti, to what he sees and hears in Italy in 1942-43.

After so long, and with so much other evidence available of Pound's commitment to Fascism, there can be no excuse for not publishing these Cantos as soon as possible.

The rest of the story is generally known. In May 1945 Pound gave himself up to the American army in Rapallo, was arrested as a war criminal and imprisoned in conditions of extreme and inhumane privation. There, turning over forty years' memories, he wrote the *Pisan Cantos* which include, in flashes, some of the finest lyrical poetry of our age. At the end of 1945 Pound was returned to America; he was judged to be insane and so unable to stand trial for treason. Then followed the thirteen years of cruelly and needlessly protracted confinement at St Elizabeth's Hospital until, in 1958, he was released and returned to Italy.

Pound was, without doubt, a dedicated if eccentric supporter of Fascism, and remained so, with perverse courage and integrity, until the very end of the Second World War. It would be aggreeable to conclude that Pound finally abandoned his convictions, once the war was over, and, in the prison-cage at Pisa, underwent the crisis and self-encounter that produced the *Pisan Cantos*. Indeed, when Pound wrote in that work, 'Pull down the vanity', and,

> Tard, très tard je t'ai connue, la Tristesse,
> I have been hard as youth sixty years

it seemed that he was abandoning former fanaticisms and accepting a late, hard-won maturity and humanity.

The truth, though, is less simple and less comforting. Pound did, in fact, maintain his former allegiances, as we see from affectionate references in the later Cantos to Mussolini and the Salò Republic. And he certainly remained anti-Semitic. Charles Olson, who was a profound admirer of Pound's art and one of his earliest visitors at St Elizabeth's, stopped coming because he was unable to take Pound's anti-Semitic remarks. The delicately lyrical texture of Canto 91, in the *Rock-Drill* sequence, is brutally broken by lines such as 'Democracies electing their sewage', 'a dung flow from 1913' and 'in this, their kikery functioned, Marx, Freud and the American beaneries'. Violent clashes between sensitivity and crudity of feeling are a recurring feature of the *Cantos,* and nowhere more disturbingly than here. In the last

Cantos, the *Drafts and Fragments*, which mark the abandonment, not the conclusion, of the entire work, Pound expressed the troubled sentiments of his old age with a new directness and refinement. The accents are close to those of Lear:

> But the beauty is not the madness
> Tho' my errors and wrecks lie about me.
> And I am not a demigod,
> I cannot make it cohere.
> If love be not in the house there is nothing.

The errors, alas, continued for a while. Back in Italy, Pound picked up with his old friends, many of whom were still unrepentant Fascists; in 1961, in Rome, he was photographed at the head of a May Day parade of 500 goose-stepping members of the neo-Fascist Movimento Sociale Italiano. As he grew older Pound sank into long periods of almost unbroken silence, and when he spoke he tended to dismiss his own writings, thereby disconcerting his admirers. In 1967 he told Allen Ginsberg: 'The worst mistake I made was that stupid, suburban prejudice of anti-Semitism. All along, that spoiled everything.' This, however late, was well said, even though it understated the offence: there was nothing 'suburban' about Auschwitz or Treblinka.

Mr Heymann sets the record down plainly, presenting sources for his assertions, and without extended comment, even though it is evident that he found parts of his task painful. If one welcomes his work it is not in a spirit of vindictiveness or witch-hunting, but simply because the truth needs to be told. For the past thirty years that record has been obscured, partly because the material was not available, and partly because of the obfuscations of the Poundians, for many of whom Pound has to be right, all the time, about everything. If pressed, Pound's admirers would probably plead madness as a defence for the worst of his ideological excesses (some, in fact, remain discreetly pro-Fascist to this day and would not admit the need of any defence).

In any ordinary sense of the word Pound no doubt was mad. As long ago as 1934, when he was bombarding Ciano and Mussolini with letters about monetary reform, an Italian government official annotated one of them: 'One thing that is clear is that the author is mentally unbalanced.' In 1941, when Pound began broadcasting from Rome, another official who had met and talked to him noted: 'There is no doubt in my mind that Ezra Pound is insane!' though acknowledging that 'he is a pleasant enough madman'. This, too, was the judgement of the American jury which found Pound unfit to stand trial, and one which he himself seems to have agreed with in old age. Setting aside the venerable romanticism that identifies the poet and the madman, one then has to ask: can a madman be a great poet? Donald Davie confronted this question in *Ezra Pound: Poet as Sculptor*, his first book on Pound, and argued that *Thrones* had something in common with Christopher Smart's *Rejoice in the Lamb* which 'though plainly the product of a mind unhinged, is none the less a work of genius and somehow a great poem'.

Other writers on Pound have been less cautious. William Cookson, for instance, writing in the summer 1976 *Agenda*, describes the *Cantos* as 'the greatest single poetic achievement of the century', surpassed in freshness and rhythmic energy only by Homer, Dante, Chaucer and Shakespeare. One of the striking things about Pound is the extent to which his personal magnetism and didactic persuasiveness have compelled uncritical discipleship.

This is particularly noticeable in America, where so many younger writers, often Jews and left-wingers, hold him in veneration. This literary admiration shades into the heavy academic explications of the Pound industry: in a poem as long as the *Cantos*, full of fragmentary but recurring references, cultural and historical, there is enough to keep the work of exegesis and scholarship going for ever.

But there is a striking lack of actual literary criticism. Greatness is assumed before the exegesis, not presumed at the end of it: what seems chaotic is shown to be coherent, what is arbitrary becomes deliberate, and what looks like improvisation is really part of a grand if subtle unity, where every word and image and reference has its place. There has also been uncontrolled abuse of Pound, notably from Robert Graves and Robert Conquest, but very little responsible criticism, which takes the work seriously but is prepared to ask awkward questions. This is in marked contrast to the treatment of Pound's old friend and collaborator, Eliot, who has been the object of some very sharp critical attention in the past twenty years or so. This means that *The Waste Land* is still argued about, in a way that the *Cantos* are not.

In other than literary matters, Eliot has been more severely treated than Pound. Some readers genuinely find Eliot's conservatism more offensive than Pound's Fascism. And Eliot has been often attacked for his anti-Semitism, which, though not defensible, did not involve more than a few expressions of supercilious distaste for Jews, whereas Pound has been quickly forgiven for his fanatical diatribes against 'kikes and kikery'. These matters are presumably part of American cultural politics, in which Eliot was never forgiven for selling out to Europe, whereas Pound was accepted as a true if wayward heir of Whitman, coming on with a new American epic.

One critic who has tried to come to terms with Pound without abnegating the critical function, and without too much special pleading, is the Englishman Donald Davie. In his two books on Pound he has taken note of the 'errors and wrecks', has made frequent limiting judgements, and rejected what he finds unacceptable as literature or ideology. Yet in both books a warm admiration for Pound emerges, despite all the qualifications; Davie, too, cannot but respond to the Poundian magnetism. Very significantly, his recent Modern Masters volume, *Pound*, contains successive chapters headed 'Ideas in the Cantos', and 'Rhythm in the Cantos', thereby separating what Pound would have thought of as indivisible. Pound, it is well known, did not want his readers 'to get through hell in a hurry': the ideas were part of the poetry, and they had to be taken together. But what if the ideas were mad or vicious? I must remark in passing that I am not equipped to say whether Pound's economic ideas make sense or not; in Canto 45, 'With Usura', they were expressed in exquisite poetry, whose beauty is not affected by the validity or otherwise of the ideas. But in other Cantos, and in his prose, these ideas seem extraordinarily crude, projecting a narrow economic determinism every bit as reductive as vulgar Marxism.

Apart from a fanatic fringe, Pound's admirers now praise him, like Davie, for his rhythms rather than his ideas. Pound's rhythm, which Davie analyses very well in his Modern Masters book is indeed fascinating, of unparalleled delicacy and fineness, so that dipping into the *Cantos* is often a rewarding experience, however obscure or rebarbative the material. It was Pound's great achievement to devise a metric which was equally effective for lyricism or argument (and to which even quoted documents could be made to adhere), and broke decisively with the dominance of the English pentameter line. He has, indeed, an angelic poetic ear.

It is this aspect above all of Pound's art that has appealed to poets like Davie and Olson and Ginsberg, and which has been so influential in recent American poetry. But one needs to ask what the rhythms do, what meanings they carry, what sense of man and the world they convey. Pound can readily be granted the ancient and honorific title of a 'poet's poet'. But although high praise this is not the finest thing one says about a poet; the greatest are not only teachers to their fellow practitioners but men speaking to men. This is true of the two masters who owed so much to Pound: Yeats, whose ideas were quite as strange as his; and Eliot, whose poetic personality was narrower and less generous, and who has never attracted a comparable devotion. They are, however, read and reread by many who are neither poets nor scholars.

Pound's rhythms are indeed admirable, if not very imitable. But his syntax is surely another matter, a restriction rather than a proper exploration of the resources of language. I am thinking of his excessive reliance on parataxis in the *Cantos* and his curious distaste for the copula, perhaps derived from Fenollosa; Pound has, in fact, tried to write English like Chinese, or his idea of Chinese. As a result, it seems to me, the rhythms move beautifully, but the syntax hardly moves at all. This is, of course an over-simplification, perhaps a crude one, but it points to a question that a truly attentive criticism of the *Cantos* would need to consider. Donald Davie is certainly aware of it, as one would expect from the author of *Articulate Energy*. Back in 1952, when he admired Pound less than he now does, he complained in *Purity of Diction in English Verse* that Pound 'pins his faith on individual words, grunts, broken phrases, half-uttered exclamations (as we find them in the *Cantos*), on speech atomized, all syllogistic and syntactical forms broken down', adding that 'the development from imagism in poetry to fascism in politics is clear and unbroken'. Davie still worries about this problem; in his Modern Masters *Pound* he concludes that it would be 'equally honourable' either to accept or to reject Pound's departures from syntactic order.

The complete *Cantos* contain much that is beautiful as well as much that is ugly or tedious. And the beauty persisted in a flickering but pure light until the very end:

> A blown husk that is finished
>   but the light sings eternal
> a pale flare over marshes
>   where the salt hay whispers to tide's change.

But the *Cantos* are also a monument to Pound's wilfulness in combining the compression of the imagistic or ideogrammatic mode with the expansions and repetitions of the epic. For the Poundians the combination is triumphantly successful; for the rest of us it is contradictory. In 1921, after he had turned *The Waste Land* from a collection of fragments into a poem, Pound told Eliot: 'The thing now runs from "April ..." to "shantih" without a break. That is 19 pages, and let us say the longest poem in the Englisch langwidge. Don't try to bust all records by prolonging it three pages further.' There are implications here that escaped the author of the *Cantos* in 800 pages.

1976

NOTE

1. William M. Chace has argued convincingly that Heymann's book is excessively dependent on other authorities, and that its scholarship is generally suspect. See his review in *Contemporary Literature*, Autumn 1976, and Heymann's reply in the Summer 1977 issue.

6

Pound and Donald Davie

Ezra Pound has been a recurring presence in Donald Davie's writing for some thirty years. He is mentioned at the beginning of the first essay, 'The Spoken Word', dated 1950, in Davie's *The Poet in the Imaginary Museum: Essays of Two Decades* (1977); since then there have been many essays and reviews on Pound, and two books, *Ezra Pound: Poet as Sculptor* (1964), and *Pound* (1975), in the Fontana Modern Masters series. And passing references to Pound often occur in his criticism. Pound is clearly important for Davie, in ways that make him much more than an object of professional academic interest. The nature of Davie's feelings about Pound is indicated in a footnote in *The Poet in the Imaginary Museum*, attached to a review-article on F. R. Leavis's *'Anna Karenina' and Other Essays*, first published in 1967. In the article Davie agreed with Leavis that Pound had no real understanding of culture and tradition, but in the footnote of 1977 he retracted this judgement: 'it is clear that when I wrote this, I was in a mood of exasperated impatience with Ezra Pound. (I know this mood very well; it alternates with another in which I revere Pound as highly as any writer of the twentieth century.)'[1] Davie has changed his mind about Pound on other occasions. In 1961, in the *Pelican Guide to English Literature*, he published an admiring essay on 'Hugh Selwyn Mauberley', reading it as a deliberate and coherent exercise in the handling of a persona. Three years later, in *Ezra Pound: Poet as Sculptor*, Davie remarked that he no longer believed that 'Mauberley' is a coherent poem; in 1975, in *Pound*, he was still more severe about it and referred to his commentary of 1961 as 'one which I now want to disown'. Nevertheless, he reprinted it in *The Poet in the Imaginary Museum*, with a footnote saying that, although he cannot accept his earlier interpretation of 'Mauberley', I'm glad and impenitent about having given it a new lease of life in print because on balance I think it still a great deal more right than wrong.'[2] The compass needle has pointed over the years in the general direction of Pound, but has often moved erratically round the dial, and on occasion it has swung right round and pointed in the opposite direction.

Davie's first sustained discussion of Pound occurs in *Purity of Diction in English Verse* (1952), and is predictably unfavourable, given the neo-classical premises of Davie's early criticism. He notes that Pound is more concerned with images than with syntax in poetry, and assumes that Pound's imagism is part of the symbolist aethetic,[3] an assumption vehemently reversed in his later criticism. Discussing a passage from *Guide to Kulchur* Davie writes of Pound:

> By hunting his own sort of 'definiteness' (truth only in the particular) he is led to put his trust not in human institutions but in individuals. Similarly he pins his faith in individual words, grunts, broken phrases, half-uttered exclamations (as we find them in the *Cantos*), on speech atomized, all syllogistic and syntactical forms broken down. His own esteem of the definite lands him at last in yawning vagueness, the 'intuitive' welcome to Mussolini (he 'plays his hunch'), or, elsewhere in *Guide to Kulchur*, the 'intuitive' perception of form as something over and above pigment, stone, chords, and notes, phrases, and words.
> It would be too much to say this is the logical end of abandoning prose syntax. But at least the development from imagism in poetry to fascism in politics is clear and unbroken.[4]

These cool dismissals represent the nadir of Davie's view of Pound. Had he persisted in them, it would have remained similar to Yvor Winters's. But thereafter his reading of Pound's work in general and the *Cantos* in particular became steadily more favourable. By the time he wrote the 1975 book, Davie had altogether accepted Pound's idea of form as existing apart from its particular embodiments in sensory phenomena. But the problems of Pound's political inclinations, and the asyntactical nature of the *Cantos*, continued to worry Davie. What is particularly striking in this extract from *Purity of Diction in English Verse* is the untroubled and sweeping assertion that the development from imagism to fascism is 'clear and unbroken'. Many readers would believe that it is nothing of the sort, and would require much more demonstration and evidence; here Davie is 'playing his hunch' suddenly leaping from a plausible argument to an extreme or even outrageous conclusion. Such rapid leaps or cutting of corners have always been a feature of Davie's criticism; they can be disconcerting or engaging, but, either way, they indicate the qualities that make him something other than a cautious academic commentator.

Elsewhere in *Purity of Diction* Davie compares the *Cantos* to *The Prelude* as a poem which is not enough of a 'made thing', and too much of an exploration of the poet's mind; in one sense, he concedes, the *Cantos*, in its formal complexity, is very much a 'made thing', but ultimately it is something other: 'it invites, as *The Prelude* does, the admiring reflection, "What an interesting mind he has"; not that older reaction, "What an interesting thing to say".' Davie was shortly to retreat from this dogmatic, rather jejune neo-classicism, and to change his mind about Wordsworth as well as Pound. But it was part of the climate of opinion of the early 1950s.[5]

Davie's second critical book, the admirable *Articulate Energy* (1955), developed hints about the nature and value of poetic syntax thrown out in *Purity of Diction*.[6] He is still critical of the *Cantos* for embodying faulty poetic principles, but is less dismissive. The *Cantos*, he says, are articulated by a syntax that is musical and rhythmical, not linguistic, and he describes the effect of the rhythm very well: 'not only the rhythm that rides through tempo and metre in the verse-paragraph, but also the rhythmical recurrence of ideas hinted at in one canto, picked up in another much later, suspended for many more, and so on.'[7] This now looks like a critical commonplace, a statement of the elementary procedure needed to read the *Cantos* at all; in 1955 it was less taken for granted. Davie is not, however, inclined to be easily persuaded by the *Cantos* as a musical analogue. He sees the frequent absence of linguistic syntax as a major disability and declares he has great difficulty in trusting to articulation by rhythm alone:

> For it is plain that the reader has to make a like act of faith before he can yield himself to the *Cantos* . . . the rhythm steps out alone and we must follow it in blind faith, with no metrical landmarks to assist us. Every reader must decide for himself whether he can make this act of faith. I confess for my part I cannot.[8]

This suggests the language of religious conversion rather than of literary criticism.

Articulate Energy, which stresses the importance of syntax in poetry, and above all the value of verbs as an energizing element, engages rationally and urbanely with Pound's theory and practice. Davie looks at one of Pound's major intellectual sources, Ernest Fenollosa's essay 'The Chinese written character as a medium for poetry', and makes the point that Pound took certain things from Fenollosa and ignored others. That is to say, Pound was excited by the Chinese ideogram as a model for imagistic precision and concreteness, but took no notice of Fenollosa's accompanying demonstration of the importance of verbs in Chinese syntax; Pound, says Davie, 'has shown himself far more interested in Fenollosa's observations on the structure of words than in what he says about the structure of sentences',[9] and attempts to substitute thinking by ideogram for thinking by sentences, leaving the work of syntax to be performed by rhythm alone. As a radical criticism of Pound's procedures this argument has always seemed to me convincing, but Davie's later writing on Pound is marked by a general reluctance to enforce it. In *Articulate Energy* Davie makes a fairly detailed comparison between Pound's poem 'The Gypsy' and Wordsworth's 'Stepping Westward', seeing the former as an example of what he still calls 'symbolist syntax' and the latter as an example of the traditional syntax of prose and ordinary speech. What Davie says is illuminating about both poems; but he is remarkably uncertain about his valuation of Pound's poem. He begins by saying, 'Wordsworth's poem is one I am very fond of; yet it is difficult to deny that Pound's is much superior'; a page later he acknowledges, 'if Pound's poem is better than Wordsworth's, it is not better because it is more "concrete" or because its syntax has become music'; after two more pages he concludes, 'When all is said and done, there is no way of deciding which is the better poem . . .'[10] The compass needle is veering wildly, but it would be superficial to complain that Davie cannot make up his mind. The uncertainty about 'The Gypsy' is a sign of the larger uncertainty Davie felt about Pound at that time, as a poet who transgressed many of his convictions about literature and life, but to whom nevertheless he was increasingly drawn.

On the evidence of *Articulate Energy*, Davie was still wrestling with his intellectual conscience and resisting the leap of faith. But another book published in the same year, 1955, suggested that he had already made it. D. J. Enright, who was teaching in Japan, edited an anthology, *Poets of the 1950s*, which was published in Tokyo by Kenkyusha. It was primarily intended for teachers and students of English in Japan, but the anthology is important in literary history as the first collection of Movement poetry, appearing a year before a similar anthology, *New Lines*, was published in England. Davie contributed a brief introduction to the selection of his poems in *Poets of the 1950's*, which began: 'I honour the poets, English, Irish and American, who revolutionized English poetry thirty years ago; and indeed it seems to me that one of those poets, Ezra Pound, has influenced me more deeply and more constantly than any other poet of the present century.'[11] It was, to say the least of it, a surprising announcement for readers who were familiar with the coolness of the comments on Pound in Davie's criticism. On the face of it, there was no direct influence by Pound on the rational, argumentative, formal, tightly syntactical verse that Davie was then writing. Davie's statement might be better understood as the act of faith itself, a surrender to Pound, disguised as the assertion of a long-standing allegiance.

Davie's subsequent commitment to Pound, though never abandoned, was not at all serene or untroubled; it might be described in Bishop Blougram's words as a life of faith diversified by doubt. In 1957 he was still trying to make his mind up about the *Cantos*. Reviewing *Rock-Drill* in March of that year he condluded, 'the great gamble continues. The method is being pressed to its logical conclusion. Either this is the waste of a prodigious talent, or else it is the poetry of the future.'[12] By July, in two broadcast talks with the title of 'The Poet in the Imaginary Museum', he was prepared to describe the *Cantos*, without reservation, as a great poem, though written in an international language.[13]

By about 1960 Davie had found sufficient reasons for admiring the *Cantos*, substantially if not unreservedly, which involved a distinct shift in his own critical attitudes. Henceforth Pound was to be no longer aligned with Eliot as an exponent of the symbolist aesthetic; he was concerned with things and sensory phenomena, whereas Eliot was concerned with words; imagism was not a development of symbolism but something in opposition to it; the *Cantos* no longer resembled music, but sculpture, and specifically sculpture as carving rather than sculpture as modelling. These oppositions were first outlined in 'Two Analogies for Poetry'[14] (1962), developed throughout *Ezra Pound: Poet as Scupltor*, and further enlarged on in 'Eliot and Pound: A Distinction'[15] (1970). They can be presented diagrammatically in this way, in an increasing order of generality:

Pound	:	Eliot
imagism	:	symbolism
painting, sculpture	:	music
carving	:	moulding
patient observation	:	objective correlative
things	:	words
externality	:	interiority

During the 1960s Davie became firmly committed to the qualities in the left-hand column, though the implied rejection of Eliot and what he stood for was strictly relative; Davie continued to admire him as a great poet and to defend him vigorously against the philistinism of people such as Malcolm Muggeridge.[16] But Pound, regarded, like Gautier before him, as *un homme pour qui le monde exterieur existe*, was preferred as poetic innovator and moral exemplar. Davie's earlier opposition to Pound's undermining of linguistic syntax in the *Cantos* was not retracted; it was simply ignored, though hints of it surfaced from time to time and Davie ultimately returned to the question in his *Pound* of 1975.

Davie's new view of Pound and his ensuing reading of the *Cantos* was based on two texts by Pound, published more than thirty years apart: *Gaudier-Brzeska: A Memoir*, first published in 1916, and reissued by the Marvell Press in 1960; and the *Pisan Cantos* of 1948. Pound's memoir of his friend, Henri Gaudier-Brzeska, the young French sculptor of genius who was killed in action in 1915, is a discursive work in which Pound reflects at large on art and literature. It is the principal product of his Vorticist phase of 1914-15, when he was closely associated with painters and sulptors, such as Gaudier himself, Wyndham Lewis and Edward Wadsworth. Under their influence Pound refined on the imagist concern to present the exact appearance of things. This concern, Davies argues, became dominant in the *Cantos*. It is true that there are passages in *Gaudier-Brzeska* that resemble extracts from an artist's sketch-book, translated into words:

> These new men have made me see form, have made me more conscious of the appearance of the sky where it juts down between houses, of the bright pattern of sunlight which the bath water throws up on the ceiling, of the great 'V's' of light that dart through the chinks over the curtain rings, all these are new chords, new keys of design.[17]

Gaudier aroused Pound's interest in the craft of stone-carving, which Pound applied to his own poetry, as he tried to present a clear, sharply defined image; Davie, in turn, developed it in his analogical view of Pound as 'poet as sculptor' who works to uncover the forms and appearances already latent in nature. And when Pound offers such perceptions as these, 'The pine-tree in mist upon the far hill looks like a fragment of Japanese armour. . . . The tree and the armour are beautiful because their diverse planes overlie in a certain manner',[18] Davie sees them as an early anticipation of the imbricated images of the late *Cantos*. From *Gaudier-Brzeska* Davie takes the idea of Pound as a keen observer of visual phenomena; in the *Pisan Cantos* he finds Pound working in a Ruskinesque tradition of precise, meticulous, disinterested perception of the natural order: the ant, the wasp, the lizard, respecting their creatureliness and otherness.

In *Ezra Pound: Poet as Sculptor* Davie discusses some celebrated and beautiful lines from Canto 83:

> and in the warmth after chill sunrise
> an infant, green as new grass,
> has stuck its head or tip
> out of Madame La Vespa's bottle
>
> mint springs up again
>   in spite of Jones' rodents
> as had the clover by the gorilla cage
>   with a four-leaf
>
> When the mind swings by a grass-blade
>   an ant's forefoot shall save you
> the clover leaf smells and tastes as its flower . . .

Neither Eliot nor Yeats possessed the sensibility that could write like this, Davie remarks. He makes an interesting and persuasive distinction between those writers who respect the natural world for being what it is, and those who incorporate it into their work as objective correlatives or symbols of their mental states:

> One is reminded rather of passages in Coleridge's and Ruskin's notebooks, in some of the letters of Keats, in the essays and poems of D. H. Lawrence, above all in the writings of Hopkins. In fact, what lies behind a passage such as this (and they occur throughout the *Cantos*, though seldom at such length) is an attitude of mind that is incompatible with the symbolist poet's liberation of himself from the laws of time and space as those operate in the observable world.[19]

Davie compares the sparrow that Keats describes in a famous letter, pecking about on the gravel, occupying a quite other realm than the human, with Shelley's skylark or Yeats's swan, birds that are transformed into emblems of human feelings and attitudes. Davie remarks of the baby wasp described in Canto 83, 'at no point does the wasp become a symbol for something in Pound's predicament, or for his ethical or other programmes, or for his personality.'[20]

This way of reading Pound is so elegantly and eloquently presented that I am reluctant to question it. Nevertheless, I have to say that I find it unconvincing. To make, first, a small but not trivial point; there is at least one place in the *Pisan Cantos* in which Pound does turn one of the natural creatures he observes into a potent symbol, vibrant with traditional Romantic feeling, of his own predicament:

> As a lone ant from a broken ant-hill
> from the wreckage of Europe, ego scriptor.
>
> (Canto 76)

In general one can agree with Davie that in the *Pisan Cantos* Pound does find solace, in the midst of the privations and humiliations of the summer of 1945, in loving, patient, disinterested observation of the small creatures around him in the prison camp, though the observation is never sustained for long, being constantly interwoven with Pound's memories, extending over many years, of other times and other places. Most readers do, I think, find this quality of observation of things actually present before the poet's eyes something new in the *Cantos*; just as the sense of personal self-discovery and humility in the midst of suffering is new; as Davie has recently written, 'the Pisan ordeal had shocked Pound into recovering a compassion and tenderness which we look for mostly in vain in the Pound of the years preceding.'[21] Both aspects of Pound's Pisan experience are linked by the concept of patience, understood with an etymological awareness of its origin in *pati*, to suffer. If I am right, and this quality of observation of natural things was new, then Davie is being disingenuous or misleading when he asserts parenthetically that similar passages to those describing ant and wasp occur throughout the earlier *Cantos*. One is entitled to ask where they occur; in fact, I would be inclined to regard them as conspicuous by their absence before the Pisan sequence. Similarly, I find little evidence in the earlier *Cantos* of the kinds of exact, painterly observations that Pound offered in *Gaudier-Brzeska*. There is, of course, a great deal of visual description in the *Cantos*, much of it exquisitely and poignantly beautiful, *phanopoeia*, in Pound's own terminology. But how much of it in fact arises from the poet trying hard to capture something that he has actually seen, as Hopkins, for instance, does in poems or notebook entries? Remarkably little, I would have thought. Pound's visual descriptions tend to arise from memories, from reading, from paintings, from whatever we mean by imagination, and to fuse aspects from some or all of these sources into visual images. These descriptions are intense but generalized:

> Wind over the olive trees, ranunculae ordered,
> By the clear edge of the rocks
> The water runs, and the wind scented with pine
> And with hay-fields under sun-swath.
>
> (Canto 20)

This is beautiful, but there is a lack of specificity about it, or of *haecceitas* in Hopkins's Scotist language. When Pound was writing the earlier *Cantos* he was an impatient man; he literally did not have the time or patience carefully to describe plants or rocks or cloud formations in the Ruskinesque tradition in which Hopkins wrote. One has to consider, too, that some of Pound's most haunting evocations are of places he had never seen: the

Chinese landscapes he had to create for himself from literature and art:

> Autumn moon; hills rise about lakes
> against sunset
> Evening is like a curtain of cloud,
> a blurr above ripples; and through it
> sharp long spikes of the cinnamon,
> a cold tune amid reeds.
>
> (Canto 49)

Davie took the notion of Pound as Ruskinesque observer of nature from the *Pisan Cantos*, where it undoubtedly exists, and projected it back on to the earlier *Cantos*, where I see little evidence of it. The comparable notion of poet-as-sculptor seems to me to have been projected forward from *Gaudier-Brzeska* on to the *Cantos*. Undoubtedly many of the local effects of imagery in the *Cantos* can suggest the sharpness of cut stone; but the nature of cut stone is to stay cut, whereas the essence of the *Cantos* is that they are metamorphic; things and images and percepts are constantly changing their identity. When Pound is describing Mediterranean sea and sky and light we are undoubtedly in the presence of a poet who could use his eyes wonderfully well; but what he sees is often transformed into aspects of classical myth, as in Canto 2, for instance; Ruskin or Hopkins would not have found this practice acceptable. Davie in his essay 'Two Analogies for Poetry' shows himself well aware that analogical descriptions have at best only limited value, even though critics have good reasons for using them. Poetry is patently closer to music than it is to sculpture, being an aural art that moves forward in time and to that extent the *Cantos* remain closer to music, as Davie suggested in *Articulate Energy*, than to sculpture. The *Cantos* are full of light, it is true, but it is as much an inner radiance as the actual blaze of the Mediterranean sun. Pound was a man who lived in the world of the senses; but he was equally *un homme pour qui le monde interieur existe*, and something of a neo-Platonist, as Davie subsequently acknowledged.[22] In *Ezra Pound: Poet as Sculptor* and the essays associated with it Davie draws a picture of Pound that is attractively coherent and morally appealing; but it leaves out too much to be plausible. Michael Alexander, in his excellent book on Pound has got the emphasis right, I think:

> Despite his frequently hearty tone, his interest in the natural object and the external world, his connoisserurship of the visual image, and his reformist attitudes to such practical issues as the nature of coin, credit and circulation, Pound's subject-matter is very often internal and symbolic. The arcane lies near the centre of his work.[23]

In the early 1960s Davie changed his mind about Pound in two important respects. The first of them was deciding that Pound was an imagist, not a symbolist. The second was to emphasize Pound as, essentially, a poet who spoke in his own voice, rather than a creator of personae. This change of emphasis is apparent in Davie's indecisions about 'Mauberley'. In his 1961 essay on that poem Davie follows other critics in making a distinction between 'E.P.' and 'H.S.M.', the poet and his persona. He assumes that Pound, like Yeats and Eliot, was given to the use of dramatic figures, 'personae' or 'masks', through which to distance feeling and achieve impersonality. Even so, he believes that Pound may at times be uncomfortably close to 'Mauberley' in feeling, just as Eliot is to Gerontion. Later Davie decided that the Mauberley-persona does not work at all and should be dismissed. 'Hugh Selwyn Mauberley' was best read as a sequence of poems undisguisedly by Pound himself. 'We have already found reasons for thinking that Pound's remarks about "personae" and "masks" are so many red herrings since his talent was not histrionic, like Yeats's, but rather took him towards speaking confessionally *in propria persona*.'[24] In a later essay Davie enlarged on this judgement:

> even in the heyday of the *persona* and of impersonality in poetry, there were poets writing who would not fit the doctrine and who came off badly in consequence. Ezra Pound, the very man who introduced the concept of *persona*, was one of those who came off badly. His *Pisan Cantos*, written late in his career, are confessional poems, and they have been esteemed by many who find all or most of the rest of Pound unreadable. Who shall say those readers are wrong?[25]

That last question is a disconcerting abandonment of critical direction on Davie's part. Nor is it clear what he means when he says that Pound 'came off badly' in his attempt to use the persona. Leaving aside the case of 'Hugh Selwyn Mauberley'—which we may agree is a less accomplished poem than it was once thought to be—we have to face the fact that in the earlier *Cantos*, particularly the first thirty, Pound consistently speaks through personae. His own voice is sometimes apparent, but it is a weaker and less commanding voice than that which comes from Malatesta or Confucius or the many other masks that Pound assumes. This is an aspect of the *Cantos* that Davie tends to ignore in *Ezra Pound: Poet as Sculptor*; his account of the Malatesta Cantos, which are superbly dramatic utterances, for all their incoherence, is perfunctory.

Wyndham Lewis's judgement, though deliberately exaggerated, seems to me essentially correct about the relation between poet and masks in the earlier Pound:

> *By himself* he would seem to have neither any convictions nor eyes in his head. There is nothing that he intuits well, certainly never originally. Yet when he can get into the skin of somebody else, of power and renown, a Propertius or an Arnaut Daniel, he becomes a lion or a lynx on the spot. This sort of parasitism is with him phenomenal.
>
> Again, when he writes in person, as Pound, his phrases are invariably stagey and false, as well as insignificant. There is the strangest air of insincerity about his least purely personal utterance: the ring of the superbest conviction when he is the mouthpiece of a scald or of a jongleur.[26]

Much later, when Pound wrote the *Pisan Cantos*, he did indeed speak with an authentic personal voice. In his discussion of Pound, Davie wants to take the *Pisan Cantos* as a norm; they contain the Pound he most admires, the patient, loving observer of nature, and the man speaking in direct, personal, even confessional tones. It is not evident how far he discovers this figure in the earlier *Cantos*, or whether he really believes it worth the attempt; or whether, in the last analysis, Davie would be prepared to give up all the pre-Pisan *Cantos*. (His attitude to the post-Pisan *Cantos* is still ambivalent, but more sympathetic, since there the personal voice is consistently heard.) His discussions of Pound in the 1960s suggest that he is prepared to place *Cantos* 1-71 in a space bounded on one side by *Gaudier-Brzeska*, an acknowledgement of the power of observation, and 'Hugh Selwyn Mauberley', a proto-confessional poem; and on the other by the *Pisan Cantos*, where both these aspects are manifest.

This is, of course, an over-simplification, but it makes explicit what is, I think, generally implicit. Davie has, in fact, by ignoring a lot of the evidence, projected, or invented, a version of Ezra Pound with whom he can feel a close affinity. His motives for doing so are deeply personal and not likely to be brought wholly into the light, though his own poetry may offer some clues.[33]

Ezra Pound: Poet as Sculptor distorts Pound in important ways, but is by no means lacking in judgement and discrimination. Like many other readers, Davie largely rejects the Cantos retailing American and Chinese history, partly because of the perversity of their method, partly because he regards the aim of including great tracts of history as insanely presumptuous: 'there is simply too much recorded history available for any one to offer to speak of it with such confidence as Pound does.'[27] Elsewhere he has referred to 'the variously cock-eyed or idiosyncratic readings of cultural history which in Pound lay waste whole areas of the Cantos';[28] in this respect, at least, Davie finds common ground between Pound, Eliot and Yeats, since all of them were given to faulty, mythologizing readings of history. In general, Davie plays down the historical dimension of the *Cantos;* he is, not surprisingly, more drawn to those aspects of the poem where Pound is orientated to geography and cartographical exactitude, which he discusses in an essay, 'The *Cantos:* towards a pedestrian reading'.[29] Davie's readiness in *Ezra Pound: Poet as Sculptor* to make limiting judgements on his subject has annoyed the ultra-Poundians, like, for instance, the editor of the 'Critical Heritage' volume on Pound who complained in his introduction that Davie's 'elegant but not particularly convincing book, is a sustained and occasionally bitter attack upon the intention behind the *Cantos*'.[30]

Davie's second book on Pound, the short 'Modern Masters' volume of 1975, is critically unsatisfactory and, in places, quite eccentric. It contains some useful observations, such as Davie's discussion of the large, overall rhythms of the *Cantos,* showing how verbal motifs recur at intervals; but they are offset by passages of coat-trailing irrelevance. Trying to make a case for the *Cantos* in a small compass, Davie becomes irresponsible. He discusses the poem via one of Pound's fundamental notions, the vortex or the cluster of energy, and uses the analogy of a sea traversed by waterspouts:

> As we start to read the *Cantos*, we float out upon a sea where we must be on the look-out for waterspouts. These, when they occur, are ideas, the only sort that this poem is going to give us. And meanwhile we can forget about such much debated non-questions as whether this poem has a structure, and if so, what it is: or again, why the poem isn't finished, and whether it ever could have been. Does a sea have a *structure*? Does a sea *finish* anywhere? The Mediterranean boils into and out of the Atlantic, past the Rock of Gibraltar.[31]

Here Davie is illegitimately making the analogy go much further than it should, and necessary questions are begged. In fact, what Davie dismisses as non-questions about the *Cantos* have continued to exercise him since 1975.

There are, however, some significant passages in this book. In one of them Davie returns to his early conviction of the importance of syntax in poetry, and faces the asyntactical nature of the *Cantos*. In *Ezra Pound: Poet as Sculptor* Davie had acknowledged that Pound, and Williams, Olson and Creeley after him, wrote a poetry 'of the noun rather than the verb'.[32] but the author of *Articulate Energy* forbore to comment further. In *Pound* Davie writes, apropos of certain of Pound's syntactical liberties,

> I am far from being unaware of the riskiness—not for the poet only, but for his culture—of playing thus fast and loose with the conventions that govern prosaic or spoken discourse. And everyone must detect the irony in the fact that the poet who came round to writing like this should have started from a conviction that poetry had to incorporate (and surpass) prosaic exactness. Just here, in fact, is a parting of the ways; either we suppose that our grasp on cultural order, as reflected in our language, is too insecure for such departures as this to be tolerated, let alone emulated; or else, we do not. For my part, a decision either way—given that the person deciding has recognized just what is at issue—is equally honourable.[33]

This is conspicuously inconclusive, but it represents the honest facing of a dilemma. As in other passages in which Davie writes of his personal commitment to Pound the language is close to that of religious conversion, or at least of major existential choice. At the end of *Pound* Davie acknowledges that for much of his life Pound had invented a public persona for himself: 'A mask worn for so long grows on the face beneath. And yet Pound in the end could throw it off; that is the meaning, surely, of the tersely self-disgusted recantations and disavowals of his last years, in moving verse as well as in conversation.'[34] Once more Davie responds to personal revelation by Pound; he is thinking of the late *Drafts and Fragments* of the *Cantos*. The *Pisan Cantos* had, indeed, been profoundly personal, but as Davie has remarked their most nakedly confessional lines had been distanced by being expressed in French: 'Tard, très tard je t'ai connue, la Tristesse. . . .'[35]

Davie's most recent essays on Pound, collected in *Trying to Explain* (1980), show that his interest is unabated and moving in new directions. Davie has written sceptically about the academic Pound industry, but he has not been able to avoid getting caught up in it, to the extent of contributing to *Paideuma* and lecturing to Pound conferences. He has lately been interesting himself in biographical aspects of Pound, and, in particular, Pound's dealings with English intellectual and literary life between 1908 and 1920, when he left England. Davie contrasts Pound's professionalism with English amateurism; he strongly approves of the former, but feels that there is a case to be made for the latter. He is struck by the absoluteness of Pound's severance of his ties with England, the country where for twelve years he seemed very much at home. The questions about English life and culture raised by Pound's departure over sixty years ago fascinate and trouble Davie, who is himself a voluntary expatriate. Davie's expatriation, however, unlike Pound's, has enhanced his preoccupation with England, evident in 'England', *The Shires* and *Thomas Hardy and British Poetry*.

Davie's latest critical writing on Pound has tended to undermine positions upheld in *Ezra Pound: Poet as Sculptor*. After having taken the imagist tenets as central to Pound's poetics, Davie now suspects that they may have been short-term tactics, even an aberration, in the course of a long-term commitment to melody and *cantabile* effect in poetry.[36] These subversive reflections are merely hints, thrown out in response to Pound's disconcerting admiration for archaic diction in others, as in Laurence Binyon's translation of Dante, and his own practice of it in passages of the *Cantos*. Davie's combination of restlessness and intellectual honesty causes him to probe away at critical positions once he has established them; more complacent critics would be willing to let well alone. But in Davie, as I have remarked, the compass needle rarely stays still. There is a particularly significant instance of it wavering in his essay 'Sicily in *The Cantos*'. This provides a scolarly discussion of the extent to which Pound's visits to Sicily between 1923 and 1925 are reflected in the *Cantos*. Davie draws a depressing conclusion from his investigation, for apart from a few lyrical lines from Canto 109 beginning 'Clear deep off Taormina', all the Sicilian references in the *Cantos* are, in Davie's words, verbal, notional, or ideological; when Pound was in Sicily, Davie sadly reflects, he seems to have moved around in that vivid landscape with his eyes closed, his ears and nostrils stopped. Yeats, who was with Pound in Sicily, appears to have used his eyes to good effect; as chairman of the Irish Senate Committee that commissioned Irish coinage, Yeats showed prospective designers photographs of Sicilian Greek coins as a model. 'Pound was to mock Yeats indulgently for seeing in Notre Dame not a physical presence in worked stone, but only a symbol; yet in Sicily Pound's seems to have been the mind that was *symbologizing*.'[37] Davie is here alluding to his earlier citation in *Ezra Pound: Poet as Sculptor* of Hugh Kenner's remark that 'Yeats's incorrigibly symbologizing mind infected much of his verse with significance imposed on materials by an effort of will.'[38] Davie continues:

> I do not like being forced to this conclusion. It pushes back, to a disconcertingly early period in Pound's life, the first signs of that aridity, that closing of the doors of perception, which — drastically arrested and reversed though it was, at Pisa and through the first years at St. Elizabeth's — reasserted itself and wreaked the desolation of *Thrones*.[39]

It is, indeed, a desperate conclusion, and one wonders how much of Davie's earlier writings about Pound would stand up in the light of it.

Davie is, I believe, the finest critic of poetry of his generation. Yet his extensive writings about Pound, because of their partiality, mutability, and inconclusiveness, are likely to be of imperfect assistance to the uninformed enquirer. One might even argue that Davie's lifelong relationship with Pound has massively deflected the development of his criticism, preventing him from adequately developing the fine insights into the nature of poetry presented in *Articulate Energy*. But in another perspective,

Davie's studies of Pound provide an extraordinarily interesting, and occasionally moving, continuous discourse, tracing, as on a cardiogram, Davie's fluctuating attitudes. Though it looks and reads like literary criticism, this discourse contains a deeply personal subtext, and its affinities are as much with Davie's poetry as with his criticism of other writers about whom he can be more disinterested. Although, as we have seen, Davie first expressed his admiration for Pound when writing as a poet, in his note in *Poets of the 1950's* as long ago as 1955, Pound has never had a direct influence on his verse in a way that Pasternak, for instance, has had. Davie's admiration has been more generally directed at Pound as an embodiment of artistic professionalism and generosity. Even so, Davie may well have found Pound an encouraging model in the matter of translation, adaptation, imitation, all the ways in which a poet can use existing literary and historical texts in his own writing. In Davie's poetry *The Forests of Lithuania* and *A Sequence for Francis Parkman* are successful examples of this process.

In certain of Davie's later poems his sense of affinity or kinship with Pound emerges clearly; indeed, Pound's public persona seems almost to have become a mask for Davie to assume and wear. In the 'Essex Poems' of 1969 occurs 'Ezra Pound in Pisa', a simple, affectionate expression of Davie's admiration for the poet of the *Pisan Cantos*. The final stanza reads:

> Sun moves, and the shadow moves,
> In spare and excellent order;
> I too would once repair
> Most afternoons to a pierced
> Shadow on gravelly ground,
> Write at a flaked, green-painted
> Table, and scrape my chair
> As sun and shade moved round.[40]

That 'I too . . .' is striking; it is apparent that the poem is as much about Davie's own perceptions and sense of excellence as about those of the imprisoned poet; Pound has, in effect, been appropriated as an objective correlative. It is revealing to compare this poem with a later one, 'Ars Poetica', from *In the Stopping Train and other poems* (1977). 'Ars Poetica' is in memory of Michael Ayrton, and Davie writes of himself in the third person in terms recalling the aged Pound:

The old man likes to sit
Here, in his black-tiled *loggia*
A patch of sun, and to muse
On Pasternak, Michael Ayrton . . .

The old man likes to look
Out on his tiny *cortile*,
A flask of 'Yosemite Road'
Cheap Chablis at his elbow.[41]

Davie was only in his mid-fifties when he presented himself in this way; but the Poundian persona seems to have been immensely appealing. The title poem of 'In the Stopping Train' is also written in the third person; in all other respects it is intensely personal, more so than any other poetry by Davie, a nakedly confessional poem in cold, disdainful language. In the first section the poet reflects bitterly on his lack of knowledge of nature, his imprisonment in a world of words:

Jonquil is a sweet word.
Is it a flowering bush?
Let him helplessly wonder
for hours if perhaps he's seen it.

Has it a white and yellow
flower, the jonquil? Has it
a perfume? Oh his art could
always pretend it had.

He never needed to see,
Not with his art to help him.
He never needed to use his
nose, except for language.[42]

These lines take on a particular poignancy if we recall how in *Ezra Pound: Poet as Sculptor* Davie praised Pound as a man who used to notice such things, who used his eyes and nose, and was fully alive to the natural world. Davie, perhaps, needed to insist that Pound, his beloved master, had these faculties, since he was so aware of his own lack of them. Needing a model for such painful self-exposures, Davie seems to have found one in those affecting, Lear-like utterances in the last *Cantos*, where Pound speaks more personally even than in the *Pisan Cantos:*

> But the beauty is not the madness
> Tho' my errors and wrecks lie about me.
> And I am not a demigod,
> I cannot make it cohere.
>
> (Canto 116)

This, it seems to me, is very much the tone and the language of 'In the Stopping Train', though Pound was some twenty years older than Davie when he wrote these lines. As I hope to have shown, Davie's feelings about Pound are not simple, and they run very deep; if love is prominent, envy and dismay and resentment are also apparent. The ultimate paradox may be that when Davie, in the course of a mid-life crisis, wanted to abandon the personae and the impacted learning and the allusiveness that are so characteristic of his poetry, and to confront himself and his feelings as nakedly as possible, it was Pound's own late example that enabled him to do so.

1983

NOTES

1. Donald Davie, *The Poet in the Imaginary Museum; Essays of Two Decades,* ed. Barry Alpert (Manchester, 1977), p.152.
2. *ibid.,* p.92.
3. Donald Davie, *Purity of Diction in English Verse*, 2nd edn (London, 1967), pp.94-5.
4. *ibid.*, p.99.
5. *See* Blake Morrison, *The Movement: English Poetry and Fiction of the 1950s* (London, 1980), pp.37-9, p.109-10.
6. My reasons for admiring it are set out in 'Syntax Now', *Critical Quarterly,* 19, No. 2 (Summer 1977), 31-9.
7. Donald Davie, *Articulate Energy: An Inquiry into the Syntax of English Poetry*, (London, 1955), p.20
8. *ibid.*, pp.128-9.
9. *ibid.*, p.40.
10. *ibid.*, pp.155-8.
11. *Poets of the 1950's: An Anthology of New English Verse*, ed D. J. Enright (Tokyo, 1955), p.47.
12. *Ezra Pound: the Critical Heritage,* ed Eric Homberger (London, 1972), p.444.
13. *The Poet in the Imaginary Museum*, p.47.
14. *ibid.*, pp.108-12.
15. *ibid.*, pp.191-207.

16. Donald Davie, *Trying to Explain* (Manchester, 1980), pp.49-51.
17. Ezra Pound, *Gaudier-Brzeska: A Memoir*, 2nd edn (Hessle, 1960), p.126.
18. *ibid.*, pp.120-1.
19. Donald Davie, *Ezra Pound: Poet as Sculptor* (New York, 1964), p.176.
20. *ibid.*, pp.176-7.
21. *Trying to Explain*, p.101.
22. Donald Davie, *Pound* (London, 1975), p.20.
23. Michael Alexander, *The Poetic Achievement of Ezra Pound* (London, 1979), p.159.
24. *Ezra Pound: Poet as Sculptor*, p.97.
25. *The Poet in the Imaginary Museum*, pp.142-3.
26. Wyndham Lewis, *Time and Western Man* (London, 1927), p.86.
27. *Ezra Pound: Poet as Sculptor*, p.204.
28. *The Poet in the Imaginary Museum*, p.118.
29. *ibid.*, pp.236-41.
30. *Ezra Pound: the Critical Heritage*, p.29
31. *Pound*, pp.73-4.
32. *Ezra Pound: Poet as Sculptor*, p.119.
33. *Pound*, p.69.
34. *ibid.*, p.114.
35. *ibid.*, p.79.
36. *Trying to Explain*, pp.130-3, 160.
37. *ibid.*, p.142.
38. *Ezra Pound: Poet as Sculptor*, p.181.
39. *Trying to Explain*, p.142.
40. Donald Davie, *Collected Poems 1950-1970* (London, 1972), p.189.
41. Donald Davie, *In the Stopping Train and other poems* (Manchester, 1977), pp.21-2.
42. *ibid.*, pp.23-4.

7

Leavis and Eliot: the long road to rejection

I

Very early in his career as a critic F. R. Leavis decided that the two major modern writers were T. S. Eliot and D. H. Lawrence; Yeats and Pound and Joyce, whatever limited merits might be granted them, did not deserve so high a place. At the end of Leavis's life in 1978 he regarded Lawrence as one of the greatest writers of all time and had the gravest doubts about Eliot; yet when he began his career, nearly fifty years earlier, his attitude to Eliot was wholly admiring and he had decided reservations about Lawrence. To say that he changed his mind about both of them would be too simple. It is true, though, that his attitude to Lawrence developed straightforwardly, from qualified to unqualified admiration. His changing approach to Eliot was less clear-cut but more interesting, involving a zig-zag progress through many different stages, of enthusiastic regard, tinged with doubt and unease, of renewed expressions of admiration, followed by exasperated swings into abusive dismissal.[1]

Eliot was much discussed in Cambridge in the late 1920s, when Leavis was trying to establish himself as an academic, and it is significant that one of his first published pieces of criticism should have been a defence of Eliot against a cool notice in the *New Statesman*. This was 'T. S. Eliot: a reply to the condescending', which appeared in the *Cambridge Review* on 8 February 1929.[2] Leavis's essay is urbane and persuasive, providing both a reasoned defence of Eliot as a poet and critic and a statement of personal indebtedness. He refers enthusiastically to the constituent poems of what was to be *Ash Wednesday*, then appearing in magazines, and this was the first sign on Leavis's part of a steady admiration; whatever his later shifts of opinion, he always regarded *Ash Wednesday* as a major poetic achievement. In this essay Leavis hints at a critical programme, heavily indebted to Eliot, that was to be developed in his two influential books on English poetry, *New Bearings in English Poetry* (132) and *Revaluation* (1936):

> If no serious critic or poet now supposes that English poetry in the future must, or can, develop along the line running from the Romantics through Tennyson, this is mainly due to Mr Eliot. But for him we certainly should not have had this clear awareness; and for this debt alone—it is a very great, though incalculable debt—the histories of English literature will give him an important place.

The tone of his admiring article is not quite that of discipleship, though that shortly becomes apparent. In 1930 Leavis published a pamphlet on D. H. Lawrence with the Minority Press, Cambridge. On the first page he writes, 'I start, then, by assuming that "genius" is the right word for Lawrence, though, in a recent "affair", an incomparably better critic than myself did this, and it did not save him from rebuke'.[3] The reasons for thinking that Eliot is the 'incomparably better critic' in this oblique reference are circumstantial but very strong. The 'affair' in question probably refers to a correspondence in the *Nation and Athenaeum* following Lawrence's death in March 1930. E. M. Forster published a tribute to Lawrence as 'the greatest imaginative novelist of our time'. On 5 April Eliot contributed a letter questioning this judgement, asking Forster exactly what he meant by such words as 'greatest' and 'imaginative' and 'novelist', though he introduces his implied dissent with a disingenuous and formal tribute: 'I am the last person to disparage the genius of Lawrence . . .' (Forster made a spirited rejoinder saying that he could not define any of those words, nor indeed 'exactly', but Eliot's letter made him feel that he would rather be a fly than a spider). The likelihood that Leavis was referring to Eliot is reinforced by the fact that in the same paragraph he alludes, though without naming it, to Eliot's essay on Blake, a text that was to be of peculiar interest and importance for Leavis.

To speak of an unnamed Eliot as an 'incomparably better critic than myself' introduces a note of coy discipleship that was picked up in the 'Prefatory note' to *New Bearings in English Poetry* where Leavis denies that his book has any real originality, describing it as 'largely an acknowledgment, vicarious as well as personal, of indebtedness to a certain critic and poet'. In *Revaluation* the chapter on Shelley is introduced by a reference to 'a critic of peculiar authority' and a quotation, without source, from that critic. The critic was Eliot and the quotation comes from *The Use of Poetry and the Use of Criticism*.

New Bearings and *Revaluation* contain some of Leavis's best and most influential criticism; I have long thought that he was much better as a critic of poetry, where he is able to respond sensitively and attentively to the 'words on the page', than of fiction, where his method all too often declines into loud adjectival praise directed at large but not closely examined quotations. The two books, taken together, contain a firm redrawing of the map of English poetry along Eliotic lines, beginning with the twentieth century, then moving back to the seventeenth century and forward to the early nineteenth. Victorian poetry, with the exception of Hopkins, is removed from the map.

New Bearings in English Poetry is a good-tempered and balanced work that can still be read with profit, given an understanding of its historical context. As Leavis acknowledges, Eliot inspired its approach and is the subject of the longest chapter in the book; indeed, he is alluded to in the very title: 'He has made a new start, and established new bearings.' The book's organizing ideas are clearly derived from Eliot's criticism and poetry: 'complexity' and the poet's need to be open to everyday modern experience recall 'The Metaphysical poets', while 'impersonality' is taken from 'Tradition and the individual talent'; the desirability of conversational tones or colloquial speech in poetry is a reflection of Eliot's own poetic practice. (Such notions are, of course, commonplaces of modernist poetics, with other sources than Eliot: Hulme and Pound, de Gourmont and Bergson, to name but a few; however, Leavis's freely admitted debt to Eliot makes him the most likely source in this context.) Leavis did have other sources in *New Bearings*, notably I. A. Richards, from whom he takes the idea of the poet as more alive than other people, and 'the most conscious point of the race in his own time', which is linked to an Arnoldian emphasis on socio-cultural health and the need for intellectual standards, and eventually applied to Eliot's own achievement:

> That Mr Eliot could be so decisive shows, of course, that he was not a mere individual in isolation: he had a more important kind of originality. He was more aware of the general plight than his contemporaries, and more articulate: he made himself (answering to our account of the important poet) the consciousness of his age, and he did this the more effectively in that he was a critic as well as a poet.[4]

In his account of Eliot's poetry Leavis briefly recognizes the modernity of 'The love song of J. Alfred Prufrock' but finds a subtler poise in 'Portrait of a lady'. In 1932 Eliot was most famous as the poet of *The Waste Land* and Leavis's commentary on the poem is conscientious and serviceable. Having praised 'Gerontion' for possessing 'the impersonality of great poetry', Leavis sees *The Waste Land* as taking impersonality to an extreme limit: 'it would be difficult to imagine a completer transcendence of the individual self, a completer projection of awareness'.[5] There is perhaps a hint of unease in this judgement, a suggestion that if the poet is the fine point of awareness of his age, and the age is radically dehumanized, then the poet may come to suffer from too much awareness. Leavis's reading of *The Waste Land* is diagnostic, in familiar ways: the poem is valuable for showing us what modern life is like in an urban world where traditional practices and sanctions are fragmented and overthrown, where sex is without meaning and where human existence is cut off from the rhythms of nature. There is no explicit cross-reference to Lawrence, but it is easy to see how Leavis found a common base for his admiration for both writers. The final judgement on *The Waste Land* is dutiful and slightly cool: 'a great positive achievement, and one of the first importance for English poetry'. 'The hollow men', which followed *The Waste Land,* seems, if anything, to explore an even deeper desolation; yet Leavis responds to it warmly as a 'marvellous positive achievement', and hints that some of its value may come from its more apparently personal nature. The hint becomes explicit when Leavis goes on to discuss *Ash Wednesday,* Eliot's most recently published poetry at that time. He praises it highly as a work of personal conviction and spiritual exploration, even if doing so meant transgressing Eliot's commitment to 'impersonality'. A certain tact was necessary:

> We remind ourselves of Mr Eliot's precept and practice in criticism: the sequence is poetry, and highly formal poetry. Yet it is impossible not to see in it a process of self-scrutiny, of self-exploration; or not to feel that the poetical problem at any point was a spiritual problem, a problem in the attainment of a difficult sincerity.[6]

On the following page Leavis expands the final phrase: 'For the poet "technique" was the problem of sincerity', and a footnote reference directs the reader to a sentence from Eliot's essay on Blake, 'And this honesty never exists without a great technical accomplishment.' The phrase about a 'technique for sincerity' often recurs in Leavis's writing about Eliot: it is a paradoxical way of bringing together opposed elements: the personal as suggested by 'sincerity' and the impersonal as suggested by 'technique'. At the end of his chapter on Eliot Leavis asserts that the poetry of *Ash Wednesday* and 'Marina'—also published in 1930—is 'more disconcertingly modern than *The Waste Land*'.

Revaluation develops Leavis's allegiance to Eliot as both critic and poet. In his 1929 essay Leavis had expressed his particular indebtedness to the readings of seventeenth-century poetry in Eliot's *Homage to John Dryden*. That slender volume contained sufficient hints and suggestions to provide a rationale for *Revaluation*, a book well known enough not to need close discussion here. Leavis sees the central tradition of English poetry running through Shakespeare to Donne and the Metaphysicals; Milton and Dryden are bypassed, but Pope is redeemed as a great poet by being essentially in the Metaphysical line. Leavis is not enthusiastic about Augustan poetry as such, but he finds things to admire in some eighteenth-century poetry, in its firmness and gravity of language, and the corresponding decency of social and moral attitudes. Wordsworth is saved for the tradition by not being a typically Romantic poet at all; at least not in the sense of being uncontrollably subjective and individualist: 'Wordsworth's roots were deep in the eighteenth century. To say this is to lay the stress again—where it ought to rest—on his essential sanity and normality.'[7] At the same time Wordsworth had a religious sense that enabled Leavis to invoke Lawrence: 'His mode of preoccupation, it is true, was that of a mind intent always upon ultimate sanctions, and upon the living connections between man and the extra-human universe; it was, that is, in the same sense as Lawrence's was, religious.'[8]

If Lawrence is explicitly invoked here, Eliot is implicitly referred to, when Leavis says that Wordsworth exhibits 'in his poetry, as an essential exhibit, an impersonality unknown in Shelley'.[9] There are references to Eliot throughout *Revaluation* and it is noticeable that in the major negative revaluations which made the book celebrated or notorious Leavis uses Eliot as a launching-pad; I have already referred to the quotation from Eliot at the beginning of the chapter on Shelley, while the chapter on Milton opens: 'Milton's dislodgment, in the past decade, after his two centuries of predominance, was effected with remarkably little fuss. The irresistible argument was, of course, Mr Eliot's creative achievement; it gave his few critical asides—potent, it is true, by context—their finality, and made it unnecessary to elaborate a case.'[10] In a scathing review of *Revaluation*, Stephen Spender observed, 'Dr Leavis rushes in (on Milton and Shelley) where the angels have already trod'.[11]

The first stage of Leavis's changing attitudes to Eliot shows not merely acknowledged indebtedness or even reverent discipleship, but a degree of psychic dependence, a need to keep hold of Eliot's hand, so to speak, before making provocatively explicit some of the bolder implications of Eliot's poetry and criticism. Such dependence might explain the compulsive quality of Leavis's later dealings with Eliot, the anfractuosities and the vehemence of rejection. At the same time, he did a good deal for his master in popularizing his work and turning academic attention to it, particularly in *New Bearings* and *Revaluation*, books which trained the critical taste of at least one generation of readers, and whose influence is still apparent.

Eliot's literary criticism of the 1920s was what he has described as 'workshop criticism', written in close relationship with his poetry. Its aim was to change the educated public's idea of poetry, so that readers who had come to have a better understanding of Middleton or Donne or Baudelaire would have a chance of appreciating what Eliot himself was writing. This summary makes the process seem altogether too deliberate; much of Eliot's motivation at the time was probably unconscious, only to be properly understood in retrospect. But when, for instance, Eliot writes in 'The Metaphysical poets', 'The poet must become more and more comprehensive, more allusive, more indirect, in order to force, to dislocate if necessary, language into his meaning', the relevance for readers of *The Waste Land* is evident. It was Leavis's considerable achievement to enlarge and systematize Eliot's personal and quite inchoate version of literary history and place it in an educational context, a process carried on in Leavis's books, his work with *Scrutiny* and his personal influence on colleagues and students. The growth and increasing prestige of English as an academic subject provided a cause and an arena where Eliot's precepts and example as poet and critic could be used in the struggle against the old forms of historical scholarship and belletrist appreciation. (There was a similar process in the United States, where the New Critics had their own taproots to Eliot, and Cleanth Brooks's *Modern Poetry and the Tradition* (1939) afforded a parallel to *New Bearings*.) What in the 1920s were revolutionary and startling ideas about poetry, confined to a brilliant coterie publication such as *The Calendar of Modern Letters* or the brightest young academics in Cambridge, had become very familiar by the 1940s; if not in total possession of the field, these ideas were confidently upheld in the educational centres where Leavis's influence was felt.

Leavis probably helped to get more readers for Eliot's poetry, though in the 1920s *The Waste Land* was certainly read and appreciated even if not properly understood (and slavishly imitated in Nancy Cunard's poem *Parallax*). This readership, however, would have been smart and fashionable in ways deplored by Leavis. He would hardly have approved of Evelyn Waugh's account in *Brideshead Revisited* of the aesthete Anthony Blanche standing on a balcony of Christ Church, Oxford, reciting passages from *The Waste Land* through a megaphone to 'the sweatered and muffled throng that was on its way to the river'[12] (based on a real-life incident when Harold Acton did this). Yet Anthony Blanche's frivolous treatment of the poem did represent a response to certain aspects of it: its quality as sheer performance, its theatricality, its affinities with those kinds of popular art that Eliot had a taste for, like ragtime and the music hall, and the qualities it shared with other manifestations of international modernism, such as Mayakovsky reading poetry through a megaphone. All these things were, no doubt, very remote from what a serious-minded, *Scrutiny*-reading undergraduate might have found in *The Waste Land* in the 1940s; but it is, I think, an index of the poem's continuing great vitality that it can generate many different readings without becoming exhausted. Leavis's version of *The Waste Land* as a diagnosis of cultural decay is not demonstrably wrong, for there is enough in the poem to support it, but it is very narrow and reductive. One can reasonably conclude that Leavis originally admired the poem without being deeply enthusiastic about it, and in later years he implied that even then he had over-rated it: 'We rightly found *The Waste Land* very impressive and very important in the 1920s, but I think we tended to make it a higher kind of achievement than it actually is.'[13]

Leavis's early criticism of Eliot tended to push him further in the direction in which he was already moving; that is to say, away from international modernism towares a firm location in English tradition. In the 1920s Eliot was regarded as a Franco-American iconoclast, with a cosmopolitan culture; conspicuously learned, he was at least as interested in Dante and Baudelaire as in Webster or Marvell; he even knew Sanskrit. *The Waste Land* was thought of as a highly provocative work, obscure certainly, perhaps a bit of a hoax, but fascinating and entertaining too, with subversive as well as solemn aspects. It drew on both popular and avant-garde culture, jazz, cinema, music-hall, *collage,* cubism, and it seemed to belong in the same world as the lively disruptions of the Futurists and Dada. These are dimensions of the poem that Leavis, we may be sure, would have intensely disliked if he had understood them. By 1930 Eliot had left behind the provocative modernism of *The Waste Land* and the transformation of personal feeling into dramatic fragments; he had also become a British subject and a member of the Anglican Church. Henceforth, his poetry, without ever being overtly autobiographical, was reflective and implicitly personal, so that it could be discussed in terms of struggle and sincerity. Leavis believed that this poetry culminated in *Four Quartets*, Eliot's supreme achievement, and, among much else, an affirmation of

English identity and allegiance. Eliot, too, believed that it was his major poetic work. His best criticism already located a vital source of English poetic tradition in the early seventeenth century, when the achievement of Shakespeare and the Elizabethan dramatists was taken over by the Metaphysical poets. In 1927 Eliot was naturalized by the British State; in Leavis's reading of Eliot he was 'naturalized' in the different sense that recent criticism has given to that word; he was removed from the uncertain and subversive context of cosmopolitan modernism and inserted firmly into the English poetic tradition. This, no doubt, was where Eliot wanted to be, and the result was to make him pedagogically more approachable. There are other ways of reading Eliot, but the remarkable and tenacious success of Leavis's version makes it difficult to grasp them.

II

We now take it for granted that Lawrence and Eliot are antithetical figures, and Leavis's later criticism exploits this polarity. But originally he did not find it difficult to admire them both, and his essay in defence of Eliot in 1929 was followed by the Minority Press pamphlet on Lawrence in 1930. Compared with Leavis's subsequent claims for Lawrence, this pamphlet is remarkably moderate and qualified. Writing soon after Lawrence's death, when he did not stand very high in critical opinion. Leavis wanted to show that he is an important if imperfect writer who deserves not to be neglected. He finds the best of Lawrence in the short stories and in passages from the novels; the novels he most admires are *The Lost Girl* and *Lady Chatterley's Lover* rather than *The Rainbow* and *Women in Love*. His treatment of the latter two, which in *D. H. Lawrence: Novelist* (1955) he takes to be supreme manifestations of Lawrentian genius, is distinctly cool. For instance, he says of *Women in Love*, 'To get through it calls for great determination and a keen diagnostic interest', and he condemns its mechanical reiteration of a specialized vocabulary: 'dark', 'pure', 'mindless', 'loins of darkness' and so on.[14] The pamphlet was reprinted in Leavis's first collection of essays, *For Continuity*, in 1933. In his prefatory note to that book Leavis suggests that he no longer agrees with all the judgements he made in 1930, but he is disinclined to rewrite the Lawrence essay, and seems to regard it as his last word on Lawrence: 'I shall never again, I suppose, be able to give the body of his works the prolonged and intensive frequentation that went to the preparing of that essay, whatever its crudities.'[15] Leavis did, of course, return to Lawrence in the 1950s. By that time he had moved far beyond the tentative reading of Lawrence in his early essay and he never allowed it to be reprinted. Nevertheless, it contains in embryonic form some of his basic ideas about Lawrence: there is the diagnostic interest in the novelist as someone who saw with painful clarity the cost of mechanized civilization and the alienation of the human spirit from the cycles and rhythms of nature. The long passage from *Lady Chatterley's Lover* beginning, 'The car ploughed uphill through the long squalid straggle of Tevershall . . .', here quoted for the first time, was to recur regularly in Leavis's writings.

In the early 1930s, Leavis's concern with literature as cultural diagnosis made him aware of what Eliot and Lawrence had in common: a feeling for tradition and continuity, a dislike of modern urban and industrial society, a corresponding nostalgia for the organic community, and some kind of religious sense. Yet these parallels were at best general and limited; Lawrence's religious feeling was strong but vague, to be summed up as 'reverence for life', whereas Eliot's was doctrinal and dogmatic. Lawrence had said that Eliot's 'classiosity' was 'bunkum', and Eliot had condemned Lawrence's ignorance and spiritual pride. Leavis was in the difficult position of someone whose two closest friends cordially dislike each other.

The difficulty was examined in an acute anonymous article published in the *New English Weekly* in January 1933.[16] The author is discussing *Scrutiny* after a year of publication but what he says of the magazine applies particularly to Leavis's own attitudes. He assumes that *Scrutiny* owes a direct debt to Eliot—'there has been little in literary Cambridge, these last ten years, which has not derived from T. S. Eliot'—but that Eliot's commitment to orthodox Christianity was an increasing cause of dissatisfaction, and that *Scrutiny* now wanted a dual allegiance to both Eliot and Lawrence is. He remarks that though a 'genuine synthesis' between Eliot and Lawrence is conceivable it has not been achieved in *Scrutiny*: 'Eliot's head and Lawrence's tail do not fit together at all. . . .' The author invokes Blake, who said that in order to redeem the Contraries we must first destroy the negation, and concludes 'really to understand Lawrence would be really to understand Lawrence-and-Eliot also; and really to understand Blake would be a direct path to both these ends at once. But to *use* Eliot to escape the reality of Lawrence, and to use Lawrence to escape the reality of Eliot is to insult both of them.' Leavis made a spirited defence of *Scrutiny* against these strictures, saying that the attitude of the responsible critic to Lawrence or Eliot could not be systematized into anything so crude as 'accepting' or 'rejecting'.[17] Nevertheless, the *New English Weekly* critic showed a shrewd insight, not only into Leavis's stance in 1933 but into its future development. His invocation of Blake is particularly interesting; whenever Leavis writes in a comparative way of Eliot and Lawrence Blake is likely to be a hovering third figure. The point of connection lies in Eliot's essay on Blake, which Leavis alluded to on the first page of the Lawrence pamphlet and often cited subsequently.[18]

This essay, first published as a review in the *Athenaeum* early in 1920 and collected in *The Sacred Wood* later that year, is one of Eliot's most curious and revealing critical pieces. Though short, it is divided into two sections, in the first of which Eliot praises Blake for being entirely his own man, and in the second finds fault with him for, in effect, not being Dante. The divisions in this essay relate to the underlying contradictions in the slightly earlier 'Tradition and the individual talent', where Eliot wants the poet to have only the degree of learning that he needs to write his poetry, and at the same time to be a highly educated man for whom 'the mind of Europe' is a reality. The first part of the essay is a valuable corrective to simplistic readings of what Eliot might have meant by 'impersonality' in the more famous essay. He praises Blake for a 'peculiar honesty, which, in a world too frightened to be honest, is peculiarly terrifying'; 'he was naked, and saw man naked, and from the centre of his own crystal' (the original version of this essay in the *Athenaeum* was called 'The naked man'). Such praise anticipates the language and attitudes of Leavis's writing about Lawrence;[19] and, as I have remarked, Leavis drew heavily on Eliot's assertion that 'this honesty never exists without great technical accomplishment'. In the second part of the essay Eliot goes on to argue that though there was nothing to distract Blake from sincerity there were also 'the dangers to which the naked man is exposed', such as eccentricity, ignorance, insularity, being cut off from Latin civilization and lacking any degree of impersonal reason. These are very much the same negative features that Eliot later condemned in Lawrence, notably in his *Criterion* review of Middleton Murry's book on Lawrence, *Son of Woman*, in 1931. Writing about Blake in 1920, Eliot remarkably anticipated both his own and Leavis's attitudes to Lawrence of later years. It is not surprising that Leavis was so preoccupied by this essay, for it cast a very long shadow; by the end of his career, Blake and Lawrence, with Dickens as a vehemently acclaimed late arrival, were enshrined in the positive wing of Leavis's personal pantheon, as forces making for life and the spirit, to be confronted on the negative wing by Eliot as a potent but malign genius.

By 1933 Leavis's admiration for Lawrence was growing and he was coming to resent Eliot's attitudes to Lawrence. Reviewing Aldous Huxley's edition of Lawrence's letters he remarks, 'For several years before the *Letters* came out one's sense that Lawrence was greater than his writings had been steadily growing, as the signs accumulated and understanding increased', and adds that this sense of Lawrence's greatness had been amply confirmed by the letters.[20] Leavis sharply rejects Eliot's judgement in his review of Murry's book that Lawrence's history was 'an appalling narrative of spiritual pride, nourished by ignorance'. He also quotes some remarks made by Eliot on Lawrence in *La Nouvelle Revue Francais* in 1927: 'quand ses personnages font l'amour . . . non seulement ils perdent toutes les aménités, raffinements et grâces que plusieurs siècles ont elaborés afin de rendre l'amour *supportable* mais ils semblent remonter le cours de l'évolution . . . jusqu'a quelque hideux accouplement de protoplasme.' The italicization of *supportable* is Leavis's, but his comment on this passage is restrained, far more so than when he later returned to it in *D. H. Lawrence: Novelist:* 'Surely the rejection of Romantic Love, Love as the Absolute, does not necessarily lead one to *this*?[21] (Eliot's analysis is not all that far from Leavis's own complaint of the 1930 pamphlet that the characters of *Women in Love* 'tend to disintegrate into swirls of conflicting impulses and emotions'.)[22] Leavis's continuing high opinion of Eliot is such that he is unwilling to make a sustained attack on him, but he cannot help unfavourably comparing his attitudes to sex with Lawrence's.

In 1934 Eliot published his 'Primer of modern heresy', *After Strange Gods*, where Lawrence is given a careful but cold examination as an outstanding modern literary heretic. *After Strange Gods* is an unbalanced and disturbing book, vulnerable both as criticism and ideology, as Eliot came to recognize, for it was never reprinted. Leavis's review, collected in *The Common Pursuit* as 'Eliot, Wyndham Lewis and Lawrence', is a finely poised and effective piece of criticism, written with the urbanity which characterized Leavis's early prose.[23] He finds certain things to approve in *After Strange Gods*, particularly Eliot's belief in tradition and continuity, but he dissents from his Christian orthodoxy, which he says has had a weakening effect on Eliot's criticism. He finds Eliot's account of Lawrence contradictory and unconvincing, and again draws disapproving attention to his attitudes to sex. The conclusion of the essay is modest in what it claims for Lawrence, but it shows that for Leavis whatever could be learnt from Lawrence was becoming a necessary balance to those aspects of Eliot that he still admired but was becoming wary of:

> for attributing to him 'spiritual sickness' Mr Eliot can make out a strong case. But it is characteristic of the world as it is that health cannot anywhere be found whole; and the sense in which Lawrence stands for health is an important one. He stands at any rate for something without which the preoccupation (necessary as it is) with order, forms and deliberate construction, cannot produce health.

This delicate balance of opposing forces was to serve Leavis for a considerable time as a means of preserving his allegiance to both Eliot and Lawrence. Leavis did not write at any length on Eliot during the later 1930s, but passing remarks indicate his increasing impatience, particularly with Eliot's editing of the *Criterion*, which Leavis saw as weakly opportunistic and a betrayal of the idea of a responsible literary review. (Spender's attack on *Revaluation* in the *Criterion* would certainly have provoked his resentment.)

III

The publication of *Four Quartets* was the occasion for Leavis to turn again to Eliot with renewed enthusiasm. The first Quartet, *Burnt Norton,* had originally been published separately in 1936 in Eliot's *Collected Poems 1909-1935,* and was reviewed very favourably in *Scrutiny* by D. W. Harding.[24] He made the suggestive observation that Eliot was formulating poetically a whole new concept, which had affinities with ideas such as 'regret' or 'eternity' but was distinct from them. Leavis said that this review by Harding 'Seems to me pre-eminently the note on Eliot to send people to'.[25] *Burnt Norton* was followed in 1940 by *East Coker* and in 1941 by *The Dry Salvages.* Leavis made the publication of the last of these the basis of an essay in *Scrutiny* in 1942, 'T. S. Eliot's later poetry',[26] which continued the discussion from the point at which he had left it in *New Bearings.* Leavis sees the *Quartets* as great poetry, to be read as poetry, not as versified doctrine, and in essence not offering propositions at all:

> The poetry from *Ash Wednesday* onwards doesn't say, 'I believe', or 'I know', or 'Here is the truth'; it is positive in direction but not positive in that way (the difference from Dante is extreme). It is a searching of experience, a spiritual discipline, a technique for sincerity—for giving 'sincerity' a meaning.

This essay first adumbrated a view of Eliot's poetry that Leavis was to hold for nearly thirty years. The poetry based on the persona and the dramatic monologue, from 'Prufrock' to *The Waste Land* is downgraded, apart from 'Portrait of a lady', which Leavis had singled out for praise in *New Bearings* and continued to admire. Eliot's major achievement is seen as the quasi-personal poetry of reflection and spiritual exploration, which begins with 'The hollow men', continues in *Ash Wednesday* and 'Marina' and triumphantly culminates in the *Quartets.* Leavis concludes the essay with unqualified praise of Eliot as poet and makes a curious gesture of bringing Eliot and Lawrence together, perhaps in a spirit of wartime reconciliation, akin to that which made Eliot, in a late addition to the manuscript, place his old adversary Milton—'one who died blind and quiet'—among the spirits commemorated in *Little Gidding.*[27]

> His relative distinction and his title to respect and gratitude are certainly not less than they were a dozen years ago. To him, in fact, might be adapted the tribute that he once paid to that very different genius, D. H. Lawrence; he pre-eminently has stood for the spirit in these brutal and discouraging years.[28] And it should by now be impossible to doubt that he is among the greatest poets of the English language.

In the *Quartets*, which move between Eliot's personal and ancestral American past and his English present, his poetic commitment to English tradition becomes total. Significantly, Leavis reprinted his essay as an appendix to *Education and the University* (1943), a book whose central pedagogic proposal is for a close study of the literature and culture of the seventeenth century, Eliot's favoured *moment privilégié* in English history.

In 1943 D. W. Harding published a laudatory review of *Little Gidding* in *Scrutiny*, very much in the vein of Leavis's essay of the previous year. Its publication led to a piquant exchange in *Scrutiny*. A reader, R. N. Higinbotham, wrote in to complain that Harding's review was not literary criticism at all, but merely an exposition or paraphrase (a judgement that seems to me broadly correct). Higinbotham's complaint was unsympathetic to Eliot, but offered an intelligent invitation to discussion of the less achieved aspects of the *Quartets*, and related his criticism to particular passages of the sequence. His conclusion was impeccably Scrutineering in tone, if possibly somewhat tongue-in-cheek: 'The unevenness and lack of homogeneity in these four poems from "Burnt Norton" onwards are therefore the result of disequilibrium in the author's feelings. If Mr Eliot's achievements were not so great and his seriousness beyond question I should use the word "insincerity" to describe the general effect.' Harding was not available for comment and Leavis undertook to answer on his behalf. He took ten pages to do so, as against Higinbotham's two-and-a-half, and his defence of *Little Gidding*, and Harding's review of it, was total and uncompromising. He was polite but severe in his rebuttal of Higinbotham, asserting that he had not read the poem properly.[29]

A few years later Leavis reviewed the gramophone records of Eliot reading the *Quartets* and was very disappointed with Eliot's poor quality as a speaker of his own major poetry. What is particularly interesting about this brief review is the way in which Leavis interprets Eliot's insufficiencies as a reader in terms of his divided personality:

> In his poetry he applies to himself a merciless standard; it is the product of an intense and single-minded discipline—for sincerity and purity of interest. In his prose he seems to relax from the ascesis he undergoes as a composer of verse. The prose-writer belongs to an external social world, where conventions are formidable and temptations are not only often not resisted, they seem not to be perceived. The reader of the poetry would seem to be more intimately related to the prose-writer than to the poet.[30]

This note illustrates a tendency in Leavis's later dealings with Eliot, to draw closer to Eliot the man and make inferences about the divisions in his nature and his faulty psychic development. Leavis subsequently remarked of a collection of academic essays on Eliot that he was reviewing: 'it seems to me calculated in sum to promote, not the impact of Eliot's genius—a disturbing force and therefore capable of ministering to life—but his establishment as a safe academic classic.'[31]

In the post-war years Eliot's critical writing became weaker and more diffuse, and there was increasing reason for Leavis's dissatisfaction with Eliot as prose-writer, particularly in so evasive a piece as the British Academy lecture on Milton. At about this time Leavis returned to the close study of Lawrence, and in 1955 published *D. H. Lawrence: Novelist*, a book which contains many comments on Eliot, harsher in tone than anything Leavis had previously produced. Eliot's disparaging observations on Lawrence from the late 1920s and early 1930s, which Leavis had once noticed urbanely and more in sorrow than in anger, are resurrected, to be bitterly denounced. Leavis still regards Eliot and Lawrence as the two masters of modern literature, but what was once a delicate poise of complementary forces is now a polarity, and an unbalanced one: 'our time, in literature, may fairly be called the age of D. H. Lawrence and T. S. Eliot: the two, in creative pre-eminence, I think, though Lawrence appears to me so immensely the greater genius, will be seen in retrospect to dominate the age together.'[32]

In the late 1950s Leavis goes beyond a sharp shift of tone and emphasis actually to change his mind about Eliot. On the face of it, he had always admired Eliot's early seminal essay, 'Tradition and the individual talent'; he often directed approving attention to it, from 'T. S. Eliot: a reply to the condescending' in 1929 to 'T. S. Eliot's later poetry' in 1942 and 'Literature and society' in 1943. But in 1958 he published 'T. S. Eliot as critic', a long review-article whose point of departure was Eliot's *On Poetry and Poets*.[33] It is pervaded by the animus against Eliot so noticeable in the Lawrence book. Leavis finds it remarkable that anyone should have taken 'Tradition and the individual talent' seriously:

> Actually the trenchancy and vigour are illusory and the essay is notable for its ambiguities, its logical inconsequences, its pseudo-precisions, its fallaciousness, and the aplomb of its equivocations and its specious cogency. Its offered compression and its technique in general for generating awed confusion help to explain why it should not have been found easy to deal with. Yet the falsity and gratuitousness of its doctrine of impersonality are surely plain enough.

Leavis is right in finding mystifying and contradictory elements in that famous essay, though he had not previously mentioned them. It is true that his frequent favourable citations had been of what Eliot says about tradition and the poet's relation with the past, in the first part of the essay; what he condemned in 1958 was the doctrine of impersonality in the second part. The condemnation of impersonality is not surprising, given Leavis's increasingly strong allegiance to Lawrence and the value of individual creativity; there were hints of reservation about it even in *New Bearings*. Nevertheless, as R. B. Bilan points out, as late as 1948 Leavis had praised George Eliot for the 'impersonality' of her presentation of Mrs Transome in *Felix Holt*;[34] he actually quotes from 'Tradition and the individual talent': 'The more perfect the artist, the more completely separate in him will be the man who suffers and the mind which creates.'[35] By the time he published 'T. S. Eliot as critic' Leavis believed the exact opposite. It reads like a substantial rejection of Eliot's criticism; not just of 'Tradition and the individual talent' and the weak late essays in *On Poetry and Poets*, but even of Eliot's early studies of seventeenth-century drama and poetry, which Leavis had always seen as the firm evidence of his critical genius. This essay, which in places seems more like a howl of rage than an exercise of the rational intelligence, shows how unstable Leavis's attitude to Eliot had become.

IV

Leavis had more to say about Eliot in public lectures that he gave in America, at Cornell and Harvard, in 1966, and in the Clark Lectures at Cambridge in 1967. They were published as *Lectures in America* (with Q.D. Leavis, 1969) and *English Literature in Our Time and the University* (1969). There is much overlapping material in these two books and they can be discussed together. The tone is more positive and accommodating than in Leavis's writings of the 1950s; Eliot's death in 1965 seems to have induced in him a spirit of *de mortuis,* or at least an elegiac mildness of manner. Certainly his remarks on Eliot as critic represent a drawing back from the extremities of the 1958 essay. 'Tradition and the individual talent' is condemned and the doctrine of impersonality firmly dismissed: 'The relevant truth, the clear essential truth, is stated when one reverses the dictum and says that between the man who suffers and the mind which creates there can never be a separation'.[36] But Leavis once more gives high praise to the essays in *Homage to John Dryden* and reaffirms Eliot's correctness in formulating the doctrine of the Dissociation of Sensibility. In the Clark Lectures he returns to the proposal outlined in *Education and the University* for an interdisciplinary study of the seventeenth century in the light of Eliot's reading of it.

Leavis draws freely on what he had already written about Eliot in *New Bearings* and 'T. S. Eliot's later poetry'; there is extensive paraphrase and sometimes direct quotation from those sources. What is new is the clearer emergence of Leavis's map of Eliot's poetry, emphasizing the sequence, 'The hollow man', *Ash Wednesday,* 'Marina' *Four Quartets,* and his increasing readiness to read it in psychobiographical terms. *The Waste Land* is allowed historical importance but gently dislodged from its former position, though Leavis continues to admire 'Portrait of a lady'. In passing, he remarks that, notwithstanding Eliot's debt to French sources, there is nothing in this poem that suggests Jules Laforgue.[37] Leavis is being extraordinarily perverse here, since

Laforgue's influence is evident and some lines are even adapted from the French poet. In 1932 he had been quite willing to acknowledged Laforgue's influence on this and other poems by Eliot,[38] and why he needed to deny it in 1969 is puzzling. Another early poem for which he displays a new enthusiasm is 'La figlia che piange', of which he says, 'Love—love in the lyrical sense, with no irony in the tone or context: where else in Eliot do you find that?'[39] It seems to me that this is in no sense a straightforward love poem, despite the Pre-Raphaelite imagery and the mellifluous expression, since it offers not an expression of love but a sad, mildly voyeuristic contemplation of the end of another person's love, and that there is a distinct irony generated by the language of the final lines. Yet one can see why Leavis praised this poem, even at the cost of misreading it, since he wanted to find *some* trace of normal human love in Eliot's *oeuvre*. After the sentence I have just quoted he goes on to say, 'The general, and pregnant, truth about him is that he can contemplate the relations between men and women only with revulsion or distaste—unless with the aid of Dante.' It is this conviction that is at the heart of Leavis's later dealings with Eliot. He regards him as a man stricken with a grave spiritual sickness and disorder, where the man who suffers and the mind which creates are inextricably linked; in so far as Eliot struggles to turn disorder into creative order he is to be admired: 'I see Eliot's creative career as a sustained, heroic and indefatigably resourceful quest of a profound sincerity of the most difficult kind. The heroism is that of genius . . . poetic technique for him is a technique for sincerity in relation to the most difficult personal strains.'[40] Leavis's admiration for the struggle is in tension with a growing conviction that Eliot's disorder is so extreme that it never could be overcome or transformed: 'The fact is that his inner disorder and his disability remained grievous and tell to its disadvantage on his concern for the spiritual.'[41]

In these lectures of the 1960s Leavis's opinion of the *Quartets* remains, on the face of it, as high as ever. He describes the *Quartets* in *Lectures in America* as 'that astonishing feat of sustained creative integrity' and quotes a paragraph from his 1942 essay in support of this judgement. A chapter of *English Literature in Our Time and the University* is called, 'Why "Four Quartets" matters in a technologico-Benthamite age', and again draws on Leavis's earlier treatment of the poem. Yet this lecture is qualified by its context; the following lecture is called, 'The necessary opposite, Lawrence', in emblematic contrast. And the preceding lecture looks forward to it with these words:

> I intend to discuss Eliot's own poetic achievement next. And I thought it well to put myself, as I have done, in a position to say that the attitude towards life and humanity defined in the work that showed how a modern poet might rival a major novelist as a serious artist is very different from that in relation to which I have associated Blake, Dickens and Lawrence. You hardly needed reminding of that. But I shall no doubt convey a strong admiration for Eliot's work as a poet, and I would rather that, from the start, you didn't suppose me to have adopted for myself the attitude, the ethos, the spirit of it. I am secure against that now, I hope.[42]

There need be no great difficulty in admiring a poem as poetry, whilst at the same time not accepting 'the attitude, the ethos, the spirit of it'. But to do so implies a broadly formalist view of literature, which has never been acceptable to Leavis. In *New Bearings* he mildly rebuked Eliot for saying that he was more interested in the way Pound said things than in what he said: 'it seems improbable that a way of saying something that can be so sharply distinguished from the thing said could do much towards reorientating English poetry.' Leavis was still committed to his earlier judgement of the *Quartets* as some of the greatest poetry of our time and a work of astonishing creativity. But he shows signs of needing to convince himself of its truth. Eliot's kind of creativity was evidently very different from that to be found in Blake and Dickens and Lawrence. Sooner or later Leavis would have to face the question: in what sense was it creative at all?

V

In the late 1940s Leavis defined his attitudes to Eliot, the divided man. The creative genius who wrote the major poetry was to be praised, and the timid, opportunistic social being who edited the *Criterion* and produced the weak later criticism and wrote plays for the fashionable theatre was to be deplored and rejected. This double focus served Leavis well for many years, during which time he had no doubt that in the succession of poems from 'The hollow men' to the *Quartets*, Eliot was a great poet, triumphantly striving to produce a 'technique for sincerity' out of personal stress. But by degrees the fact of division in Eliot became in itself a cause of scandal to Leavis. He dwelt increasingly on Eliot's inner disorders as he saw them: the disgust and self-loathing, the wrong attitudes to sex, the alienation from the rest of humanity. He came to doubt if such negative attitudes could ever be the basis for major poetry, however heroic the struggle to contain and transform them. By the early 1970s Leavis's doubts were undermining his immensely high valuation of the *Quartets* and he even applies the word 'failure' to them: 'The failure is a failure of the courage of self-knowledge—that is, a weakness of the disinterested "identity", and the consequence manifests itself in the poem as a basic nullifying contradiction.'[43] The 'heroism of genius' is now less apparent than weakness and lack of courage.

In *The Living Principle* (1975) Leavis engages in the large-scale revaluation of Eliot that he has been hinting at, in a close commentary on the *Quartets* of over a hundred pages. In 1942-3 he and Harding had acclaimed *Four Quartets* in *Scrutiny* without nuance or qualification, and when the unfortunate R. N. Higinbotham asked for Eliot's sequence to be given more responsible literary-critical attention, which would consider weaknesses as well as strengths, he was silenced by a tide of Leavis's rhetoric. Leavis's subsequent discussions of the *Quartets* tended simply to recycle what he had written in the 1940s. In *The Living Principle* he looks at the poem in great, even laborious detail, and seems to see it with fresh eyes. The result is a change of mind at least as striking (and as unacknowledged) as the more familiar change about Dickens. Leavis would, no doubt, have denied that he was doing anything so simple as 'rejecting' the poem. In fact, he goes to some lengths to avoid saying that *Four Quartets* is *not* a great poem, and stresses the things in it that he still admires, such as the opening lines of *East Coker* and *The Dry Salvages* and the Dantean 'All Clear' section of *Little Gidding*. (Though he now sees Harding's 1943 essay on *Little Gidding*, which he had once totally endorsed, as a 'disastrous misreading'.) Eliot is still permitted ambiguously positive qualities:

> Eliot, to whom nevertheless we find that we can't deny major

> status, remains a 'case'; his inescapable dividedness is an incapacitating malady. We can't call him anything but a major poet because of the impressiveness of his astonishingly daring and original heuristic creativity—the creativity in which the drive has its clear association with his desperate need.[44]

But this creativity Leavis has already described as having radically negative implications: 'creativity actually employed by Eliot to discredit the creativity of life'.[45] Here, as often elsewhere in this long examination of the *Quartets*, Leavis's favoured terminology seems to collapse as he uses it. There are many instances of local contradiction. For instance, Leavis writes of Eliot's 'American blindness to the nature of languages, and to the implications of his creative use of a given one as essential to the pursuit of his quest'.[46] But within a few pages he calls him 'a "practitioner" whose genius manifests itself in his practice as a rare intelligence about the language in which he works.'[47]

A larger contradiction appears in Leavis's final judgement on the poem. There is a suggestion that having—as he was quite entitled to do—changed his mind about the *Quartets*, Leavis no longer regards the poem as a triumphant expression of heroic individual genius, but as something to be read diagnostically, as he had once read *The Waste Land*, so that Eliot's personal disorders are themselves representative of the disease of modern civilization: 'The genius and those conditions together make his involuntary testimony challenging in a highly significant way; that is, consideration of the plight his poetry reveals sharpens our understanding of our civilisation.'[48] Leavis does in fact go on to compare the *Quartets* with *The Waste Land*, but only to deny culturally diagnostic value to the latter; both the early poem and the late, it seems, are to be read simply as evidence of Eliot's personal sickness:

> The earlier work invites the criticism that it is in a limiting way more personal than the form and the notes suggest. The 'waste land' is not that of western man or the 'modern sense of the human situation' but the peculiar personal 'waste land' of T. S. Eliot who (inevitably, one may say) assumed it to be, in its significance, representatively human.[49]

One of the most disturbing aspects of the essay is Leavis's

willingness to push his psychobiographical reading of the *Quartets* to extreme and wounding lengths. He seems, at times, to be pursuing Eliot down its labyrinthine ways, scarifying what he calls the poet's 'intellectual weakness, his imprisonment in his own sick plight'.[50]

In discussing particular passages Leavis often overturns his own former judgements. Previously he had commented on the small extent to which *Four Quartets* makes doctrinally Christian affirmations, and had discussed the moment in *The Dry Salvages* where Eliot does, very tentatively, make such an affirmation:

> These are only hints and guesses,
> Hints followed by guesses; and the rest
> Is prayer, observance, discipline, thought and action.
> The hint half guessed, the gift half understood, is Incarnation.

In *English Literature and Our Time and the University* Leavis makes what seems to me a just comment on these lines:

> Is that last sentence non-affirmative? Isn't it explicit affirmation? In form, certainly, and no doubt in the poet's intention too. But the context, it seems to me, gives it something of an interrogative force—or (shall I say) imparts to it something of that element of appeal which characterises a judgement: 'This is so, isn't it? And the point I want to make is that I don't think the word comes so charged by what has preceded that it has the clinching inevitability the poet hopes for.[51]

Discussing these same lines in *The LivingPrinciple* Leavis has nothing to say about the way the apparent sense of the words is acted upon and qualified by the context. He refers bluntly to 'the emphatic theological pronouncement' that Eliot intended to make. Leavis is now willing to read the poem not with a critical awareness of separation between text and intention but entirely in terms of assumed intention, so as to be in a better position to reprobate the latter. In his summarizing remarks on the lines, Leavis's tortuous late-Jamesian syntax, which in the past had been used to convey judgements of a finely subtle and elusive kind, here appears to conceal either contradiction or total uncertainty:

> It is one thing to say, as I have just done, that Eliot's arrival at the long-deferred decisive affirmation, clear and unequivocal, doesn't prompt one with the idea that charges of insincerity might be in place. But actually the positive attribution of 'sincerity' *could*, I think, propose itself only to be judged out of the question; it would imply something about the poet, in relation to this after all basic issue, that one's commentary is bound to negate.[52]

In his previous writings on *Ash Wednesday* and *Four Quartets*, Leavis had insisted time and again that these poems of spiritual exploration could not be reduced to analysable separate propositions, which conveyed doctrine to be abstracted from the whole. His entire critical emphasis—to which many readers were and are indebted—had been to show that 'meaning' in this poetry is continually affected and modified by context and verse movement and music. At their best, these poems do not convey or reproduce familiar ideas; as Harding said of *Burnt Norton*, they create fresh ones, to be apprehended poetically, not philosophically or doctrinally. It is remarkable how in *The Living Principle* Leavis reverses his previous critical precept and example in order to deal with passages from the *Quartets* simply as propositions, to be argued with or questions: 'It is well, then, to remind ourselves, and to be reminded, that there *are* questions that, if we were attending duly to the "music", we should have to ask—questions to which we should be right in thinking that we ought, ultimately, to find answers.'[53] Leavis picks up lines and phrases from the *Quartets*, such as 'human kind/Cannot beat very much reality', or 'Ridiculous the waste sad time/Stretching before and after', and treats them as propositions illustrative of Eliot's spiritual plight, to be denounced. The questions Leavis directs at the poem are crude, even philistine: 'What, when it is said of words ("after speech"), we may ask, does "reach into the silence" mean? What is it meant to convey?;[54] 'How, we ask, does Eliot know that prayer in the church of Little Gidding has been valid?[55] One might expect such simplistic demands from a critic like Yvor Winters, whose whole approach to poetry was to look for propostitions to be agreed or disagreed with; but Leavis's superiority as a critic lay precisely in his conviction and practice that no such reductive method could ever be applied to poetry. What we see in his revaluation of *Four Quartets* is Leavis abandoning his integrity as a critic in order finally to cut loose from Eliot.

A different way of making this point would be to say that if the function of the literary critic is that of a judge, whether severe or benign, then here Leavis has abandoned it for the role of prosecuting counsel. Much the same conclusion has been drawn by writers on Leavis who are quite sympathetic to his position. R. B. Bilan refers to 'one's sense that he is determined to make a case against Eliot',[56] while David Holbrook has written:

> I find his analysis perverse—perverse in the sense that he seems to be writing a piece of literary criticism *à these*. I don't feel that the conclusions follow from a response to the text as art, but rather come from an intense scrutiny which is seeking to find faults to substantiate a case against Eliot: to inhibit himself in not being the music while the music lasts. Moreover, the psychology and philosophy on the basis of which the analysis is done seem to me based on unsubstantial ground.[57]

On a particular passage of the poem, Holbrook offers the piquant spectacle of a critic of Leavisite training answering his teacher not with the expected 'Yes, but', but rather, 'No, in Thunder!' In *The Living Principle* Leavis examines in some detail the opening lines of *Little Gidding*, with a view to showing how poor they are; Holbrook flatly disagrees—'The texture of the opening lines of *Little Gidding* is surely superb?'—and presents his own counter-analysis. In the same issue of the *Universities Quarterly* in which Holbrook wrote in 1975, Andor Gomme also disagreed with Leavis about *Four Quartets*; his dissent is all the more striking in that it occurs in the course of an account of Leavis in general and *The Living Principle* in particular that is fulsomely favourable.[58] He prefers Leavis's earlier estimation of *Four Quartets* and compares his late opinion of it to George Orwell's:

> for all the colossal differences in critical acumen and technique, there is a distressing affinity in some of their conclusions—distressing in that Orwell made it quite plain that his dislike of the poem came from an inability to take seriously some of the fundamental attitudes or beliefs without which the poem is hardly conceivable.

Gomme poses the central question, 'why, if Eliot's case is so personal and the effect of this on his poem so damaging, does *Four Quartets* bulk so large in Leavis's thinking?'

The question invites speculation rather than convincing answers. R. B. Bilan has remarked that Leavis's late concern with Eliot was 'almost an obsession'.[59] The word seems appropriate, but I want to stop this discussion at the frontiers of psychobiography. Certain facts have, I hope, been established; as Leavis at one time freely acknowledged, what he owed as a critic to Eliot was immense—even, perhaps the fact that he was a critic at all—and this is apparent not only in his map of English poetry, but in his method and terminology. Eliot's early essay on Blake preoccupied Leavis all his life; he took from it not just critical language, but an idea of Blake as the 'naked man', secure in his creative identity. Something very like this image of Blake later emerges from Leavis's readings of Lawrence, so that, in a bitter irony, Leavis was then able, in his later years, to use both Blake and Lawrence as weapons against Eliot. Another factor may have been that Eliot was, as Leavis often insisted, a great poet and a creative genius, and Leavis was not. His final treatment of Eliot recalls Harold Bloom's cloudy typologies about the anxiety of influence and the function of symbolic parricide. Certainly, what Leavis does to Eliot in *The Living Principle* looks like a mode of psychodrama, involving rituals of explusion and exorcism and ultimate destruction. Striking the father dead may be a necessary part of achieving maturity and independence, but it usually occurs near the beginning rather than at the end of the son's career.

1984

NOTES

1. There have been a number of previous studies of Leavis's relations with Eliot. Michael Black's 'A kind of valediction: Leavis on Eliot 1929-75' appeared in the *Universities Quarterly* in 1975 (vol. 30, pp.78-93) as one of a group of articles published to commemorate Leavis's eightieth birthday. It is a detailed survey of Leavis's writings on Eliot over forty-six years, but its value seems to me limited by Black's total identification with all of Leavis's attitudes and judgements and the corresponsing lack of any critical distance. This is also true of the short and fairly superficial chapter on Eliot in Ronald Hayman's *Leavis* (London, 1976) and of the scattered remarks on the subject in William Walsh's hagiographic *F. R.*

Leavis (London, 1980). There is a more discriminating discussion in R. B. Bilan's *The Literary Criticism of F. R. Leavis* (Cambridge, 1979), though the force of Bilan's comments is constantly muffled by the limpness of his style and his general reluctance to draw firm conclusions.

2. It has been reprinted in E. Homberger, W. Janeway, S. Schama (eds.) *The Cambridge Mind* (London, 1970), pp.235-41.
3. F. R. Leavis, *For Continuity* (Cambridge, 1933), p.111.
4. F. R. Leavis, *New Bearings in English Poetry* (2nd edn, London, 1950), pp.157-8.
5. *ibid.*, p.80.
6. *ibid.*, p.98.
7. F. R. Leavis, *Revaluation* (London, 1936), p.174.
8. *ibid.*, p.165.
9. *ibid.*, p.172.
10. *ibid.*, p.42.
11. *The Criterion,* XVI (January 1937), pp.350-3.
12. Evelyn Waugh, *Brideshead Revisited* (Harmondsworth, 1951), p.32.
13. F. R. Leavis, *Lectures in America* (London, 1969), p.29.
14. *For Continuity*, pp.121-2.
15. *ibid.*, p.2.
16. 'Ille Ego', *New English Weekly*, 5 January 1933.
17. *For Continuity*, pp.176-89.
18. See *New Bearings in English Poetry,* p.99n; *For Continuity*, p.151; *English Literature in Our Time and the University* (London, 1969), p.106; *Nor Shall My Sword* (London, 1972), p.26; *The Living Principle* (London 1975), p.189n; *The Critic as Anti-Philosopher* (London, 1982), pp.2-4.
19. In 1932 Leavis wrote, 'Mr Eliot might have found in an essay on Blake included in a book called *The Sacred Wood,* some admirably said things that might have been said of Lawrence'; *For Continuity,* p.151.
20. *ibid.*, p.151.
21. *ibid.*, pp.156-7.
22. *ibid.*, p.121.
23. F. R. Leavis, *The Common Pursuit* (London, 1952), pp.240-7.
24. The review was reprinted in D. W. Harding, *Experience into Words* (London, 1963), pp.104-11, and in part in Bernard Bergonzi (ed.), *T.S. Eliot: Four Quartets: a Casebook* (London, 1969), pp.29-31.
25. F. R. Leavis, *Education and the University* (2nd edn, London, 1948), p.88n.
26. *ibid.*, pp.87-104.
27. See Helen Gardner, *The Composition of Four Quartets* (London, 1978), p.203.
28. I do not know the source of the words that Leavis attributes to Eliot, unless it is based on a passage about Lawrence in *After Strange Gods* (London, 1934): 'Against the living death of modern civilisation he spoke again and again . . .'; p.60.
29. The contributions by Harding, Higinbotham and Leavis are reprinted in *Four Quartets: a Casebook,* pp.64-80; Harding's review is also included in

Experience Into Words, pp.121-5.
30. F. R. Leavis (ed.), *A Selection from Scrutiny* (Cambridge, 1968) vol. 1, p.88.
31. *The Common Pursuit*, p.292.
32. F. R. Leavis, *D. H. Lawrence: Novelist* (London, 1955), p.303.
33. F. R. Leavis, *'Anna Karenina' and other Essays* (London, 1967), pp.177-96.
34. Bilan, *op. cit.*, p.167.
35. F. R. Leavis, *The Great Tradition* (London, 1948), p.54.
36. *Lectures in America*, p.33.
37. *English Literature in Our Time*, p.81.
38. *New Bearings in English Poetry*, p.69.
39. *Lectures in America*, p.42.
40. *ibid.*, pp.30-1.
41. *ibid.*, p.50.
42. *English Literature in Our Time*, pp.107-8.
43. *Nor Shall My Sword*, p.26.
44. *The Living Principle*, pp.248-9.
45. *ibid.*, p.231.
46. *ibid.*, p.222.
47. *ibid.*, p.227
48. *ibid.*, p.197.
49. *ibid.*, p.208.
50. *ibid.*, p.233.
51. *English Literature in Our Time*, p.131.
52. *The Living Principle*. p.248.
53. *ibid.*, p.173.
54. *ibid.*, p.227.
55. *ibid.*, p.256.
56. Bilan, *op. cit.*, p.279.
57. David Holbrook, 'F. R. Leavis and "Creativity",' *Universities Quarterly*, vol. 30 (1975-6), pp.66-77.
58. Andor Gomme, 'Why literary criticism matters in a technologico-Benthamite age', *loc. cit.*, pp.36-53.
59. Bilan, *op. cit.*, p.277.

8

Eliot's ghostly voices

In essentials, T. S. Eliot's *oeuvre* is binary: *Waste Land: Quartets*. Some readers are strongly attracted to one pole, some to the other. It is possible, though not easy or usual, to feel a perfect and equal regard for both poems; it is probably more common to veer, according to mood or circumstance, between the two. A few years ago Mrs Valerie Eliot's edition of the *Waste Land* manuscripts made that poem an object of new critical interest. It began to look more confessional, less historical and 'impersonal' than earlier readers had supposed. Indeed, by now the tendency to read *The Waste Land* in deeply personal, even autobiographical terms has gone far enough. Dame Helen Gardner's book on *Four Quartets*[1] may do something similar in directing fresh readings of the latter masterpiece. It is a dexterous and enlightening work of scholarship; the book production, in the presentation of texts, drafts, commentary and critical apparatus, is both elegant and functional.

Although we habitually speak of *Four Quartets* as a unified sequence, even a single poem, it was never planned as one. *Burnt Norton* grew out of some lines discarded from *Murder in the Cathedral* in the course of production, and for several years stood alone as the last poem in Eliot's *Collected Poems 1909-1935*. The outbreak of war in 1939 turned Eliot's thoughts away from drama and back to lyrical and meditative poetry; the result was *East Coker* in 1940, consciously modelled on *Burnt Norton.* For a time Eliot was thinking in terms of a trilogy; *The Dry Salvages* followed in 1941 and it was not until *Little Gidding* came out, after some delay, in 1942 that the familiar quadripartite structure was established. In tracing the stages of composition Dame Helen has been through many manuscripts, typed drafts and early printed versions, most of them now at Cambridge, in the John Hayward collection at King's or in the papers that Eliot himself presented to Magdalene. There is not a lot of material pertaining to *Burnt Norton,* but for the other three *Quartets* the deposits are rich and complex: several manuscript or typescript drafts for each poem; the first printed versions in the *New English Weekly*; the first separate publication as Faber pamphlets; and the collected sequence brought out by Faber as *Four Quartets* in 1944. Dame Helen uses this 1944 edition for her texts, while also collating them with the *Collected Poems* of 1963, and the recent paperback edition of that published in 1974.

Students of bibliography and editorial method will find much meat here; but the general reader may need Dame Helen's assurance in her preface that 'the study of the creative process, however interesting, has far less to give us than a study of the object created'; she adds, though, that in this case her four years of labour on the *Quartets* has only increased her understanding and enjoyment of them. Her book is not an edition of the *Quartets,* but it provides much material essential to a future editor. She pinpoints those places where there is evidently something wrong with the existing texts, and this aspect of her book will be immediately useful to readers of Eliot. For instance, there are the well-known lines in *East Coker:*

> In my beginning is my end. Now the light falls
> Across the open field, leaving the deep lane
> Shuttered with branches. . . .

All the drafts and the proof of the *New English Weekly* text read 'open fields'. Dame Helen suggests that the final 's' may have been accidently dropped in the magazine publication and that the error was never noticed and corrected. The published reading seems to me impoverished compared with the poetically suggestive sense of light falling over a whole countryside conveyed by the plural 'fields'.

Later in *East Coker* we have:

> Whisper of running streams, and winter lightning.
> The wild thyme unseen and the wild strawberry. . .

All the drafts and printed texts before the 1944 *Four Quartets* have a comma after lightning. As Dame Helen says in her commentary this is clearly the right reading and should eventually be restored.

There is a further instance in *Little Gidding*. The opening paragraph ends with the lines:

> Where is the summer, the unimaginable
> Zero summer?

Four out of five drafts and the first printed text in the *New English Weekly* read:

> Where is the summer, the unimaginable
> Summer beyond sense, the inapprehensible
> Zero summer?

Again, this is evidently preferable to the established text, a delicately modulated conclusion where 'inapprehensible' leads on deftly to the otherwise abrupt 'Zero'. The middle line disappeared from the supposedly final draft from which the pamphlet was set up. Dame Helen thinks it possible that the omission was accidental; in fact, John Hayward pencilled the line in on the draft as if he suspected just that. Here again a future editor will have to consider whether or not to restore the reading.

There is plenty of evidence in this book of how easily errors could creep into the text, particularly in the successive printed versions. There is one crass instance in *East Coker,* where 'Here or there does not matter' became the meaningless 'Here and there does not matter' in the 1944 edition; Eliot acknowledged the error when it was pointed out to him, but it was not finally corrected until the 1974 paperback edition of the *Collected Poems*.

In a less problematical area Dame Helen puts Eliot right about the supposed etymology of 'The Dry Salvages'. Like many other readers I have always believed, following his note, that it meant 'presumably *les trois sauvages'*. On the authority of no less than the distinguished naval historian, Rear-Admiral Samuel Eliot Morison, U.S.N. (Ret.)—a great admirer, incidentally, of the passages about the sea in *The Dry Salvages*—we learn that Eliot was wrong. 'Dry' means simply 'dry', because the rocks in question were above the sea at high water, in contrast to the nearby 'Little Salvages' which were covered twice daily. 'Salvages' does have something to do with 'sauvages' or 'savages', though the connection remains obscure.

These are matters on which Eliot's readers will want to pencil in a few queries and corrections on their text of *Four Quartets*.

Turning to the substance of the drafts and the process of composition, one makes interesting if inconclusive discoveries. *Little Gidding* gave Eliot most trouble and is full of false starts and abandoned possibilities. He wrote to John Hayward while he was working on it in 1941: 'My suspicions about the poem are partly due to the fact that as it was written to complete a series, and not solely for itself, it may be too much from the head and may show signs of flagging. That is a dilemma.' The dilemma was most acute with *Little Gidding,* though it had been present from *East Coker* onwards, after Eliot resolved to write a related sequence of poems, with the same structure. Most of the difficulties in *Little Gidding* were overcome, partly by Eliot's own tact and self-critical insights, partly by the good advice of John Hayward who read and commented on the drafts. Hayward was no Pound; his comments were sometimes over-literal and pedantic, but he was generally very useful to Eliot in getting the poem into shape.

Eliot himself decided not to end Part III of *Little Gidding* with a version of the traditional prayer, *Anima Christi sanctifica me:*

> Soul of Christ, sanctify them,
> Body of Christ, let their bodies be good earth,
> Water from the side of Christ wash them,
> Fire from the heart of Christ, incinerate them.

The excision was well judged, since the *Quartets* are effective as religious poetry without being too explicitly or exclusively Christian. Earlier in this section Eliot's thoughts move out from the chapel at Little Gidding to the illustrious dead of the seventeenth century, in the lines beginning 'If I think of a king at nightfall'; the line referring to Milton, 'And of one who died blind and quiet', was, it appears, inserted in the manuscript as an afterthought. Yet it is a very significant insertion, indicating Eliot's personal reconciliation with the poet whom he had long regarded with antipathy, perhaps reflecting the wartime feeling that all factions should be brought together, 'folded in a single party'.

Dame Helen's account of *Little Gidding* is particularly interesting on the Dantean 'air-raid' section which Eliot said 'cost me far more time and trouble and vexation than any passage of the same length that I have ever written'. The drafts reproduced here show vividly the kind of trouble he ran into, for as Dame Helen puts it, 'He was here attempting to sustain a style consistently over a long span, whereas his natural genius was towards the paragraph.' That part of the poem originally finished with a rather weak catalogue of images or 'essential moments', concluding with a deliberate harking-back to 'La figlia che piange':

> He turned away, and in the autumn weather
> I heard a distant dull deferred report
> At which I started: and the sun had risen.

Then, happily, fresh inspiration came and Eliot substituted the magnificent lines that begin: 'But, as the passage now presents no hindrance/To the spirit unappeased and peregrine. . . .' One of the most powerful phrases here, 'the laceration/Of laughter at what ceases to amuse', is thanks to a suggestion by John Hayward which Eliot gratefully adopted.

Such insights into Eliot's creative activity are illuminating, though they are not numerous in Dame Helen's book. It does not transform one's ideas of the *Quartets,* but the process of comparing the 1944 text—printed at the top of the page—with the drafts, and following the editorial commentary, does provide a uniquely valuable experience of reading the sequence carefully and slowly and patiently. Dame Helen's introductory chapters—on the documents in the case, and on the growth and sources of *Four Quartets*—succinctly marshal a lot of relevant information. But they seem to me deficient, by omission, in one major respect.

Nearly thirty years ago, in *The Art of T. S. Eliot*, she remarked that the structure of each quartet 'is essentially the same as the structure of *The Waste Land'*. It is indeed; *Burnt Norton* in particular is noticeably close to *The Waste Land.* The rose-garden parallels the hyacinth-garden, and the phrase 'heart of light' occurs in the first section of each, while there are London settings and place-names in the third sections. It seems that when Eliot was developing *Burnt Norton* from the lines removed from

Murder in the Cathedral he must have been consciously using *The Waste Land* as his model, though unfortunately the manuscript remains are too sparse to offer any supporting evidence. The model was reproduced three more times when the other quartets were written between 1940 and 1942, and to this extent *The Waste Land* affects the whole sequence, however different the poetry. I find it strange that Dame Helen, having made the point so long ago, ignores it in her new study, where one might have expected it to be developed.

There is another and much smaller question where she passes over a link between the *Quartets* and Eliot's earlier poetry. As she reminds us, and as Eliot reminded John Hayward, 'the children in the apple-tree' at the end of *Little Gidding* echo 'the hidden laughter of children in the foliage' in *Burnt Norton* and both recall 'Children's voices in the orchard', the first line of 'New Hampshire'. But that line was itself adapted from 'Children singing in the orchard', from the suppressed 'Ode', published for the first and last time in *Ara Vos Prec* in 1920. Eliot was a careful salvager of his own discarded fragments and this particular *topos* clearly meant much to him over many years.

So, in the end, when the process of composition has been carefully inspected and the panels are screwed back into place and the text stands more or less as we always knew it, with smooth and continuous surfaces, what remains? *Four Quartets*, a difficult poem. More difficult, certainly, than Eliot thought, since he genuinely believed that it was simpler and easier to understand than *The Waste Land*. In a superficial way it is, since there are fewer allusions and phrases in foreign languages, and no disconcerting shifts in space and time. But *The Waste Land* is a dramatic poem: the voices may weave in and out in an elusive way, but they have names and recognizable intonations and even, sometimes, personal identities. *Four Quartets* has many voices—reflective, lyrical, lecturing, praying, preaching—but we cannot easily identify and separate them. Nor can we be sure how to hear them.

Like many other critics I have condemned the flatter and duller expository passages of the *Quartets*; Dame Helen herself is unhappy about such things as the 'regrettably defensive' lines in *East Coker*. 'You say I am repeating/Something I have said before, I shall say it again', or what she describes as the 'lame close' of *The Dry Salvages*. Some critics have claimed that in the *Quartets* Eliot abandoned the fragmentary but intense art of *The Waste Land*, which was dramatic, imagistic, and intuitive, in favour of merely relaxed or empty discourse. C. K. Stead has argued this case, urbanely in *The New Poetic*, and much more sharply in a lecture I heard him deliver in 1977. For years I have been half-convinced by it; now I tend to doubt it. Critically it may not be acceptable to quote a few lines and simply dismiss them as 'flat' or 'thin'. They may indeed seem so in isolation, but the contexts can redeem them, or 'recuperate' them in structuralist terminology. This isn't always so—some flatness is irredeemable—but increasingly I hear the *Quartets* as an interplay of ghostly voices, some rich, some thin, but interacting polyphonically.

It is not an easy music to pick up or listen to—I find *The Waste Land* far solider and more approachable—but it grows upon one. And in the end the music seems to draw the poem out of the contexts that are evident in *The Composition of Four Quartets*: Possum in middle age; John Hayward's pedantic learning; Faber and Faber; the Anglican Church; England in wartime; memories of the sea and an American childhood. Eventually the voices *are* the poem, as it floats in space, a pure linguistic entity. This is not just my own personal response; something similar has been argued by recent critics who are happy to recuperate the *Quartets* in neo-symbolist terms as a great self-referring exploration of their own langauge; I am thinking of Peter Ackroyd in *Notes for a New Culture* and Michael Edwards in *Eliot/Language*. Such a reading can account for everything, the flattest discourse as well as the most intense lyricism. All is language, all belongs. My own view is more cautious than this, since I still incline to believe that the *Quartets* do not finally and completely hang together; not everything fits. I find too many resistances to complete recuperation; the poem remains hard, not properly *lisible*, modern.

1978

NOTE

1. Helen Gardner, *The Composition of Four Quartets*

9

The 1930s: types and myths

Recent studies of literature and society in the 1930s have shown a common concern with the typology and mythology of the period. If the representative literature, such as the poetry of W. H. Auden and Louis MacNeice or the early novels of Graham Greene and George Orwell, is acutely responsive to contemporary social realities, the society presents itself in recurring images and archetypes. Auden, above all, has a sharp, categorizing vision of the world:

> Their splendid People, their wiseacres,
> Professors, agents, magic-makers,
>   Their poets and apostles,
> Their bankers and their brokers too,
> And ironmasters shall turn blue
> Shall fade away like morning dew
>   With club-room fossils.

Such lists abound in Auden's poetry; this one, from an early poem originally called 'A Communist to Others', has acquired a new twist of meaning with the passing of time: 'poets and apostles' now suggests the Cambridge Apostles and what we have learnt of their divided loyalties in the thirties. Lists and catalogues of representative types of people and things, strings of nouns and phrases prefaced by the placing definite article, were part of the literary idiom of the time. Then, on 1 September 1939, as the Second World War began, Auden wrapped up and dismissed the whole decade in a magisterial phrase that was to become famous: 'As the clever hopes expire/ Of a low dishonest decade.' It is satisfyingly comprehensive, but one must resist it. 'I do not know the method of drawing up an indictment against a whole people,' said Edmund Burke, and one can say the same thing about indicting a whole decade.

It would be far too simple to claim that Auden alone was responsible for our subsequent view of the thirties; but his broad typifying view was and remains immensely influential. Types became archetypes, and archetypes turned into myths; indeed, the writers of the Auden generation were inclined to mythicize their experience from the very beginning. Auden's *The Orators,* published in 1932, shows the process at work. *The Orators* is a melange of verse and prose of, so to speak, dazzling obscurity, which includes some of Auden's most brilliant writing. It is supposedly a revolutionary text, though it also contains many private jokes and allusions which mythologize the author and his friends. At its centre is the potent figure of the airman-as-hero, supposedly an embodiment of left-wing ideals, but ideologically ambiguous, since the lonely airman was as much a fascist emblem as a revolutionary socialist one. In later years Auden felt very alienated from *The Orators* and confessed that it seemed to him that it might have been written by a young Nazi. When the Spanish Civil War broke out literary myths moulded a complex historical reality, as was exemplified in Andre Malraux's *Days of Hope (L'Espoir).* This novel is directly based on Malraux's experience in the early months of the war of organizing the Republican air force; it was written soon after the events it describes and deliberately embodied a propagandist myth. Towards its conclusion Malraux presents an impressive tableau as the Republican aircraft triumph over their fascist enemies at the battle of Guadalajara. But an uninformed reader might get a misleading sense of the course of the war if he was not aware that soon after the victory that Malraux describes the Republican air force lost its ascendency and never regained it. Myths appeal profoundly to the imagination and the feelings; but they are not history, however much they draw on it. The First World War for instance, was a terrible and enormously complicated set of events. Literary readers obtain a vivid but mythicized image of the war if they rely solely on the poetry of Wilfred Owen and Siegfried Sassoon, or the song-and-dance routines and arresting slogans of *Oh What a Lovely War!*

To take another example from the thirties. Christopher Isherwood has memorably recorded pre-Hitler Berlin in *Mr Norris Changes Trains* and *Goodbye to Berlin,* to the extent that he seems not only the recorder but the inventor of that doomed time and place; the captivating myth of Sally Bowles hangs over everything (particularly if we consider its successive transformations, from the novella of *Sally Bowles* to the play of *I am a Camera* to the film of *Cabaret*). Isherwood's deadpan pretence of photographic realism might suggest that he truly is a camera, passively recording the stuff of history. But attentive reading soon reveals that the Berlin stories embody an art of caricature and careful selection, a network of heightened effects and significant omissions.

Recently, in the course of teaching a graduate seminar on the fiction of the thirties, I asked the members of the class to contribute, quickly and without time for reflection, their pre-existing impressions of the period. The responses were predictable: the Slump, hunger marchers, Jarrow; fascism; the war in Spain; the poetry of the Auden generation. All of these things existed and were important, but their significance is both reinforced and distorted by their autonomous importance as literary myths. Books such as Walter Greenwood's *Love on the Dole* and George Orwell's *The Road to Wigan Pier* provide images of English life in the thirties which are so strong and so appalling that they colour many readers' apprehension of what was in fact a very diverse period, when social decay coexisted with new forms of social development. Not all of England experienced the misery and destitution of Salford or Wigan. What is presented in literature gets further focused by the visual images from old newsreels, which are regularly shown in television documentaries. I find them invariably fascinating; but they are also predictable; the hunger marchers, battles between blackshirts and workers in the East End; and, above all, Spain; the barricades, the bombing of Madrid; the defiant militiamen, the odious fascists; the rallying of the International Brigades ('They floated over the oceans; / They walked the passes: they came to present their lives' wrote Auden in his supremely mythological poem, 'Spain 1937'). The verbal and visual rhetorics were directed to one single, irresistible end: to see the Spanish War as a simple, clear-cut struggle between democracy and fascism. If there is one lesson to be learnt from the wealth of subsequent historical writing about the Spanish Civil War it is that there was nothing simple about it; what was presented as a battle between the international powers of darkness and light was in fact a bitter struggle between opposed forces deeply rooted in Spanish history and tradition.

The difficulty with myths is that they are fixed, static, ahistorical; whereas historiography is always provisional and changing, liable to be affected by new evidence or challenging interpretations. The dominant literary images of the 1930s retain their emotional power, unaffected by noises from the next room of social and economic historians currently arguing over revisionist versions of the period. Not all the myths have persisted. We now have no illusions about Russia, for instance. Devotion to the Soviet Union was common at the time though not often reflected in the literature that is still read. C. Day Lewis was an active member of the Communist Party for some years, but his son remarks in his recent biography that Day Lewis was quite uninformed about Russia and had little real interest in it.[1] Day Lewis was unusually insular, perhaps; even so, Republican Spain attracted many more writers in person than the Soviet Union, the latter being visited, as a rule, only by dedicated party members or fellow-travellers. Yet Day Lewis, an amiably English and unideological figure at heart, was at least casually acquainted with Guy Burgess and Anthony Blunt. The subsequent revelations about Burgess and Blunt, Philby and Maclean, have inevitably affected attitudes to the ideological movements of those years, in the light of what we now know about Stalinist terror. Given the global crisis and near-collapse of capitalism in the early thirties it was reasonable that intellectuals might turn to socialism as an ideal; what was a lot less reasonable or even intelligible was their readiness to take at face value the assertion that the socialist ideal was already embodied in the Soviet Union (not all of them did, of course; André Gide and George Orwell got into trouble for heresy on this point). With the menacing rise of fascism the comforting principle that 'my enemy's enemy is my friend' offered sufficient reason for embracing still more warmly the Soviet Union, which also called itself a democracy, even of a different kind from the West. The myth of the Russian Revolution, the 'ten days that shook the world', had so strong an attraction for Western intellectuals that it made the Soviet Union virtually immune to criticism. In fact, quite a lot was already known about Soviet realities, if not the whole horrifying story, from the reports of refugees and some Western journalists; but, in Eliot's words, 'Human kind cannot bear very much reality', and people were very ready not to hear what they did not want to hear. Stephen Spender, in his autobiography, describes Edward Upward, there called 'Chalmers', as responding to the Moscow Trials by saying 'I've long ago given up thinking about such things.'

Intellectual commitment to the Soviet system is one thing, actively working for it as a spy is another. We now know that a number—just how many remains uncertain—of well-bred and well-educated young Englishmen began as idealistic socialists and ended as Soviet agents. There are some interesting literary hints of this state of mind, not in any of the major canonical texts of the period, but in one of Eric Ambler's urbane, fast-moving spy stories, written in the Buchan tradition but underpinned by impeccably left-wing assumptions. *Case for Alarm* (1938) describes the adventures of an innocent abroad, a young, apolitical English engineer called Nicholas Marlow who is sent to Mussolini's Italy to do a job and, despite himself, gets caught up in the intrigues of German and Italian secret agents. He is helped out of bad trouble by a good Samaritan whom he shortly discovers to be a Soviet agent called Zaleshoff, a bluff, amiable figure who speaks perfect American English; he is described as having brown curly hair, blue eyes, a prizefighter's nose and hefty broad shoulders. Zaleshoff emerges as the true hero of the story, in the literal sense of appearing as an heroic figure out of Soviet iconography. Marlow recalls their hard time together on the run from their enemies: 'Looking back now on those days together with Zaleshoff one thing makes me marvel above all else—my complete and unquestioning belief in Zaleshoff's superior powers of endurance. It was always Zaleshoff who coaxed me into making a further effort when no further effort seemed possible.' Stalin himself could have done no better. And Zaleshoff is not just a tough and inventive secret agent; he is also well grounded in Marxist doctrine, which he does not hesitate to expound: 'You can't change human nature, buddy. Bunk! Human nature is part of the social system it works in. Change your system and you change your man.' Despite his early doubts Marlow comes to see things in Zaleshoff's way and agrees to work with him: 'Zaleshoff was a Soviet agent—I had come without effort to take that fact for granted—and he had his work to do, he had the business of his extraordinary government to attend to. I supposed that, strictly speaking, I too was a servant of that government. Oddly enough, I found that idea no worse than curious.' We are not too far from the mental world of the Cambridge spies, though with the crucial difference that Ambler's character is ideologically naive, as indeed is his creator (or was, in 1938). *Cause for Alarm* ends with a paragraph, supposedly quoted from a French periodical but suggesting authorial approval, that expresses the hope that a rift may appear in the Rome-Berlin Axis, provided there is co-operation between the 'three great European democracies', Britain, France and the Soviet Union . . . Ambler's novel remains a highly competent and readable thriller, but it also offers a curious memento of a particular phase of historical consciousness in the late thirties; it presents an abortive myth—the tough, genial, omnicompetent Soviet agent saving the muddled Westerner—that did not survive the history of the next few years. Zaleshoff is a figure from Soviet self-mythologizing briefly transposed into a Western literary context.

The encounter between literature and politics in the 1930s has been well and thoroughly discussed by Samuel Hynes in *The Auden Generation* (1976), a work that has been criticized as offering too much of its own myth of the thirties, though no one has yet given a convincing alternative interpretation. In my own book, *Reading the Thirties* (1978), I suggested that the approach in terms of politics had been taken about as far as it profitably could, and that a different view of the period shows it as responding, often in troubled and contradictory ways, to the impact of mass technology. In some respects technology fed directly into myth, as in the 'helmeted airman' that fascinated Auden and other writers. Most technological influence was less direct but still very pervasive. I suggested in *Reading the Thirties* that two of the most important presences were the cinema and the fear of aerial bombing; one an enhancement of life, the other a desperate threat to it; and both products of new technology. I provided a range of examples of both from the literature of the thirties, and since then I then come across many more. The prevalence of images of bombing has been discussed in an excellent essay, 'Popular fiction and the next war, 1918-1939' by Martin Ceadel, in *Class, Culture and Social Change: A New View of the 1930s,* edited by Frank Gloversmith (1980). In 1936

George Orwell made Gordon Comstock, the gloomy hero of *Keep the Aspidistra Flying,* look forward with apocalyptic relish to the bombing of London. That was in fiction, but in real life David Gascoyne, standing on Hampstead Heath in October 1936, reflected, 'What a heart-shaking spectacle it will be from this height some night soon to come, when the enemy squadrons blackening the skies rain down destroying fire upon these roofs' (*Journal 1936-37,* first published 1980). Aerial bombing had already become familiar in Abyssinia and Spain, but such intensely literary ways of responding to it showed that the fear could take a mythic shape. References to bombs and air-raids occur in unlikely places, like small, half-hidden clues to a prevalent state of mind. For instance, in a description of an industrial landscape early on in Walter Greenwood's *Love on the Dole* we read, 'A double row of six smaller chimneys thrust up their steel muzzles like cannon trained on air raiders'; while in a later novel of the thirties, different in every possible way in subject and treatment, Elizabeth Bowen's *Death of the Heart,* occurs this sentence: 'Appalling as the talk with Daphne had been, it had not been so finally fatal, when you looked back at it, as an earthquake or a dropped bomb'. In both these novels, too, there are references to cinema-going; in the former as a weekly treat for the people of Salford when they are in work, and as something they can no longer afford when they are unemployed; in the latter as a detailed account of a visit to a sumptuous West End cinema. People go to the cinema all the time in the novels of the thirties, as they did in real life.

The cinema was a universally present sign of the new world of mass civilisation and technological advance that co-existed with the depression and industrial decline along with the new housing estates, the chain stores, the arterial roads, the motor car, the radio. The spread of this new world was a steady process, not a matter of arresting or dramatic events that could be captured on newsreels or mythicized in literature. Significantly, *The Road to Wigan Pier,* that observant though very subjective anatomy of social and industrial decay, looks not only at the slums but at the results of slum clearance; the new council housing estates, decent but utterly bleak, on the fringes of industrial cities. Orwell makes a thoughtful assessment of the loss and gain involved in such displacements; he noted that the destruction of slums also involved the loss of a close-knit community, long before this became a common insight. Returning to fiction in *Coming Up for Air* Orwell made a dispirited attack on the new England, the product of spreading suburbia and light industry and growing consumerism; exemplified in Hayes, Slough, Dagenham: 'The kind of chilliness, the bright red brick everywhere, the temporary-looking shop-windows full of cut-price chocolates and radio parts.'

D. H. Lawrence had made similar attacks on the emerging new world in the twenties. But by the late thirties that world, with all its potential for promise or destruction, had really arrived. It was dominated by the internal combustion engine, that technological invention of the late nineteenth century that has so transformed collective and individual life. As early as the turn of the century W. E. Henley had described the thrill of riding in a motor car in 'A Song of Speed', and the motor car became a conspicuous entity in Edwardian texts such as *The Wind in the Willows* or *Howards End.* But it is not until the thirties that writers convey the recognizable experience of sitting at the wheel and actually driving a car. I am thinking of Louis MacNeice's poem 'Birmingham', or the wonderfully vivid evocation of driving a car at night in the rain in part XIV of his *Autumn Journal:*

> The wheels whished in the wet, the flashy strings
>   Of neon lights unravelled, the windscreen-wiper
> Kept at its job like a tiger in a cage or a cricket that sings
>   All night through for nothing.

Much of the writing of the thirties has lost its original impact in terms of political reference and social attitude. But MacNeice, in this passage written over forty years ago, is showing us something that has not changed at all in essentials: windscreen-wipers are not the stuff of myth, but the familiar, modest and, in more than one sense, necessary part of a universal experience. In 1938 only a restricted segment of society knew about driving cars; now nearly everyone does.

For readers concerned with the interpenetration of literature and history the 1930s seem endlessly interesting. But the study has its dangers. Some social historians very reasonably use literature as a source of knowledge, but they need to be alert to the distorting effects of personal or social myths, whether in Isherwood's Berlin or Graham Greene's Brighton; conversely, students of the literature of the thirties should not deceive themselves that they have a good understanding of its historical context when what they are acquainted with are the potent but ahistorical myths that are partly generated by the literature itself.

1982

NOTES

1. Nevertheless Day Lewis wrote with confident praise of the Soviet Union in his poem, 'On the Twentieth Anniversary of Soviet Power', published in *Russia Today* and reprinted in 1938 in the anthology *In Letters of Red.* Representative lines are:

> Twenty years have passed
> Since a cry, All Power to the Soviets! shook the world.
> We have seen new cities, arts and sciences,
> A real freedom, a justice that flouts not nature,
> Springing like corn exuberant from the rich heart
> Of a happier people. We have seen their hopes take off
> From solid ground and confidently fly
> Out to the mineral north, the unmapped future.
> U.S.S.R.! The workers of every land
> And all who believe man's virtue inexhaustible
> Greet you today: you are their health, their home,
> The vision's proof, the lifting of despair.
> Red Star, be steadfast above this treacherous age!
> We look to you, we salute you.

10
Poets of the 1940s
(Bernard Spencer, Alun Lewis, G. S. Fraser)

Bernard Spencer, who was born in the same year as Stephen Spender and was a frequent contributor to *New Verse*, might have been remembered as a poet of the 1930s if it were not for the accident that his first book, *Aegean Islands and other poems*, did not appear until 1946. By then his experience of England in the 1930s had been enlarged by life in Greece and Egypt in the 1940s. But his basic style and stance did not change; the continuity of Spencer's poetry shows just how arbitrary is the convenient periodization in surveys of modern literature, where the 'social realist' 1930s are instantly replaced in 1940 by the 'neo-romantic' 1940s. Spencer published only one other collection of poems in his lifetime, *With Luck Lasting* (incorporating some poems which had first appeared in a limited edition published at Reading University in 1960), a few months before his accidental death in Vienna in September 1963. His first *Collected Poems*, published by Alan Ross in 1965, contains his two published volumes and a group of poems written in the last year of his life. That work is now superseded by Mr Bowen's fine edition, which includes a valuable critical and biographical introduction.[1] He has done a thorough editorial job, checking the printed texts of the poems with Spencer's manuscripts at Reading, recording variants and adding explanatory notes. He has added to the text of the 1965 volume some twenty or so previously uncollected poems, from magazines or manuscripts, plus a selection of Spencer's undergraduate poems written at Oxford in the early 1930s. Mr Bowen is a scrupulous and unobtrusive editor who has served his subject well.

Spencer was an amiable, recessive personality, who floated round the fringes of London literary life before the war without making any great impact on anyone, like a minor character in Anthony Powell, perhaps, or a faint carbon copy of the urbane and elegant MacNeice, who had been his older contemporary at Marlborough. But a real personality comes through Spencer's poetry of the 1930s; he offers the particular interest of a poet who uses a common style in recognizably original ways. One of his best, and best-known, pre-war poems, 'Allotments: April', is in some respects a quintessential period piece, an exact observation of a time and place that firmly locates it in history ('The wireless voice repeating pacts, persecutions'), in an Audensque idióm, replete with definite articles and a catalogue of the contents of the age. Yet the poem is unified by a nervious, very personal rhythm which is, for me, uniquely Spencer's. In poems such as 'A Thousand Killed' and 'A Cold Night' he responds to public crisis—particularly the Spanish Civil War—with conscientious anxiety, aware of his own impotence and, in the end, guiltily returning to private satisfactions. Yet he knows that history cannot be shut out for long, as in 'A Cold Night', which moves to a quietly eloquent conclusion that I find immensely effective:

> I turn back to my fire. Which I must.
> I am not God or a crazed woman.
> And one needs time too to sit in peace
> Opposite one's girl, with food, fire, light,
>
> And do the work one's own blood heats,
> Or talk, and forget about the winter
> —This season, this century—and not be always
> Opening one's door on the pitiful streets
>
> Of Europe, not always thinking of winter, winter, like a
> hammering rhyme
> For then everything is drowned by the rising wind,
> everything is done against Time.

Spencer's poise and intelligence may recall MacNeice, but he is less concerned to strike attitudes. He was never a copious poet but a few of his poems from the late 1930s can, I think, stand comparison with anything by his better-known contemporaries.

In 1940 he began working for the British Council and went on doing so for the rest of his life, in a series of Mediterranean exiles; in Greece in 1940-41, then in Egypt after the Germans occupied Greece; then, after the war, in Italy, Spain, Greece again, until the final move north to Austria, for the last year of his life. In Greece he met Laurence Durrell, who became a close friend, and Durrell's Mediterranean hedonism evidently modified Spencer's northern anxiety. Roger Bowen suggests that Spencer's southern exile meant for him a welcome departure not only from England, but from the whole 1930s literary ethos. His poem, 'Aegean Islands 1940-41', written after his departure from Greece and nostalgically retrospective, crystallizes his new attitudes:

> Where white stares, smokes or breaks,
> Thread white, white of plaster and foam,
> Where sea like a wall falls;
> Ribbed, lionish coast,
> The stony islands which blow into my mind
> More often than I imagine my grassy home . . .

This poem suggests Durrell's influence, in style as well as in feeling. But its structure is characteristic of the 1930s, a list of separate observations and notations, brought together only in the final lines:

> The dark bread
> The island wine and the sweet dishes;
> All these are element in a happiness
> More distant now than any date like '40,
> A.D. or B.C., ever can express.

Spencer may have turned away from England but he could not wholly sever his links with the northern world. 'The Ship' delights in the simplicity and directness and sensuous immediacy of a beach in Palestine:

> Scarlet of flags, a children's see-saw, swings,
> Like elementary shapes a child has drawn;
> And the mind grasps them in a stride.

But the poem ends with a metaphorical acknowledgement of the dark, buried power of the north:

> No wonder mind should find this scenery bland
> as lotions are to eyes;
> our loves being mostly natives of a land

mountainous, hung with forests, loud with storms:
and our thoughts climb
to light like things the digger's spade has struck,
a broken dish, a ring,
confused with dark and roots and time.

'The Ship' is one of several poems in which Spencer celebrates ships or boats, modest Mediterranean craft, exemplifying human skill and a human scale; other examples are 'Yachts on the Nile', 'The Boat', and 'Boat Poem'; in 'Aegean Islands 1940-41' he had lovingly recalled 'the gear and grace of sailing,/The drenching race for home and the sail-white houses'. Spencer admired the tough, functional elegance of these simple vessels, a quality which characterizes his own poetry. Describing such things was a way of conveying his own feelings, in an economical embodiment of the objective correlative. Spencer was always a strongly personal poet, who attempted no other poetic form than the brief lyrical expression of a moment's feeling, and he was prepared to wait for the feeling to come, which is why his poems are both short and infrequent. Understatement and irony were evidently part of his temperament as well as being common in the public style of the Auden generation. Personal feeling and historical predicament come together with laconic intensity in one of his most moving poems, 'Letters', which reflects his wartime separation from his wife:

Letters, like blood along a weakening body
move fainter round our map. On dangerous wings,
on darkenss-loving keels they go, so longed for;
but say no memorable things. . . .

Now public truths are scarcer currency,
what measure for the personal truth? How can
this ink and paper coursing continents
utter the clothed or the naked man?

As one of the remarkable and gifted collection of English poets, military and civilian, who had been brought together in Cairo by the accidents of war, Spencer would have been well aware of the ebb and flow of the battles in the Western Desert; in

'Libyan Front', which is a little untypical in style, he presents a spectator's impression of the battlefield. Spencer was a civilian and cannot quite be called a 'war poet', though in the Second World War the distinction between civilian and combatant responses was much less clear-cut than in the First. In wartime Cairo—whose atmosphere was vividly evoked by another of its inhabitants, the late Olivia Manning, in *The Levant Trilogy*—Spencer was friendly with a young officer who survived the desert war only to die in Normandy, and who is now remembered as the finest poet of the Second World War: Keith Douglas. His poetry and Spencer's have a comparable wryness and irony in their attitudes to war and to experience at large.

Alun Lewis served as a soldier for four years and is generally regarded as a 'war poet', though he was never under fire and his death in Burma in 1944 remains mysterious. Discussing Lewis's *Selected Poems* together with Spencer's volume involves me in a conscious effort to resist the invidiousness of comparison; I have known and enjoyed Spencer's poems for many years, and have had a long-standing suspicion that Lewis was not such a fine poet as his admirers claim. Going back to their work has confirmed both the enjoyment and the suspicion. Lewis's most celebrated poem is 'All day it has rained . . .' which renders the sombre miseries of life in camp:

> All day it has rained, and we on the edge of the moors
> Have sprawled in our bell-tents, mody and dull as boors,
> Groundsheets and blankets spread on a muddy ground
> And from the first grey wakening we have found
> No refuge from the skirmishing fine rain . . .

This poem deserves its fame, as the sharp evocation of a characteristic experience of the Second World War, though I think it would have been a better poem if it had ended a little before it does, on the lines: 'Tomorrow maybe love; but now it is the rain/Possesses us entirely, the twilight and the rain.' There is an echo here of Auden's 'Spain', but Lewis has integrated it into his own response; the remaining few lines, with their concluding invocation to Edward Thomas, seem to me conventional and anticlimactic. Jeremy Hooker, in his intelligent afterword to this selection,[2] acknowledges the quality of the poem but says it is not really typical of Lewis's poetry in its realistic observation and muted sense of human solidarity. Lewis, he says is 'essentially a poet of feeling, frequently unrestrained in expressing his bewilderment or ecstacy or anguish or depression; a tender love poet; and one who insisted on seeking the answer to ultimate questions at a time when for many survival meant restraint and resignation.' This is well put, and Mr Hooker goes on to acknowledge that Lewis took many risks; his intensities of vision and feeling were often too much for the inadequacies of his poetic technique; as Mr Hooker says, he had 'a weakness for debased romantic diction and rhetoric'. The romanticism is not all debased and in places it is stiffened by Audenesque idioms. Yet it is not difficult to find examples of the kind of writing that gives 1940s poetry a bad name:

> Did the anxious eye of pain
> Bravely bear the stigmata
> Of the christ in us, the livid
> Weal of history bleeding in us again?

The romantic and subjective feeling in Lewis's best poems is far superior to such inauthentic lines; but they remind us that Lewis, as a war poet and victim, is closer to Sidney Keyes than to the ironic and tough-minded Keith Douglas. Keyes and Lewis shared a devotion to Rilke, who was a patron-saint of poetic subjectivity in the 1940s. I find Lewis most congenial in the sober, human observations of 'A Welsh Night', a formally tighter poem than most of his, though Mr Hooker is uneasy about it. I agree with him that 'The Jungle' is Lewis's most sustained and perhaps his most impressive poetic achievement. It uses the Indian jungle as a symbolic landscape where Lewis enacts his sense of personal and historical crisis. Mr Hooker, having found quite a lot to criticize in Lewis's poetry, somewhat overstates a plausible case when he says that 'The Jungle' 'should be placed with Auden's "September, 1939" and David Gascoyne's "Farewell" as one of the great poems signalling the end of an era of illusions in "the humming cultures of the West" '. This is a loose use of 'great' and it does not allow for the extent to which Lewis, in this poem, not only has affinities with Auden but in places is excessively influenced by him:

> The willingness to please that made a wound,
> The kneeling darkness and the hungry prayer;
> Cargoes of anguish in the holds of joy,
> The smooth deceitful stranger in the heart,
> The tangled wrack of motives drifting down
> An oceanic tide of Wrong.
> And though the state has enemies we know
> The greater enmity within ourselves.

Lewis was a clearly gifted writer, though his real talent may have been for fiction rather than poetry. Contrary to common assumptions, I do not believe he was very much closer to poetic maturity when he died at twenty-eight than was Sidney Keyes, who was killed just before his twenty-first birthday.

The collected poems of George Sutherland Fraser make a substantial and elegant collection, very agreeably produced by Leicester Univerity Press.[3] It is, sadly, a posthumous work, for Fraser died in January 1980 at the age of sixty-four, soon after taking early retirement from the English Department at Leicester, where he had taught for twenty years. The quantity of poetry in this volume may surprise readers who think of Fraser as a poet only in the context of the wartime Cairo school and London bohemia in the immediate post-war years. He was a freelance literary journalist until the late 1950s, and thereafter an academic, and was a productive and versatile critic in both these phases of his life; he was more widely known as a critic than as a poet. The greater part of his poetry was, indeed, written in the 1940s and appeared in his first two collections, *Home Town Elegy* (1944) and *The Traveller Has Regrets* (1948). But Fraser never gave up writing poetry and in the 1970s he experienced a remarkable revival of poetic activity, the results of which are generally available for the first time in this book. The editors, Ian Fletcher and John Lucas, have done an excellent job, bringing together most if not quite all of Fraser's poems, collected or uncollected, of four decades, and providing unobtrusively helpful notes. The one place where they have significantly gone astray is in publishing a poem in French called 'Rhétorique Sentimentale du Temps d'Hiver' without comment, as if Fraser had written it in that language. In fact, as an introductory note to *The Traveller*

Has Regrets makes clear, the French version was a translation by a friend of an early poem by Fraser. He preferred the French version to the English original, which can be found in the New Apocalypse anthology of 1941, *The White Horseman,* and is not included in the present collection.

Fraser's earliest poems go back to the mid and late 1930s, when he was a student at St Andrews and then a young journalist in Aberdeen. They reflect the idiom and interests of the times; at their simplest, Audenesque diction and anxiety about approaching war. But though they make their gestures towards history and public crisis, their inspiration is personal and local. As a young poet Fraser was self-absorbed and often self-pitying, though his great skill with metre and stanzaic forms, which was evident from the beginning, enabled him to distance his feelings sufficiently to prevent them coming across as merely egotistical or mawkish. A recognizable persona emerges from the early poems: the clever, clumsy, lonely young Scotsman, awkward at parties and on the dance floor, fascinated by girls but never quite knowing what to say to them. From these situations Fraser drew poetic feelings that were sad and elegiac and regretful, shortly to be refined into the wartime exile's nostalgia and longing for home. The titles of his first two books were characteristic; *Home Town Elegy,* in addition to the title poem, contains several other poems called 'elegy' and another called 'lament'. The elegies and the regrets were not simply personal, for they also involved Fraser's sense of Scottish identity. As a very young man, still living in Scotland, he felt merely provincial. In 'Sonnet' he writes:

> My simple heart, bred in provincial tenderness,
> And my cold mind, that takes the world for theme
> With local pain, with universal remedy,
> Avert the real, disturb the noble dream . . .

(Later in the poem Fraser employs the idiom of the time: 'the loud guns laughing over Europe' and 'the pages of history'.) Some of the pre-war poems bring together doubts about personal and national identity. 'To Hugh MacDiarmid', infused with polite self-deprecation, projects warm admiration for the Nationalist poet but in the end rejects his exclusiveness and fanaticism:

What a race has is always crude and common,
And not the human or the personal:
I would take sword up only for the human,
Not to revive the broken ghosts of Gael.

In 'Meditation of a patriot' Fraser adopts an angrier attitude to the myths and realities of his country:

The posters show my country blonde and green,
Like some sweet siren, but the travellers know
How dull the shale sky is, the airs how keen,
And how our boorish manners freeze like snow.
Romantic Scotland was an emigrant,
Half-blooded and escaped from sullen weather.
Here, we toss off a dram to drown a cough
And whisky has the trade-mark of the heather.
My heart yearns southwards as as the shadows slant,
I wish I were an exile and I rave:
With Byron and with Lermontov
Romantic Scotland's in the grave.

The refrain directly imitates Yeats's 'September 1913', and is an early sign of Fraser's lifelong devotion to Yeats. Elsewhere in *Home Town Elegy* are poems called 'For Yeats' and 'Elegy for Yeats and Freud'. Later Fraser wrote several critical essays on Yeats—some are included in his *Essays on Twentieth-Century Poets* (1977) and others remain uncollected—and in his poetry he often engaged with Yeats, by reference, allusion or imitation. The relationship looks like what Harold Bloom has called the 'anxiety of influence', where a young poet finds in an admired older poet something of a father-figure whose influence has to be thrown off before he can discover his own identity. For Fraser Yeats seems to have embodied a cultural nationalism that was rich and viable in a way that the crude philistinism of Scottish Nationalism was not. Yeat's gestures of heroic assertion and mythic resonance were captivating to an intelligent, empirical, self-conscious young Scot, whose own attitudes were tinged with nostalgia but basically bourgeois and urban. The literary influence of Yeats seems to have kept Fraser a traditionalist. As a critic he had an intelligent and sensitive understanding of modernism—he was one of the first British critics to respond sympathetically to Ezra Pound—but as a poet he was not profoundly affected. Yet his traditionalism was far from being a mere neo-Georgian survival; it was rooted in Fraser's wide knowledge and deep love of past English poetry, particularly of the seventeenth century. His short lyrical or elegiac poems successfully re-enact the form and feeling of the Caroline lyric, while the epistles of Ben Jonson and Dryden are an evident model for the verse letters that contain some of Fraser's best poetry of the 1940s. Behind the English poets stand Latin ones. Fraser was a competent Latinist, who could read and respond to Catullus and Horace in particular as if they were his contemporaries. The editors of the *Poems* write in their introduction of Fraser's poetic voice: 'It is the voice of a man at once wrily witty, capable of anger, but modest, knowledgeable though, curious, vulnerable; most valuably, perhaps, it is a voice that is marked by a kind of off-hand conversational eloquence, an eager desire to communicate. In short, it is the true Horatian voice.' There are translations from Horace in *The Traveller Has Regrets* and in the group of translations from Latin poets that concludes the *Poems*. Among them occurs Fraser's version of Catullus's 'Vivamus mea Lesbia', a poem that attracted Campion and Jonson and many other English poets I think that Fraser's translation can stand comparison with its distinguished predecessors; it shows the metrical deftness that was one of the characteristics of his poetry:

> Dear Lesbia, let us live and love,
> Never thinking twopence of
> All these grumbling grim old men,
> Suns go down, come up again:
> Down but once goes our brief light
> Into one perpetual night.
> A thousand kisses, then a hundred,
> Then a thousand and a hundred,
> A hundred on a thousand pour!
> When we've many thousand more
> Let us muddle up the score.
> Bad men might count every kiss
> And might envy us our bliss.

The Second World War introduced Fraser to the southern exile for which he had yearned in 'Meditation of a patriot'. He served in the army as, on his own admission, a very unsoldierly NCO, engaged in writing propaganda and official journalism in Egypt and Eritrea. In Cairo, he was one of a distinguished collection of English poets, civilian or military, who included Keith Douglas, Laurence Durrell, Bernard Spencer, and Terence Tiller. Fraser's 'Egypt', like other poems by the Cairo poets, catches the mingled fascination and distaste that they felt for the county in which they were exiled; in 'Monologue for a Cairo evening' he presents a more extended reflection on their way of life, including vignettes of literary friends and acquaintances. The Cairo writers made an important contribution to the literature of the Second World War, though it has yet to be properly described and assessed. Fraser's wartime poetry, though authentically personal, expressed many of the common preoccupations of their situation. Away from Egypt and the relatively clean fighting in the desert the war could show far crueller aspects. In 'S.S. City of Benares' Fraser writes of drowned refugee children, and the carefully formal diction and verse movement barely contain the intolerably painful subject:

> Think what you will, but like the crisping leaf
> In whipped October, crack your thoughts to grief.
> In the drenched valley, whimpering and cold,
> The small ghosts flicker, whisper, unconsoled.

After the war, in the late 1940s and 1950s Fraser wrote fewer poems, though he kept his hand in by making excellent translations of poetry from several languages, most of which have yet to be collected, though one hopes they will be. In his original poems the Yeatsian note is evident and sometimes over-insistent, as in 'Poetic generations'. Another poem from about 1950 is interestingly and promisingly different; this is 'Mannerist poem', where Fraser attempts a subtler music, influenced perhaps by Pound's 'Lustra' and 'Mauberley'.

> Images of tears induce
> actual tears, and rhetoric
> A kind of ghost gesture:
> talk of bodies,
> how they moved and with what beauty,
> will not bring them back again . . .

It is an attractive and memorable poem, but, for whatever reason, Fraser did not pursue this style.

He did not publish another volume of poetry until *Conditions* came out in 1969, which contains a fairly slim selection of his best work of the past twenty years. The dedicatory poem, 'For my wife on her fiftieth birthday', is a delicate *cantabile* piece that suggests without quite echoing the phrases and cadences of Shakespearean song. It is a good example of the way in which Fraser's poetry could be at its most literary when it was most personal; for him, the experiences of literature and living did not need to be dichotomized. One of the most striking poems in *Conditions* is 'For Tilly, sick, with love', an affectionate address to a sick, much-loved woman friend, and a lament for a vanished past, where the Horatian *Eheu fugaces* finds an equivalent in the sad, recurring refrain, 'People don't give such parties now'. The editors call this poem a great example of Fraser's metrical dexterity, 'a poem of consumate craft'; this may well be so, but as with certain poems by an earlier accomplished metrist, Hardy, the exact scansion is not easy to establish.

When not particularly advanced in middle age Fraser tended to adopt the persona of someone older than his years, possibly following the example of Yeats and his 'aged man', and Eliot—whom he admired immensely but never imitated—and his 'aged eagle'. The often impressive poetry of the last ten years of Fraser's life shows the mould of Horatian compsure breaking, as when he speaks in the accents of a man not merely aged but bitter, as in 'Colleagues and students' and 'Older'. At the same time, 'Home thoughts on Ireland' is a triumph of the Horatian conversational, reflective manner, fusing personal and public experience: Fraser's Irish honeymoon in 1946 recalled before travelling to lecture to a Yeats summer school in 1972, against a background of terrorism and violence. The lifelong devotion to Yeats becomes a matter of theme as well as manner:

> I shall go to Sligo this August and lecture on
> 'The Influence of Yeats'. And if they shoot me,
> Or blow me up, in the Town Hall, in mid-quotation,
> It will be after all a nice last touch.
> For an otherwise tepid *Times* obituary!

The most remarkable of Fraser's late poems is surely 'A napkin with Veronica's face not Christ's', an elegiac sequence in memory of Veronica Forrest-Thomson, a brilliant young colleague who died young in 1975. The sequence is densely literary, using the *terza rima* of Shelley's 'Triumph of life', and thick with allusions, in ways intended to illustrate Forrest-Thomson's structuralist idea of poetic language; Fraser's review of her posthumous critical book, *Poetic Artifice* (Manchester University Press, 1978), published in *Encounter* in July 1979, provides a helpful gloss on the poem. The poem achieves not only eloquence but power, of a kind that Fraser did not often achieve or indeed aspire to. In section 4 he deliberately employs Yeatsian pastiche to express his own sense of loss, a daring but successful device:

A broth of learning seemed to blur her mind,
A rich aroma, and but one stir more,
One pinch of herb, and surely she would find

The great elixir and the hidden lore
To make her the immortal Harlequin
Of death-blue profile on Picasso's shore

And all her thoughts were angels on a pin
Or plunging horses on a carousel,
Whirling around, or weaving out and in,

Were webs of tapestry she knew so well
She'd stretch it wide to make the world her maze,
That mighty maze one word that she could spell

And cast a spell on, till the blinding ways
Of worlds, by words, she'd bind in nights and days.

Poems of G. S. Fraser makes the best possible memorial to his own life, which was dedicated to poetry in many ways, as critic and editor and teacher, as a sponsor and encourager of younger writers, and, above all, as a practising poet himself. Though not a major poet he was the kind of excellent minor poet on which a tradition depends for its vitality and continuation. This collection should slightly but perceptibly alter out understanding of the English poetry of the past forty years.

1982

NOTES

1. Bernard Spencer, *Collected Poems,* edited by Roger Bowen (Oxford, 1981)
2. *Selected Poems of Alun Lewis,* edited by Jeremy Hooker and Gweno Lewis (London, 1981).
3. *Poems of G. S. Fraser,* edited by Ian Fletcher and John Lucas (Leicester, 1981).

11

Davie, Larkin and the state of England

In the early 1950s Donald Davie and Philip Larkin were both exiles in Ireland. Davie was a lecturer at Trinity College, Dublin; Larkin, a librarian at Queen's University, Belfast. Davie's years in Ireland resulted in a dozen or so poems, some inspired by Dublin architecture. In 'Belfast on a Sunday Afternoon', he described an Orange March with an outsider's appalled fascination and hinted, with unwitting prescience, at the desperate future of Ulster:

> Pipe bands, flute bands, brass bands and silver bands,
> Presbyter's pibroch and the deacon's serge,
> Came stamping where the iron Maenad stands,
> Victoria, glum upon a grassy verge.
>
> Some brawny striplings sprawled upon the lawn;
> No man is really crippled by his hates.
> Yet I remembered with a sudden scorn
> Those 'passionate intensities' of Yeats.[1]

He reflected on his personal situation in 'Demi-Exile. Howth':

> Division of loyalties, dolour of exile,
> Do you command a quizzical smile
> Here, at the roof that once defended
> Jonathan Swift's demented head?
> Here, in the suburb that Hopkins visited,
> Strangled in sand of its famous dead? *(CP, p.8.)*

(Hopkins was another English poet, academic, and exile, whose life in Dublin was probably unhappier but certainly more creative than Davie's.)

Larkin, unlike Davie, is a poet of typical rather than specific landscapes and localities, and he seems not to have written any poems directly about Ireland. The charming, elegiac 'Dublinesque' in *High Windows*[2] appears to have been inspired by accounts of a Dublin funeral early in the century, or even by old photographs, rather than by direct observation; it evokes a milder mood than 'Samuel Beckett's Dublin' by Davie (CP, p. 51). In one poem, however, Larkin comments, briefly but significantly, on his experience of exile:

> Lonely in Ireland, since it was not home,
> Strangeness made sense. The salt rebuff of speech,
> Insisting so on difference, made me welcome:
> Once that was recognised, we were in touch.
>
> Living in England has no such excuse:
> These are my customs and establishments
> It would be much more serious to refuse.
> Here no elsewhere underwrites my existence.[3]

By the late fifties, Davie and Larkin were back in England, having found self-definition and a new perspective on English life in their Irish exile. The two poets seemed to have much in common, as socio-cultural commentators of the time remarked. They were born within a few days of each other in 1922 and had similar educations. Their background was provincial and middle class; they attended local grammar schools—Davie at Barnsley in Yorkshire, Larkin at Coventry—and went on to university to read English—Davie at Cambridge, Larkin at Oxford. Academic life (for Davie as a teacher, Larkin as a librarian) followed. (Davie also had several years' wartime service, whereas Larkin was exempted on medical grounds.) Although Larkin published his first book of poems, *The North Ship*, as early as 1945, this volume of juvenilia and apprentice work attracted no attention; indeed, little was known of it until it was reprinted in an enlarged new edition in 1966. His first mature collection, *The Less Deceived*, published by the Marvell Press at Hull in 1955, aroused wide interest and appreciation. In the same year Davie brought out his first collection of poems, *Brides of Reason*, from another small publisher, the Fantasy Press, which operated from a cottage near Oxford.

In 1955 Larkin left Belfast to become librarian of the Brynmor Jones Library at the University of Hull, a post he still holds.

Davie, on the other hand, has moved extensively; since leaving Trinity, Dublin, he has been a college fellow and university lecturer at Cambridge, Professor of Literature at the University of Essex, and, since 1968, Professor of English at Stanford, thereby embracing a new exile. These shifts in career are not of merely biographical interest, since there are parallels in poetic development. Davie's *Collected Poems, 1950-70* is a substantial volume that includes nearly everything previously published; it shows that Davie soon moved on from the quasi-Augustan formality he had cultivated in the fifties, and since then has written in many styles and been open to a wide range of poetic influences, mostly American and Continental European. Larkin, in the two volumes he has published since *The Less Deceived*—*The Whitsun Weddings* (1964) and *High Windows* (1974)—has refined and purified his style but has not really altered it.

I shall say at once that Larkin seems to be a 'better' poet than Davie; that is to say, I find more poems to move and console me in Larkin's three slender volumes than in Davie's much more extensive body of work. This is partly a matter of inherent skill; though possessing none of Davie's intelligent experimentalism, Larkin is a more naturally assured craftsman. He is a narrower but deeper poet. In each of his three mature books there is a striking poem, longer than the rest, that provides a centrepiece and that dwells on large and perennial human themes: death and religion in 'Church Going' in *The Less Deceived*; love and marriage in the title poem of *The Whitsun Weddings*; death again in 'The Building' in *High Windows*. Davie has never quite achieved this centrality, either in subject matter or in his own poetic tactics. Once, in an eassy on his early poetry, I wrote that his poems 'seemed to be buttressing a major composition which hadn't, so far, been written'.[4] After more than twenty years this still seems broadly true, however much I value individual poems of strong and direct feeling, such as 'The Garden Party', 'Wood-pigeons at Raheny', 'Time Passing, Beloved', 'The Wind at Penistone', and 'After an Accident'. Yet if David is a lesser poet than Larkin, he is also, to invoke an impure but beguiling category, in some respects a more interesting one.

The interest arises less from the character of Davie's poems, taken separately, than from the total impression one gets from all his writing of a powerful literary personality struggling with obsessions and endeavouring, with unexpected success, to balance or combine attitudes usually thought of as contradictory. Thus, Davie is emphatically a moralist, imbued with the rigorous spirit of the Cambridge English school of the forties and fifties. His first critical book, *Purity of Diction in English Verse* (1952), found admirable moral qualities in the lexical restraint and controlled syntax of eighteenth-century poetry and was offered as a lesson in the neo-classical virtues to Davie's contemporaries. In his own poetry Davie embodied this lesson in the sharp, cool, ironic observations of *Brides of Reason*. Yet he is also an aesthete, who believes with Henry James that 'it is art that *makes* life, makes interest, makes importance.' He was unable to remain satisfied for long with exclusively moral and social criteria for poetry; its significance, in the end, was ontological:

> The metaphysicality
> Of poetry, how I need it!
> And yet it was for years
> What I refused to credit
> ('Or, Solitude', *CP*, p.202)

Davie's ideal in these matters is that pure realm where art and morality become indistinguishable. Few of us, however, can inhabit it for long.

In one allegiance Davie is, unashamedly, a provincial Englishman, strongly attached to his Yorkshire roots and the nonconformist religious tradition in which he was brought up, even if he is no longer a believer. This allegiance is personally exemplified in his affectionate memory of his father, to whom he has devoted several poems. In poetic terms it shows itself in Davie's admiration not just for minor eighteenth-century poets in general, but for hymn-writers such as Isaac Watts and Charles Wesley, in particular. Against this aspect of Davie—English, provincial, traditionalist—one must set quite different allegiances, which are cosmopolitan, global, and modernist. It is this, above all, which soon marked Davie off from the unambitious poetics of the Movement. He admires and imitates Pound and Pasternak, and is drawn to the heroic style, in life and art, of the early masters of modernism. However much his imagination is rooted in Pennine landscape, it constantly turns to the large unpeopled spaces of America and Russia. Davie spent some time in Russia during the Second World War, learned Russian, and later came to read and translate Pasternak's lyric poetry. Its influence is noticeable in *Events and Wisdoms* of 1964, which I think is Davie's best single collection of poems. Martin Dodsworth, an acute English critic who reads Russian, has praised the quality of Davie's translations of the *Dr Zhivago* poems and has described the effect of Pasternak in helping Davie to find a looser, though still formal, mode of verse after his tight poetry of the fifties.[5] Pasternak's short lines, regular but not stiff stanzaic forms, and frequent exclamations are a noticeable feature of *Events and Wisdoms*.

Pound's influence on Davie is more pervasive. Indeed, Davie's interest in Pound, deeply admiring but never wholly approving, would be worth a study in itself. It has so far resulted in several articles and two books—*Ezra Pound: Poet as Sculptor* in 1964 and *Pound* in the Fontana Modern Masters series in 1975. As early as 1952 Davie was taking issue with Pound about the improper fragmentation of syntax in the *Cantos*, and in 1975 he was still worrying about the problem, though now concluding that it would be equally honourable to reject or accept Pound's procedures. In 1955 Davie wrote, 'I honour the poets, English, Irish and American who revolutionized English poetry thirty years ago; and indeed it seems to me that one of those poets, Ezra Pound, has influenced me more deeply and more constantly than any other poet of the present century'.[6] Davie revers Pound for taking the art of poetry with true seriousness, as opposed to English amateurism. He finds, too, in Pound's imagist poetics a regard for the integrity of nature, seen and respected as something non-human, and accepted in its quiddity. He finds forerunners of this attitude in Ruskin and Hopkins and Hardy, and prefers it to the symbolist procedures of Eliot, in which the world of things is swallowed up in the all-embracing consciousness of the poet.

Pound's influence is explicitly and happily evident in two extended sequences adapted from existing literary sources: *The Forests of Lithuania* (1959) and *A Sequence for Francis Parkman* (1961). The former is a free and shortened version of the Polish national epic, Mickiewicz' *Pan Tadeusz. The Forests of Lithuania* is, I think, a remarkably successful work, particularly in view of its exotic provenance and material, and suggests that Davie, like Pound, can find particular inspiration in an earlier writer. The sequence contains some magnificent verse, energetic yet demonstrating all of Davie's characteristic syntactical control. If Mickiewicz' poem fired Davie's imagination it was not just to provide a rather recherché poetic exercise; he has also written affectionate and sensitive poems about a visit to Poland, such as 'In Chopin's Garden' and 'A Meeting of Cultures'. Yet, more profoundly, the plains and forests of Eastern Europe and Russia form an integral part of Davie's mental and emotional world, fed partly from experience, partly from his reading of Polish and Russian literature. As he writes in 'Behind the North Wind', recalling his service in northern Russia in 1942:

> More than ever I need
> Places where nothing happened,
> Where history is silent,
> No Tartar ponies checked, and
> Endurance earns repose. (*CP*, p. 208)

Davie reveals a similar feeling about North America in *A Sequence for Francis Parkman*, which, as he acknowledges, draws heavily in a Poundian way on Parkman's *France and England in North America*. Davie has made effective poetry out of the appropriation. In a note in his *Collected Poems* Davie remarks, 'When this was first published, Philip Larkin in an amiable review speculated that Francis Parkman was "one of Mr Davie's American friends" '. He adds, 'Unlikely as it may seem, the sequence represents my response to North America on my first visit, from September 1957 to August 1958.' The last poem is not adapted from Parkman but is wholly original; it points to a fascination with the alienness of North America that has remained a major preoccupation with Davie:

> But I only guess,
> I guess at it out of my Englishness
> And envy you out of England. Man with man
> Is all our history; American,
> You met with spirits. Neither white nor red
> The melancholy, disinherited

> Spirit of mid-America, but this,
> The manifested copiousness, the bounties.
>
> ('A Letter to Curtis Bradford', *CP,* p. 128)

This is a key passage for understanding Davie's development and his later obsessions, both as poet and critic. The *Sequence* is a very successful result of the fusion of separate elements of experience: Pound's demonstration of the possibility of making one's own poetry out of other people's prose; the reading of Parkman; and a first visit to America. It is the first treatment of a theme to which Davie has since returned frequently in his poetry: the opening up of North America and the Pacific by British, French, and American explorers and seamen. Several late poems reflect this deep and tenacious preoccupation and seem, too, to bear an obscure relationship to Charles Olson's *Maximus Poems*, though of rivalry or correction rather than emulation. But none of them, in my view, shows anything like the distinction of the Parkman sequence. In so far as they are Poundian in spirit, but not in prosody, they recall the dull stretches of Chinese and American history in the *Cantos*.

From the early sixties Davie became increasingly concerned with America as a poetic subject. Like his Russia, Davie's North America was something of a landscape of the mind: empty, vast, silent, uncluttered with humanity—the pristine vision of the first explorers rather than the contemporary USA. He envied the American poets their freedom of imagination, reversing the traditional American envy of Europe for its cultural achievements and possibilities. At the same time, Davie, in his second, Californian exile, cannot forget England, as we see in his sequence *The Shires* (1974). In some recent poems Davie's concern with England is less ideal or metaphysical, and more overtly political. Davie's politics, though, are quite other than the left-liberal, social democratic variety professed until recently by most English intellectuals. His distaste for contemporary England has a heroic-modernist basis and is directed at many things: the drab complacency of post-imperial Britain; an industrialized and polluted landscape; social egalitariansim; civic philistinism; and the fatuities of the 'Swinging London' cult of the sixties. In 'Epistle. To Enrique Caracciolo Trejo', Davie brings together his cultural and personal discontents at the end of four unhappy years at the new University of Essex and hints at his own further expatriation:

Still in infested gardens
The year goes round,
A smiling landscape greets returning Spring.
To see what can be said for it, on what
Secure if shallow ground
Of feeling England stands
Unshaken for
Her measure to be taken
Has taken four bad years
Of my life here. (*CP*, p. 213)

In some poems Davie's attitudes harden into a cold right-wing disdain; as, for instance, 'New Year Wishes for the English':

May the humanitarian
Blackmail be paid no longer;
Instead may you work a little.

May you have, against the incessant
Rain of the new, the all-new,
Indifference as an umbrella. (*CP*, p. 210)

In 'England', a not very successful long poem written on the occasion of his departure to California, we find similar thoughts, combined with fragments of autobiography, and historical and geographical references inspired by the transpolar flight. Once he had embraced a new expatriate condition, though, Davie was able to write about his country in a more affectionate and relaxed way, in *The Shires*.

Poetry is an imperfect, even misleading guide to a man's actual opinions, and Davie's poems of the sixties tend to dramatize attitudes rather than develop arguments. There is a better expression of his ideas in *Thomas Hardy and British Poetry*, a book of criticism published in 1973[7]. Like most of Davie's criticism, it is closely related to his poetry; and it covers more ground than its title suggests. I will not concern myself here with the book's central argument, which asserts that Thomas Hardy has been a central, if unsuspected, influence on British poetry throughout most of this century, except to say that it is persuasively advanced but not really convincing. All the same, *Thomas Hardy and British Poetry* is full of interest and intellectual excitement in a personal, opinionated, and urbanely polemical way. For Davie, Hardy is a major, perhaps a great, poet; and, at the same time, an admired adversary. One of the virtues of this book is that Davie is able to deal explicitly with questions that occur only fleetingly in his poems as asides or allusions. Considering Hardy as a cultural force, Davie sees him as embodying those qualities in English life which are exasperating but necessary: humanitarianism, moderation, ironic acceptance, rational pessimism. If he finds these qualities exasperating it is because they exclude others associated with the heroic energies of the modern movement: aesthetic commitment, imaginative boldness, a willingness to explore and experiment and take chances, a concept of art as transforming experience rather than simply annotating it. Davie tends to deal in sharp, emblematic oppositions in this book, so that Hardy is set against the poets whose achievement means so much to him: Yeats, Eliot, and Pound. *Enfin Larkin vint*; for Larkin is the contemporary poet whose debt to Hardy is most explicit and manifest; he has written that he believes Hardy to be by far the greatest poet of the twentieth century.[8] So, inevitably, Davie has to concern himself with Larkin. Here, as on other issues, Davie's attitude is divided. Though admiring Larkin as a poet, he deplores his implied attitudes, his acceptance of the social democratic, egalitarian, philistine, anti-heroic ethos of post-war England. Nevertheless, his recognition of Larkin's achievement is generous even if reluctant. At the end of his book Davie forces himself to accept the England that Hardy and Larkin embody, the England of civic philistinism and civic responsibility. The alternatives, whether in the forms of 'heroic' quasi-fascism or bohemian antinomianism, are not, in the end, acceptable to a Yorkshire nonconformist. In the last sentence of his book Davie recommends Larkin to American readers, who have much difficulty in appreciating him: 'What he represents is British poetry at the point where it has least in common with American, a poetry which consciously repudiates the assumptions, and the liberties, which American poets take for granted; a poetry in short which is, for the American reader, exceptionally challenging.'[9]

And not only for the American reader, I believe; *Thomas Hardy and British Poetry* itself, and much of Davie's own late poetry, can be read as a response to the challenge which Larkin, and the spirit represented by Larkin, present to Davie. I must add that the structure of oppositions governing Davie's book sometimes makes him distort Larkin. One of his principal assumptions is that Larkin is interested exclusively in humanity and not in nature as something other and self-subsistent; so, Davie complains, Larkin can respond to nature only when it is tamed and transformed by man, a point he argues in what is probably a misreading of one of Larkin's finest poems, 'Here'. He further accuses Larkin of resignedly accepting the industrial pollution of English landscape. Davie's timing was unfortunate, for a year after his book appeared, Larkin published *High Windows* containing 'Going, Going', an impassioned complaint about the spoliation of nature and the disappearance of traditional English countryside.

Again, Davie accuses Larkin of lacking any sense of the past or capacity for historical perspective; he even calls him the least nostalgic of poets. For Davie, Larkin lives in the present, glumly accepting whatever an industrialized, suburbanized, egalitarian society offers. Yet this judgement is demonstrably untrue. 'MCMXIV' in *The Whitsun Weddings* offers a poignant evocation of a world that vanished forever in 1914:

> Never such innocence
> Never before or since,
> As changed itself to past
> Without a word—the men
> Leaving the gardens tidy,
> The thousands of marriages
> Lasting a little while longer:
> Never such innocence again. (*WW*, p. 28)

And in 'Going, Going' Larkin is as concerned, in his own way, as Davie is about the present condition of England:

> And that will be England gone,
> The shadows, the meadows, the lanes,
> The guildhalls, the carved choirs.
> There'll be books; it will linger on
> In galleries; but all that remains
> For us will be concrete and tyres. (*HW*, p. 22)

Moreover, contra Davie's assertion that Larkin is uninterested in 'pure' nature untouched by humanity, one notes throughout Larkin's poetry a recurring vein of imagery drawn from the most elemental of all natural forms: water.

Yet even if Davie sometimes misreads or misunderstands Larkin, he still has good reason to feel exasperated with his contemporary's ideas and responses. That exasperation boiled over in 1973, soon after the appearance of *Thomas Hardy and British Poetry*. In that year Larkin published *The Oxford Book of Twentieth-Century English Verse*, an anthology which he had been invited to edit in order to supersede W. B. Yeat's highly idiosyncratic *Oxford Book of Modern Verse, 1892-1935* of 1936. This new anthology is, indeed, imperfect; Larkin is not in sympathy with much recent poetry but he has tried to be fair in a halfhearted way. He does provide a full and well-chosen selection of the kind of poetry he really likes; that is to say, poems written by British poets born towards the end of the nineteenth century who came to maturity early in the twentieth and who, in Alan Brownjohn's words, 'have either pre-dated modernism or evaded it'.[10] With later poetry, however, his taste is capricious and uncertain. Davie's enraged review of the book is a splendid polemic, of Johnsonian authority and vigour. Davie accused Larkin of including innumerable poems of no poetic value at all, thereby perpetuating a *trahison des clercs*, one more surrender to English philistinism and amateurishness:

> To be, as Philip Larkin is, the author of many poems generally esteemed and loved brings with it certain responsibilities. And in this anthology Larkin shirks those responsibilities quite shamefully. The poems that we have loved, that we love and cherish still, turn out to have been written by a man who thinks that poetry is a private indulgence or a professional entertainer's patter or, at most, a symptom for social historians to brood over. It is a grievous misfortune that in him an exquisite talent for poetry seems to go along with a mocking scepticism about the possibility of critical discrimination among poems. Perhaps the right word is not scepticism but cynicism.[11]

Later in the review Davie remarks that 'there is plenty of evidence that any talk of poetry as a calling (some have thought it a sacred one) pains and infuriates him, as so much much pompous hypocrisy.'[12]

It is true that Larkin remains a man of the English fifties in not liking heroic gestures or large statements and in not taking too exalted a view of poetry or art in general. He believes that art should give pleasure rather than communicate ultimate truth, in contrast to Davie's hieratic dedication. And he openly derides the modernist masters who mean so much to Davie. Larkin has written very little literary criticism apart from occasional reviews, but he has left a pugnacious statement of his aesthetic in the introduction to a collection of jazz reviews that he contributed to the London *Daily Telegraph* between 1961 and 1968:

> To say I don't like modern jazz because it's modernist art simply raises the question of why I don't like modernist art; I have a suspicion that many readers will welcome my grouping of Parker and Picasso and Pound as one of the nicest things I could say about him. Well, to do so settles at least one question: as long as it was only Parker I didn't like, I might believe that my ears had shut up about the age of 25 and that jazz had left me behind. My dislike of Pound and Picasso, both of whom pre-date me by a considerable margin, can't be explained in this way. The same can be said of Henry Moore and James Joyce (a textbook case of declension from talent to absurdity). No, I dislike such things not because they are new, but because they are irresponsible exploitations of technique in contradiction of human life as we know it. This is my essential criticism of modernism, whether perpetrated by Parker, Pound or Picasso: it helps us neither to enjoy nor endure.[13]

Although, as I have said, Larkin's poetry did not significantly develop between 1955 and 1974, *High Windows* received the warmest reception of his three mature collections and, more important, enabled one to see *The Less Deceived* and *The Whitsun Weddings* in a fresh light. In the fifties and sixties, praise of Larkin was often qualified by a sense of his limitations. Critics complained about Larkin's 'surburban mental ratio', and A. Alvarez, in a review of *The Whitsun Weddings*, gave praise where he thought it was due, but concluded with a firmly dismissive image: Larkin, he remarked, had chosen 'a kind of suburban hermitage, with plenty of books and records, bottled beer in the cupboard and all mod. con. On the wall is a poker-work motto which reads: 'You'll never have it any better." '[14]

There is that side of Larkin, of course, and for a time it seemed dominant; but from the beginning there was another aspect, evident in condensed, somethimes cryptic lyrics of near-symbolist obliquity. For instance, 'Coming', 'Dry-Point', 'Going, Going', 'Age', 'Absences', 'If, My Darling', 'First Sight', from *The Whitsun Weddings* (*WW*, pp. 20, 27, 44, 36). These need to be set against the poems of depression, irony, and exact social comment. There are more poems of this obliquely lyrical kind in *High Windows*, Clive James, a critic given to hyperbole, coupled Larkin with Montale and described them as 'the two master poets at present alive in Europe'. After this initial flourish, James developed a singularly penetrating essay on Larkin, remarking that the total impression of *High Windows* is 'of despair made beautiful'. At the end, James moves Larkin out of his surburban hermitage and into a Mallarméan void: 'Larkin is the poet of the void. The one affirmation his work offers is the possibility that when we have lost everything the problem of beauty will still remain. It's enough.'[16]

There are other signs of fresh assessment of Larkin, though not everyone sees him in the same light as James. Another critic, J. R. Watson, has argued that Larkin is concerned with preserving and restoring a sense of ritual and the sacred in a wholly secularized world; is even, in a certain sense, *homo religiosus*.[17] Further interpretations will surely be forthcoming, no doubt to Larkin's own sardonic amusement; but their general effect will certainly be to make him seem a more varios poet than was once thought. Whether Americans will ever learn to like him is another question; one American critic has remarked, appropos of *High Windows,* 'The good grey Larkin has risen again from his ashes with another thin volume of defeats—technical as well as thematic.'[18] As Clive James argues, however, Larkin turns his defeats into triumphs.

Larkin is rejected, too, by those English writers whose literary allegiances are American. Thus, to take an example that came to hand just before I began this essay, I found in a student magazine published at King's College, University of London, an interview with Eric Mottram, Reader in American Literature at King's College and himself a poet in an impeccably American neo-modernist manner. Mottram dismisses the weary survivals of the fifties spirit and the, to him, quite unacceptable notion of Larkin's centrality as a poet; he refers, like others before him, to 'cosy middle-class irony'. Significantly, though, in the same magazine there is a note by a young, little-known English poet Steve Turner, which ends with high praise for Larkin who, he says, 'marks the key to the road ahead'.[19]

Questions of literary ideology apart, I believe that American difficulties with Larkin may arise partly from his references, partly from his linguistic tactics. Larkin began life as a novelist—in the forties he published two accomplished novels, *Jill* and *A Girl in Winter,* before abandoning fiction—and many of his poems show a novelistic feeling for social data. This gives a particular pleasure of recognition when one knows what he is writing about but must lead to confusion and wild guessing when one does not. Thus, I imagine American readers might need help if they are to construe accurately poems so heavily dependent on varities of socio-cultural reference as 'Mr. Bleaney' or 'Essential Beauty' or, indeed, 'The Whitsun Weddings' (*WW*, pp. 10, 42, 21) itself, marvellous poem though it is. Again, many of Larkin's effects come not just from playing the tones of the speaking voice against his prosodic and stanzaic structures, but from a constant play between linguistic registers in a manner characteristic of educated but *déclassé* English speech; more emphatically, he can move between low, even obscene colloquialism to high 'poetic' utterance and back in the compass of a single poem. I suspect that many American readers cannot 'hear' Larkin, just as many British readers cannot tune in to William Carlos Williams and all the poetry that stems from him. Perhaps, even, Larkin expresses feelings that are common enough in Britain but do not exist in America. A great poet, certainly, would transcend such cultural particularity, but I would not claim that Larkin is a great poet, just a very good one.

I will try, though, to say something in particular about a Larkin poem which I think is both good and characteristic: 'Sad Steps', from *High Windows*. On the level of technique, the poem shows Larkin's quite remarkable capacity to play a syntactically elaborate sentence structure against a comparably elaborate stanzaic pattern; in this case, one that he seems to have invented for the occasion, which links each pair of stanzas by the rhyme scheme: *aba bba*. This capacity is a permanent legacy from Yeats to Larkin, even if Larkin claims to have quickly shaken off the Yeatsian influence that was so conspicuous in *The North Ship*.[20] The title of the poem nicely illustrates the danger of taking Larkin's pronouncements as a reliable guide to his practice. In 1955 he wrote that he had 'no belief in "tradition" or a common myth-kitty or casual allusions in poems to other poems or poets, which last I find unpleasantly like the talk of literary understrappers letting you see they know the right people'.[21]

Even at the time, Larkin found it hard to stick to the letter of this last prescription—in 'Lines on a Young Lady's Photograph Album' from *The Less Deceived* (p. 11), there is a deft allusion to *The Princess*—and in 'Sad Steps' he does not try to. The title refers to a plangent line from Sir Philip Sidney's *Astrophel and Stella*, 'With how sad steps, O Moon, thou climbs't the skies', and establishes the theme of the poem, which is that the moon is as much a literary object as an astronomical one. The first line of the poem, 'Groping back to bed after a piss', is in Larkin's coarsely colloquial vein, but only in respect to its diction; syntactically, that kind of hanging participle belongs to the written rather than the spoken language. By the third line Larkin is writing in his own recognizable idiom: we are given an evocative abstraction instead of the concrete image that we might expect—'moon's cleanliness' rather than 'clean moon'. Then, in line four, after the isolated phrase 'four o'clock', that echoes Eliot's 'Rhapsody on a Windy Night', the poem returns to imagistically precise description of the windy, moonlit scene for two more stanzas. In the seventh line the syntax opens out on to a long, intricate sentence without end-stopping, whose rapid movement mimes the apparent dashing of the moon through the fast-moving clouds:

> Four o'clock: wedge-shadowed gardens lie
> Under a cavernous, a wind-picked sky.
> There's something laughable about this,
>
> The way the moon dashes through clouds that blow
> Loosely as cannon-smoke to stand apart
> (Stone-coloured light sharpening the roofs below)
>
> High and preposterous and separate—
> Lozenge of love! Medallion of art!
> O wolves of memory! Immensements! (*HW*, p. 32)

In stanza four, Larkin turns from description to confront the essential literariness of the moon: 'Lozenge of love! Medallion of art!' The words are ironic, since they carry two senses: 'lozenge' is technically a heraldic term, referring to a kind of shield, though in modern English usage it generally means the kind of tablet that one sucks for a sore throat; again, 'medallion' originally meant a large imposing medal or a decorative panel or a portrait—one remembers the last poem of Pound's *Mauberley*—though its current sense is rather the opposite—of a small and trivial medal or a trinket.

Stylistically, too, this and the following line are remarkable; they are not in any clearly descriptive register, either colloquial or literary. Larkin is, in fact, imitating a characteristic construction of French symbolist poetry; the appositional phrases in the vocative, the exclamations, are a noticeable feature of, for instance, Laforgue's *Derniers Vers*. Larkin claims never to read foreign poetry, but I regard such claims as part of his habitual pose of self-deprecatory mystification. Or, to put it another way, I do not think he wrote these lines pointlessly or by accident. 'Immensements!' is a particularly sphisticated invention; there is no such noun in either English or French, but it impressionistically parodies Laforgue or Rimbaud. The intention here is satirical, but elsewhere Larkin has used such constructions in a serious and effective way as in 'Absences': 'Such attics cleared of me! Such absences!' (*LD*, p. 38); or 'The Card-Players': 'Rain, wind and fire! The secret, bestial peace!' (*HW*, p. 23).

In 'Sad Steps' these formal allusions recall symbolist poetry and its frequent invocations to the moon, only to dismiss them decisively with the negation at the end of the twelfth line. The poem ends as many traditional English poems end, with a qualified assertion of human community, a Wordsworthian rather than a Laforguian note. 'The strength and pain/Of being young' is a bleak phrase, but it is movingly right. This poem, at least, is not despairing, nor even defeated. And technically, it is remarkably adroit. One notes, for instance, how the concluding two stanzas contain no sensory impressions at all, but present concepts, like 'hardness', 'brightness', 'singleness', 'strength', and 'pain', that work in the same way as images. As he does so often, Larkin achieves a striking overall effect not by vivid or arresting tropes, but by subtly combining images and concepts in a highly controlled syntax that disolves the differences between them. It is, in fact, the kind of poetry that Davie called for in his critical book of 1955, *Articulate Energy*, which tried to overthrow the modernist assumption that 'images' were good and 'abstractions' bad. Conversely, Larkin can sometimes end an argumentative or dramatic poem with a single unexpected image, like the 'arrow-shower' at the end of 'The Whitsun Weddings' (*WW*, p.23); or 'the deep blue air, that shows/Nothing, and is nowhere, and is endless' that concludes 'High Windows' (*HW*, p.17) in a pure, intensely symbolist way, with a corresponding upward shift of stylistic register.

Larkin, like other good poets before him, makes poetry out of negative feelings. He also speaks to the contemporary English in their own way, about what most concerns them in their crisis-ridden culture. To some extent he has a middle-aged audience who have grown up with his work, but the tribute of the young poet Steve Turner suggests that he is able, too, to appeal to a newer generation. In Larkin there is, I think, a fine balance between the personal and the cultural: he writes about his own dilemmas and reflections and despairs, but he conveys them in the common codes of his time and society, and commands a wide and soberly delighted recognition. His poetic vision is, as I have remarked, deep but narrow; and his exclusions have proved exasperating, whether to unsympathetic critics or to as sympathetic and admiring a reader as Davie. Davie is right, moreover, in asserting that Larkin's ideas about poetry are unworthy of the poetry he writes; the mental habits of the fifties are, perhaps, ineradicable. We also need the less assured but more ranging poetry of Davie. He, too, is much concerned with English culture and its fate, but from the vantage point of chosen expatriation and exile. I see a necessary, emblematic relationship between these two poets. Larkin stays still, does not travel, rereads Hardy; and writes about what he sees. Davie moves on, reads many literatures—though returning constantly to Pound, the master voyager of modernism—and longs for the heroic and the imaginatively possible, as well as what is actually and inescapably there.

Davie likes and cultivates the 'open-minded' poem that does not return neatly and predictably to its starting point but moves onward and outwards like an arrow-shower or a river flowing into the sea. I shall conclude this essay in a similar way, suggesting a new and perhaps far-fetched comparison, drawn not from poetry but from war and public affairs and not from England or America, but from France. During the Second World War Charles De Gaulle and Henri-Philippe Pétain mutally repudiated and condemned each other as traitors to their country. In the more generous perspective of history, however, it has been said that each was serving France in his own way: one as the sword, one as the shield. Energy: endurance.

1977

NOTES

1. *Collected Poems, 1950-1970* (London, 1972), p.14. Parenthetical page references in the text, preceded by *CP* are to this edition.
2. Philip Larkin, *High Windows* (London, 1974), p.28. Parenthetical page references in the text, preceded by *HW,* are to this edition.
3. Philip Larkin, 'The Importance of Elsewhere', *The Whitsun Weddings* (London, 1964), p.34. Parenthetical page references in the text, preceded by *WW,* are to this edition.
4. See my 'The poetry of Donald Davie', *Critical Quarterly,* 4, No. 4 (Winter, 1962), pp.293-304.
5. Martin Dodsworth, 'Poetry in the grass', *The Review,* No. 14 (December 1964), pp.23-30.
6. *Poets of the 1950's: An Anthology of New English Verse,* ed D. J. Enright (Tokyo, 1955), p.47.
7. Donald Davie, *Thomas Hardy and British Poetry* (London, 1973).
8. Philip Larkin, 'Wanted: good Hardy critic', *Critical Quarterly,* 8, No. 2 (Summer 1966), pp.174-9. Reprinted in *Required Writing* (London, 1983), pp.168-74.
9. Davie, *Thomas Hardy and British Poetry,* p.188.
10. *Philip Larkin* (Harlow, 1975) p.31.
11. Donald Davie, 'Larkin's choice', *Listener,* 29 March 1973, pp.420-1.
12. Davie, 'Larkin's choice', p.421.
13. Philip Larkin, *All What Jazz: A Record Diary, 1964-68* (London, 1970), pp.16-17.
14. *Beyond All This Fiddle: Essays, 1955-1967* (London, 1968), p.87.
15. Philip Larkin, *The Less Deceived* (Hessle, 1955), pp.15, 17, 19, 28, 38, 40. Parenthetical page references in the text, preceded by *LD* are to this edition.
16. 'Wolves of Memory', *Encounter,* 42, No. 6 (June 1974), pp.65, 71.
17. 'The other Larkin', *Critical Quarterly,* 17, No. 4 (Winter 1975), pp.347-60.
18. Frederick Busch, 'The day of the digital clock', *Stand,* 17, No. 2 (1976), p.4.
19. *Jam,* No. 2 (January, 1976), pp.26, 11.
20. *The North Ship,* 2nd edn (1945; reprinted London, 1966), p.10.

12

George Steiner: on culture and on Hitler

I

George Steiner's T. S. Eliot memorial lectures[1] have been given prominent but unfavourable reviews, indicating his ambivalent place in English literary culture. He is a conspicuous irritant, a necessary licensed jester in our low-powered intellectual life. The hostile reception of these lectures cannot have surprised Steiner; indeed he must have been bracing himself to meet it. In a long essay, 'The Language Animal' *(Encounter,* August 1969), which rehearses many of the ideas later developed in the lectures, he wrote: 'To a philosopher-linguist most of what a Sartre or an Ernst Bloch produces is simply non-sense.' So if English readers, all sturdy empiricists if not professional philosopher-linguists, find Steiner's writing mostly 'non-sense', he can console himself with the hypothetical but probably accurate reflection that greater men might get a similar treatment. His early Continental education and his breadth of interests have made him something of a conscious outsider, even an internal emigré politely despising the provincial narrowness that surrounds him.

As a literary critic, he aspires to be something radically un-English (and, less emphatically, un-American, too), namely, the kind of writer for whom criticism is not distinguished from the pursuit of ideas and confident high-level speculation about the state of the world. He would no doubt die happy if he had earned the title of an English Sartre or Lukács or Adorno. But he has a way to go, and not just because of the apparent intellectual insecurity that makes him parade his admittedly extensive reading. Far more important is the fact that the Continental masters whom he admires and emulates have a great capacity for argument, for roughly seizing hold of ideas and dragging conclusions out of them, whereas he tends to remain happily bedazzled by their sheer brilliance. Compared with the generality of English literary critics, who are more concerned with the 'tone' or 'feel' of arguments than with their content and meanings, he knows an important idea when he sees one and is prepared to tell the world about it. Here lies the value of his writing, and the English cultural climate is not so rich in intellectual stimulus that it can afford to be quite so instantly dismissive about him. But compared with the Continentals he has very little capacity for dialectic, for making his ideas work. Arguably—to use a favourite locution of his—the arresting Continental styling of his manner conceals a critic in the twentieth-century Anglo-American mainstream, who is more at home with metaphor than with logic, and who develops his argument by associative leaps, where one thing is likely to 'suggest' or 'recall' another thing, where it is 'no accident' that events fall out as they do, and where strikingly contradictory elements of experience are likely to be juxtaposed in 'significant contrast'.

On the face of it, though, Steiner has no time for this mainstream. In his first critical book, *Tolstoy or Dostoevsky,* published in 1959, he made it clear that he was not concerned with what he regarded as the narrow literary analysis of the New Criticism, and that he was prepared to draw on any form of humane learning when writing about literature. *Tolstoy or Dostoevsky* succeeds in its aim, even though it was written, as he admitted with large modesty, in ignorance of the Russian language. It remains the most immediately usable of his works, and amply fulfils the basic function of literary criticism, which is to make its subjects more available to the reader. It is thorough, perceptive, and fairly unpretentious; yet there is a cause for unease in the too-simple binary patterning suggested by its title: the design of the book is to show Tolstoy and Dostoevsky as emblematic of the major polarities of existence: the epical versus the dramatic, the progressive versus the reactionary, the rationalistic versus the religious. In places Steiner tended to reduce the specificity of the particular novels he was discussing in order to preserve the purity of these oppositions.

His next book, *The Death of Tragedy,* promised more but achieved less. It moved with easy assurance along a familiar highway, from the Greeks, via Shakespeare and Racine and German Romantic tragedy, to Ibsen and Strindberg, and ended with the strangely limp conclusion that tragedy was now either dead, or still flickering with a little dim life, or about to burst forth in a glorious rebirth. In essence a wide-ranging and high-flying survey, *The Death of Tragedy* was readable but insubstantial, offering little for the mind to engage with or remember once the book was finished. Its flaws of argument and errors of fact were discussed in a long review by the American critic, John Simon (reprinted in his collection of essays, *Acid Test*).

Perhaps wisely, Steiner has not attempted another sustained book. Most of his energy now goes into critical essays, a substantial collection of which appeared as *Language and Silence* in 1967. They showed both his breadth of reading in several European languages and a provokingly pretentious manner. English reviewers tended to concentrate on the manner and ignore the learning, though the fact remained that if he had only really read—or properly understood—half of the books he mentioned he was still doing much better than most Eng. Lit. academics. Some of his essays had a directly informative value, at a time when English cultural insularity was beginning to open up a little, notably the section of *Language and Silence* that dealt with European Marxist criticism. And one of the essays, 'Night Words', which takes issue with the tight liberal consensus on pornography, is even more timely now than when it was first published in 1965. Yet despite the coolness of the literary establishment *Language and Silence* has sold well; it has evidently been a source of intellectual excitement to many readers to whom conventional academic criticism, or ordinary literary journalism, has nothing to say; and, remarkably for a critical book, it has been translated into many languages.

The essays in *Language and Silence* were somewhat repetitive and overlapping, but they were given a degree of unity by Steiner's recurrent preoccupations, notably the topic indicated by its title: the point at which language, as a humane activity, has to give up, either because of the speechlessness induced by the mass public terror of our times, or because it has been supplanted by non-verbal modes of communication of a symbolic or mathematical kind. In *Language and Silence* his discussion of these questions was controlled by the fact that, in writing as a critic, he had to relate his preoccupations to particular works and authors. In his new book the same themes proliferate with little check and visible direction; although Steiner is still writing with the methods and attitudes of a literary critic his material is now not literature, or even writing in general, but that most tenuous and unresisting of all subjects, 'culture'.

In all of Steiner's criticism there has been an element of story-telling, a desire—not at all uncommon among critics—to give his discourse something of the pace and density of fictional narrative. (One may compare Leslie Fiedler, who has described *Love and Death in the American Novel* as itself a further instance of the kind of book he is writing about.) In 1964 he ventured into fiction proper with *Anno Domini,* a book of three long stories about aspects of the Second World War, which he was too young to have experienced at first hand; their horrified pressing on the raw nerve of violence and atrocity points to a central facet of his sensibility. Some words of his own from *In Bluebeard's Castle* offer an apt comment: 'Bending too fixedly over hideousness, one feels queerly drawn. In some strange way, the horror flatters attention, it gives to one's own limited means a spurious resonance.' In *Anno Domini* the horror remained untransmuted by the imagination; it remained at the level of sensationalism, conveyed in slack and careless prose.

Since then Steiner has made no further ventures into 'official' fiction writing. Yet *In Bluebeard's Castle* is patently devised as a work of literature, endeavouring to persuade the reader by a complex of metaphor and myth and a pervasive verbal rhetoric, at the same time as it is packed with references to real events and persons and books. An understandable inability to see how its 'fictional' and 'truth-telling' elements are meant to connect undoubtedly underlies much of the hostile response it has received. Certainly, few of its statements seem easily verifiable or falsifiable. The way Steiner himself would like to see the book may be guessed from his own description—surely quite accurate—of Freud's *Civilization and its Discontents*: 'Freud's essay is itself a poetic construct, an attempt to devise a myth of reason with which to contain the terror of history.'

'Poetic' is not a word one would instantly apply to Steiner; his writing, however metaphorical and image-laden, is sometimes clumsy and inflated. Nevertheless, there is more than mere curiosity value in recalling that his first literary appearance was as a poet, in a slender pamphlet of poems published by the

Fantasy Press, Oxford, almost twenty years ago. There the mode of high-cultural lament that pervades *In Bluebeard's Castle* is already apparent:

> No reference—but high blind Tiresias
> gone mad in a crippled lighthouse.

The note is developed in an immaculate pastiche of Pound:

> If their banality these warnings mar,
> and twenty years behind the times,
> recall what trafficants the moderns are
> and how alone a Landor dines!

The allegiance to Pound has remained constant; some elegiac lines from the late *Cantos* conclude *In Bluebeard's Castle.* Steiner refers to Pound as the 'master voyager of our age', and the honorific reference, though not misplaced, is in curious contrast with his sharp and ungenerous treatment of Eliot for the latter's anti-semitism, mild though it was: Pound was far more virulent an anti-semite, and as late as 1944 was writing in open defence of fascism. But consistency is not one of Steiner's more obvious qualities. His admiration for Pound may have affected the form of *In Bluebeard's Castle,* which is an apocalyptic voyage through recent history, where a mass of cultural fragments takes on the outlines of myth, and which is far more like the *Cantos* in spirit than it is like *Notes Towards the Definition of Culture.*

Short though it is, *In Bluebeard's Castle* is a strikingly uneven work. Steiner is at his best in the first lecture, 'The Great "Ennui"', a brilliant impressionistic survey of nineteenth-century cultural history, which he sees as the 'imagined garden of liberal culture'. His survey is no doubt open to correction on points of detail, but it is a considerable achievement to give a unified view of such a complicated and contradictory period, where, as he puts it, 'for every text of Benthamite confidence' of proud meliorism, we can find a counter-statement of nervous fatigue'. In his attitude to liberal culture Steiner is characteristically ambivalent. He knows well enough that it was often a veneer, covering great depths of exploitation and neglect and cruelty:

> We are given to understand that the crust of high civility covered deep fissures of social exploitation; that bourgeois sexual ethics

> were a veneer, masking a great era of turbulent hypocrisy; that the criteria of genuine literacy were applicable only to a few; that hatred between generations and classes ran deep, if often silent; that the safety of the *faubourg* and of the park was based squarely on the licensed but quarantined menace of the slum.

But it is a feature of Steiner's intellectual method to acknowledge, in a spirit of scrupulous fair-mindedness, quite radical objections to his developing argument, but having done so to pass on without further discussion, as though stating difficulties was much the same as answering them. If he had truly grasped and felt the tenuousness of nineteenth-century liberal culture, in the spirit of this quotation from the first lecture, then he could hardly have been so outraged by the violent collapse of that culture in the twentieth century.

As *haute vulgarisation,* Steiner's view of the nineteenth century could hardly be better done; when he focuses on the disasters of our age his approach is more predictable and less assured. As in some of his previous writings, he is transfixed by the coexistence of traditional high culture and Nazi barbarism in the Europe of thirty years ago, epiphanized in the topographical and spiritual juxtaposition of Weimar and Buchenwald. He is driven to seek a meaning for that juxtaposition, but can find none that really offers the mind any purchase, in spite of his reiteration that 'we know of personnel in the bureaucracy of the torturers and the ovens who cultivated a knowledge of Goethe, a love of Rilke'. There are facts that the mind can do nothing with, and this seems to be one of them: by itself it offers neither condemnation nor vindication of Western liberal culture. So much of Steiner's writing on such themes is in the spirit of Adorno's observation, 'To write poetry after Auschwitz is barbaric. And this corrodes even the knowledge of why it has become impossible to write poetry today.' But that statement, too, has become falsified; poetry *has* been written after Auschwitz, even at the cost of proving that we are living in a barbaric age, though less barbaric than Hitler's.

If Steiner cannot cope with this juxtaposition on the level of reason and dialectic, he has devised his own model for understanding it. He argues that at crucial moments of history the Jewish people have confronted Western man with intolerable calls to transcendence: in the emergence of Hebrew monotheism, in primitive Christianity, and in the largely Jewish development of messianic socialism in the nineteenth century: 'Three times, Judaism produced a summons to perfection and sought to impose it on the current and currency of Western life. Deep loathings built up in the social subconscious, murderous resentments.' Hence, in the end, the Final Solution. One may, if one is in sympathy with Steiner's state of feeling, respond to the imaginative boldness of this formula, as one might to a poem or an aphorism, but it is not a convincing explanation of anything. It remains a charm or fetish of the intellect against the inexplicable terrors of history.

In the last two lectures, 'In a Post-Culture' and 'Tomorrow', Steiner offers a characteristic mixture of sharp *aperçus* and deep intellectual confusion. As in *Language and Silence* he is preoccupied with the possible end of language, the replacement of speech and writing with music or mathematics. He dwells with horrified fascination on the way in which young people thoughout the world live in a cocoon of rock music, and wonders, 'What are the sweet transistorized hammers doing to the brain at key stages in its development?' Meanwhile the cultivated live out their lives to the sound of classical LPs, where the Baroque chamber ensemble has reassumed its original function as *Tafelmusik,* or gracious background noise. But the essential point about our culture, which Steiner seems reluctant to accept, is that one thing does not drive out another: if there is more music and more mathematics, there are also more and more words. The celebrated terminal silences of Wittgenstein or Beckett have themselves generated many thousands of words, spoken in seminar discussion, or written in commentary. More to the point is the fact that so little is said that is ultimately worth hearing. Steiner is convincing when he shows how far contemporary culture is polarized between the scholiasm of the academy and the populism of the mass media, with little room for real humane discourse. Nevertheless, his general discussion of culture is affected by a deep irresolution between geneticist and environmentalist views, which is notably apparent in his remarks on language. In his article, 'The Language Animal' he showed himself very ready to accept Noam Chomsky's view of linguistic performance and syntactic disposition as innate human universals, so that man is essentially a 'language-animal. But in *In Bluebeard's Castle* Steiner argues that Western grammar is a reflection of cultural modes: 'The sinews of Western speech closely enacted and, in turn, stabilized, carried forward, the power relations of the Western social order.' No doubt one can make virtuoso efforts at combining different approaches, but in the end one has to choose and so exclude.

It is Steiner's major intellectual vice that once having seized on a bright idea he is unable to let go of it, apparently in the conviction that irreconcilable ideas can be disposed of by placing them side by side like the two terms of a metaphor or the juxtaposed images of a Poundian ideogram. Thus, on one page he can write: 'As anthropologists remind us, numerous primitive societies have chosen stasis or mythological circularity over forward motion, and have endured around truths immemorially posited.' On the immediately following page he argues that the pursuit of knowlege and intellectual understanding is not merely a 'contingent error embarked on by Western man at some moment of élitist or bourgeois rapacity', but part of the basic human neural equipment, imprinted on the 'impulse-net of our cortex'. So that if some human groups seem to have opted out of the pursuit, that was merely an accident of circumstance. 'The partial absence of this questing compulsion from less-developed, dormant races and civilizations does not represent a free choice or feat of innocence. It represents, as Montesquieu knew, the force of adverse ecological and genetic circumstance.' Or, when is a choice not a choice?

Those trained in tougher intellectual disciplines, who know a contradiction when they see one, may smile tolerantly at the spectacle of a literary critic who has waded into deep waters and is patently out of his depth. But is takes some courage, some determination, to go into the water at all. George Steiner has imprudently exposed himself in these lectures; their principal offence is that they contain such an intricate combination of sense and non-sense that an excessive amount of gleaning is necessary to separate the two. But the effort is worth making.

1971

II

In this short novel,[2] his first published fiction since *Anno Domini* in 1964, George Steiner has seized on, or been seized by, an idea that might have launched a sensational thriller with global appeal. Imagine that Adolf Hitler had not, in fact, perished in Berlin in the last days of the Third Reich; that a double had been killed in his place, and the dental evidence which provided the only certain identification of the Führer's body had been faked; and that, like many lesser Nazis, he had escaped to South America. Thirty years later he is still alive, an old man in his eighties, hidden in a desperately inaccessible spot in the Amazonian jungle, where he is eventually caught by a search-party of determined Jews, master-minded by a veteran Nazi-hunter in Israel, who have been on his track for years. The news of the capture spreads round the world, as the Jews' weak radio signals are picked up; the political implications of Hitler's reappearance cause discreet consternation in official circles in Britain, the United States, France and Russia; and the world's media prepare to descend on South America. The story, as Steiner tells it, concentrates on the Jews' task in transporting Hitler back to civilization, fighting against a lethal environment and their own exhaustion and illness. This basic narrative is counterpointed with recollections of the Final Solution that Hitler had willed into being, and the arguments going on round the globe as the incredible news filters out of the jungle. The Jews themselves are uncertain if their messages to base, sent in an easy code based on the Old Testament, have been received, and they are well aware of the many forces that will try to stop them taking Hitler to Israel for trial, as Eichmann had been.

Their discussions provide a philosophical dimension to Steiner's narrative and make it something more than a simple, action-packed tale. As they struggle back through the jungle, with Hitler, who is remarkably spry for his years, keeping up with them quite well, the Jews debate the nature of revenge. Given the crimes Hitler was responsible for—and Steiner reminds us of them in some elliptical but horrendous pages—what, reasonably, can be done with their perpetrator? The youngest member of the party, who has a personal motive for revenge since his father was killed in an earlier, unsuccessful attempt to find Hitler, starts talking about ingenious tortures and physical humiliations. But an older man tells him that crude vengeance would be fatal:

> To torment him, to hang him, would be to pretend that something of what he has done can be made good, that even a millionth of it can be cancelled. If we hang him history will draw a line. Accounts settled. And forget even faster. That's just what they want. They want us to do the job for them and put the whole guilt on him. Like a great crown. *He's* the one to blame. Let the Jews hang him high. *He* did it all. They must be the ones who know. We're acquitted now. First they nailed up Christ and now Hitler. God has chosen the Jew. For his hangman. Let them carry the blood. We're in the clear.

Reflections about guilt, about the nature of justice and vengeance, about the meaning of the Holocaust and the historical relations of the Jewish people and their persecutors, provide the central themes of Steiner's novel. They come to an extraordinary climax in the final pages when, as helicopters are about to descend on the party, Hitler speaks at length, retaining a hint of his old, spell-binding oratory. The Jews have discussed on their journey a rumour, never finally dispelled, that Hitler himself may have had Jewish blood. Now, as he speaks, he confesses that many of his own ideas about a divinely ordained master race with a unique historical mission were of Zionist inspiration. He admits that he attempted to cleanse the world of the Jews, since they represented an intolerable challenge to the rest of humanity. Steiner's Hitler ingeniously elaborates the argument Steiner himself advanced ten years ago in *In Bluebeard's Castle* about the triple challenge that the Jews have presented to mankind: a demanding monotheism in Jehovah; an impossible call to love and forgiveness in Christ; and the assertion of absolute social justice in Marx. Hitler claims that he tried to save mankind from the Jew's unbearable blackmail in transcendence: 'Three times he has infected our blood and brains with the bacillus of perfection.' Hitler tried to remove the burden from mankind, and what was the result? The fulfilment of Zionist dreams in the state of Israel, which would never have been established without the Holocaust.

Steiner's treatment of Hitler ultimately moves him from history to myth. He has been brave in writing this book, since literal-minded Jewish readers may find it objectionable, missing the subtler dimensions and seeing it simply as an attempt to whitewash Hitler. I hope not. Two readings have convinced me that this is a fiction of extraordinary power and thoughtfulness, despite much that is tiresome and inept in the writing. Steiner's account of the jungle portage—largely derived, one imagines, from written sources—is immensely vivid and compelling. But passages of kitsch are disconcertingly liable to surface. This trilingual polymath has never had an easy relationship with the English language, and he reveals a tin ear when it comes to writing everyday dialogue. For instance, he makes an American pilot say, 'Keerist, I've landed on some crummy strips in my day. But this field takes the cake. I almost cracked up taxiing in. And get a whiff of the joint. No drains?' Describing a minor secret agent Steiner lapses into the register of the Forsyth saga that his novel might have been (its knowingness seems to blend easily with the knowingness of Steiner's critical writings):

> He knew how to coax the metal prongs through the stiff paper in a Danish driving licence so as not to betray a change of photograph. Or where the gum loosened in a *Livret militaire* (he had carried one in Metz). The filigree of an Irish passport enchanted him and he retained in his left thumb the remembrance of the perforations, so intricate yet easy to counterfeit, of a Moroccan *permis de séjour.*

None of this rings very true. Still, there is more to writing well than writing well all the time, and it is power rather than elegance or consistency of performance that characterizes this remarkable novel.

1981

NOTES

1. *In Bluebeard's Castle: Some Notes Towards the Redefinition of Culture.* (London, 1971).
2. *The Portage to San Cristobal of A. H.* (London, 1981).

13

The decline and fall of the Catholic novel

They are in the same Department, English, and talk books for a while. Michael's favourite novel at the moment is 'The Heart of the Matter', and Polly's, 'Brideshead Revisited.' 'But Greene's awfully sordid, don't you think?' says Polly.

'But Waugh's so snobbish.'

'Anyway, it said in "The Observer" that they're the two best English novelists going, so that's one in the eye for the Prods.'

This passage from *How Far Can You Go?,* David Lodge's new novel, is precisely located in history. The conversation takes place at a party given by the undergraduate Catholic Society of a London University college on St Valentine's Day, 1952. At that time English Catholics still maintained the exclusive and defensive attitudes that were later to be deplored as 'the ghetto mentality'. All notable achievements by Catholics, whether on the battlefield—where Catholics were said to have won many more VCs than their numbers would warrant—or in sport or in literature were triumphantly proclaimed to Protestants or unbelievers.

By the early 1950s non-Catholic readers were beginning to take 'the Catholic novel' seriously. Graham Greene, it was said, had begun it with *Brighton Rock* in 1938, followed by *The Power and the Glory* in 1940. Then came Evelyn Waugh's *Brideshead Revisited* (1945) and Greene's *The Heart of the Matter* (1948) and *The End of the Affair* (1951). Waugh loyally promoted Greene as 'a Catholic novelist', even though Greene preferred to call himself a Catholic who wrote novels; in later years Waugh came to regret these efforts, though he and Greene remained good friends. Greene, meanwhile, was discovering earlier French versions of the Catholic novel, and, as a director of Eyre and Spottiswood in the late 1940s, had the works of the distinguished

French Catholic novelist, François Mauriac, translated and published in England. Mauriac and Greene wrote admiring essays on each other's work.[1] The idea of the Catholic novel was further explored and defined in Conor Cruise O'Brien's mannered but penetrating critical study, *Maria Cross: Imaginative Patterns in a Group of Modern Catholic Writers,* published in 1953 under the pseudonym of 'Donat O'Donnell'. O'Brien related Greene and Waugh and the Irish novelist Sean O'Faoláin to French Catholic writers: Mauriac, Georges Bernanos and Léon Bloy among novelists, and Charles Péguy and Paul Claudel among poets.

Critics, whether Catholic or not, were in general agreement about the characteristics of the Catholic novel. The novelist whose Catholic beliefs were explicit in his work was working against the grain of the novel form, with whatever advantages and disadvantages that could bring. The novel as it had developed since the eighteenth century was *bürgerlich,* this-worldly, realistic, empirical, phenomenological; unlike the romance, which it had partly replaced, it was not well adapted to miraculous or supernatural happenings. If religion appeared at all it was as a matter of social behaviour or ethical conviction. The Catholic novelists occupied a world that was less solid and complacently materialistic; it was partly transparent to other worlds, revealing the flames of Hell or, less frequently, the radiance of Heaven. Their creations were not merely characters in a tale but immortal souls with an eternal destiny, either for damnation or salvation; if damnation seemed closer or more likely that was no more than one might expect, given the corruption of the world and the fallen state of human nature.

Yet nothing was certain until the end; moment by moment life was a battle between the opposed forces of Good and Evil; Divine intervention was always possible though quite unpredictable. Characters in Greene's novels, like Pinkie and Scobie, died in mortal sin and seemed destined for Hell. And yet, as the old priest tells Rose at the end of *Brighton Rock,* 'You can't conceive, my child, nor can I or anyone—the . . . appalling . . . strangeness of the mercy of God.' Unbelieving readers may have rejected the world-view but they had to admit that Catholic novels offered a particular intensity and recurring high drama lacking in their counterparts; man was poised, most precariously, on the isthmus of a middle state.

At the heart of the matter lay grace, the free and unmerited gift from God that man needs for sanctification and salvation. To show the workings of grace without violating psychological or physical credibility was a delicate business for Catholic novelists. In *Brideshead Revisited* Lord Marchmain is on his death-bed after a sinful life and years of separation from the Church; he has already once refused to see a priest, but on a second attempt, when he is *in extremis,* he slowly, laboriously makes the sign of the cross, indicating his repentance and reconciliation with God. Soon afterwards his daughter, Lady Julia, returns to the practice of Catholicism.

In *The End of the Affair* the once adulterous Sarah Miles unexpectedly dies when she is on the point of becoming a Catholic. Then strange things are reported, which may be miracles though they may also have natural explanations; a small boy is suddenly cured of acute appendicitis; a lifelong atheist finds that a disfiguring birthmark on his face has disappeared overnight. Grace, we are invited to assume, has intervened in the natural order; Catholic readers, accepting the invitation, were edified; but sceptics might have felt that the principal intervention was the busy novelist's, making things come right in the end. There is, incidentally, a subtler and less obtrusive tracing of the action of grace on a Catholic soul in danger in a much earlier version of the Catholic novel, Mrs Wilfrid Ward's *One Poor Scruple,* published in 1899, and very popular for a time.[2] This is an engrossing story of life among the Catholic upper classes, divided between a remote country house and fashionable *fin-de-siecle* London. Mrs Ward—a grand-daughter of the Duke of Norfolk—was intimate with the world of the old Catholic families that Waugh later wrote about in more superficial and bedazzled terms in *Brideshead Revisited.*

English Catholic writers were relatively restrained and tentative in showing the manifestations of the supernatural in the natural. The French were more whole-hearted; in Bernanos's *Sous le Soleil de Satan* the Devil himself appears to the humble country priest, Abbé Donnissan. Greene has said of it:

> How I wish I could have been one of those who read *Sous le Soleil de Satan* for the first time when it appeared in 1926. With what astonishment, in this novel unlike all novels hitherto, they must

> have encountered *le tueur d'ames* when he intercepted the curé on the dark road to Boulaincourt in the guise of a little lubricious horse-dealer with his sinister gaiety and his horrible affection and his grotesque playfulness.[3]

Greene is surely wrong in saying that the Satanic apparition had no antecedents in novels, for Ivan Karamazov had experienced it long before.

Two points need to be made about the English Catholic novel, once instantly evoked by the names of Greene and Waugh. It declined quite rapidly; and the novels in question did not dramatize Catholic theology *tout court,* for there is no such single entity, but a particular and extreme theological emphasis, where religious beliefs were caught up with literary attitudes and conventions. After *The Quiet American* (1955), where the frame of reference is political and ideological, and the light-hearted and cynical entertainment, *Our Man in Havana* (1958), it became evident that Greene's Catholic novels represented a phase in his personal development as a writer between 1938 and 1951 rather than a lifelong existential concern. Waugh, too, did not attempt a large-scale Catholic novel after *Brideshead Revisited,* a work which, as he subsequently admitted, was permeated by the mingled nostalgia and anxiety engendered by the war, and where, as some dissatisfied readers had the bad taste to point out, Catholicism was intimately connected with the threatened *mores* and customs of the Catholic aristocracy; in Conor Cruise O'Brien's words, 'hardly separable from a personal romanticism and a class loyalty'. Catholic pieties and practices are conspicuous in *Sword of Honour,* Waugh's fine trilogy about the Second World War, but more as a part of Guy Crouchback's personal code and myth than as an element informing the whole work.

Greene's *A Burnt-Out Case* (1961) disconcerted some Catholic readers, Waugh among them, for it seemed to repudiate the values of his Catholic novels. Its central figure, Querry, is a famous Catholic architect, who has designed many churches and cathedrals; but he has lost his faith and retreated to a leper colony in what was then the Belgian Congo to get away from his admirers and recover his peace of mind. The equation 'famous Catholic architect = famous Catholic novelist' may have been too reductive, but there were elements in Querry's thin, diagrammatic story that seemed to insist on it; character and author had received similar acclamations, even to the extent of having their pictures on the cover of *Time*. Waugh was badly shaken by the book, as he recorded in his diary:

> It emphasises a theme which it would be affected not to regard as personal—the vexation of a Catholic artist exposed against his wishes to acclamations as a 'Catholic' artist who at the same time cuts himself off from divine grace by sexual sin . . . It is the first time Graham has come out as specially faithless—pray God it is a mood, but it strikes colder and deeper.[5]

Greene briskly disposed of Waugh's objection in a recent interview: 'When I wrote *A Burnt-Out Case* he said I was the lost leader because I'd exhausted my faith. But I hadn't lost faith, my character Querry lost *his* faith. Nothing to do with me.'[6] This sounds a little disingenuous, but there is no point in further speculation about how far Greene can be identified with his character. What is more interesting about *A Burnt-Out Case* is its early awareness of the new directions given to Catholicism by Pope John XXIII and, a year or so after it appeared, by the Second Vatican Council; it is surely significant that there are recurring mentions of a photograph of the recently elected Pope.

Greene's Catholic novels proper had emphasized the separation between Nature and Grace, the exclusiveness of Catholicism, and the insufficiency of ordinary human virtue. In *A Burnt-Out Case* a more humanistic Catholicism is presented, particularly by the Father Superior of the leper settlement. Querry, no longer a believing Catholic, still thinks in the old categories, even if he sees them from the outside. Arguing with the Father Superior, he tries to insist on the separation between religious and human virtues: 'You try to draw everything into the net of your faith, father, but you can't steal all the virtues. Gentleness isn't Christian, self-sacrifice isn't Christian, charity isn't, remorse isn't.' But the Father Superior asserts the exact opposite when he preaches to his flock in pidgin-French:

> 'When you love it is Yezu who loves, when you are merciful it is Yezu who is merciful. But when you hate or envy it is not Yezu, for everything that Yezu made is good. Bad things are not there—

> they are nothing. Hate means no love. Envy means no justice. They are just empty spaces, where Yezu ought to be. . . . Now I tell you that when a man loves he must be Klistian. In this village do you think you are the only Klistians—you who come to Church?'

This spirit has been prominent in Catholic theological developments over the past twenty years, stressing that all good things come from God, that nature and grace are interdependent, and that there is a virtual and implicit Christianity as well as a doctrinally informed and committed Christianity. All this is in sharp contrast to the dramatic oppositions in Greene's earlier novels. In *Brighton Rock*—a much better novel, alas, than *A Burnt-Out Case*—the lapsed Catholics, Pinkie and Rose, are conscious of Good and Evil, as opposed to the stupid, good-natured humanist, Ida Arnold, who is concerned only with Right and Wrong. For Pinkie Catholicism conveys, above all, a sense of the closeness of Hell; Heaven is only a pale, remote possibility, and a loving God is a conspicuous absentee from the world.

David Lodge suggested in a radio interview in 1968 that the Catholic novel originating from Huysmans and developed by Bloy, Bernanos, Mauriac and Greene, was largely a thing of the past:

> I don't think that one can talk of the Catholic novel in quite such sharply-defined terms any more, partly because Catholicism itself has become a much more confused—and confusing—faith, more difficult to define, mainly in the last ten or fifteen years as a result of Pope John and the Vatican Council. The Church no longer presents that sort of monolithic, unified, uniform view of life which it once did.[7]

More recently, Lodge, reviewing Mary Gordon's novel, *Final Payments,* described it as steeped in nostalgia for the vanished forms of authoritarian, exclusive Catholicism, even though revolting against them: 'the undoubted distinction of its writing owes much to the high-cultural equivalent of the Catholic ghetto—the "Catholic novel" of Greene, Mauriac, Bernanos, Bloy, with its characteristic fondness for aphorisms that are subversive of liberal, materialistic assumptions.'[8]

Martin Green, in a hostile discussion of this tradition—himself writing as a liberal, humanistic Catholic—has remarked of its earlier French practitioners: 'In the nineteenth century this Catholic sensibility was quite recognisably and even crudely a species of Romanticism. These novelists' work usually belonged within the Romantic sub-species, Satanic melodrama; rhetorical in language, violent in action, bitter and extremist in spirit.'[9]

The Catholic novel in France and England was as much the embodiment of a literary convention as the enactment of religious experience. This is peculiarly true of Graham Greene; by the 1940s he had become a convinced admirer of Mauriac and Bernanos, but an earlier French influence seems to have been Baudelaire, who can be seen as both a Romantic satanist and a serious if heterodox Catholic moralist. Greene's Baudelaire was mediated by T. S. Eliot's influential essay of 1930, which asserted that moral Good and Evil are quite different from natural Good and Bad or Puritan Right and Wrong. In an interesting and revealing essay, 'Henry James: the religious aspect', first published in 1933, Greene quotes Eliot on Baudelaire:

> It is true to say that the glory of man is his capacity for salvation; it is also true to say that his glory is his capacity for damnation. The worst that can be said of most of our malefactors, from statesmen to thieves is that they are not men enough to be damned.[10]

Greene's essay is more enlightening about Greene than about James. He argues that James was a naturally religious writer, despite his lack of overt Christian commitment; he had a strong sense of the supernatural, and an acute responsiveness to Evil; though, like Baudelaire and the characters in Greene's own subsequent novels, he was more aware of damnation than of salvation. Some of James's characters, argues Greene, *were* men enough for damnation: 'both Densher and the Prince have on their faces the flush of the flames'. So did Pinkie, who distorts the words of the Creed to *'Credo in unum Satanum'* and who dies violently: 'He looked half his size, doubled up in appalling agony: it was as if the flames had literally got him. . . . ' In this phase of Greene's work Catholic doctrine was, as Martin Green rightly says, incorporated into Satanic melodrama. It is a phase to which *A Burnt-Out Case* marked a formal farewell. Now, it has been suggested, Greene no longer believes in Hell.[11]

David Lodge is a Catholic writer who started his literary career at about the time the Catholic novel was declining; he has retained a professional interest in it and has written studies of Greene and Waugh for Columbia Essays on Modern Writers. His work falls into two distinct kinds, perhaps as a way of conveniently coping with divisions in his own personality. His academic literary criticism—in books such as *Language of Fiction* (1966) and *The Modes of Modern Writing* (1977)—is predominantly formalist, though making saving gestures towards the mimetic and representational aspects of literature. His fiction is predominantly realistic, though his later novels make gestures towards self-reflectiveness. Lodge's best-known novel is *Changing Places* (1975), a marvellously funny and inventive satire on Anglo-American academic life. It is also, as it happens, his only novel in which Catholic themes play no part at all. In three of them, *The Picturegoers* (1960), *The British Museum is Falling Down* (1965), and *How Far Can You Go?* (1980), Catholicism is central. Here Lodge transforms the Catholic novel, as it existed when he was growing up, into something quite other: the Catholic anti-novel perhaps.

His first novel, *The Picturegoers,* was published when he was twenty-five, but was written when he was only twenty-two. Though it tends to sentimentality, it is a remarkably mature and ambitious work for so young a writer. It is set in an unfashionable South London suburb and focuses on several lower-middle-class families or groups, mostly Catholic, whose lives and fortunes interact at their regular Saturday outings to a large neighbourhood cinema; at that time, the mid-fifties, cinema-going had briefly recovered something of its pre-war popularity, before succumbing to television and bingo. Kingsley Amis reviewed *The Picturegoers* favourably in *The Observer.*

> *The Picturegoers* is a Catholic novel, but written without the nose-to-the-grindstone glumness, all sin and significance, that the phrase often implies. On the contrary, Mr David Lodge is on easy equal terms with his characters, seeing them and their lower-middle-class suburban habitat with a social eye, impatient of abstractions. He shows originality in his perception that a young lapsed Catholic, digging with a conventionally religious family

> that includes an attractive ex-novice daughter, may be drawn back to the faith because of its associations, not with any heavily orchestrated splendours and miseries, but with ordinary, decent, cheerful domesticity.

Amis's points are well taken. In Lodge's fiction the Catholic characters are indeed ordinary; there are no dissolute aristocrats like Lord Marchmain, or Satanic teenage gangsters like Pinkie, or men undergoing spiritual intensities in exotic parts of the world, like the whisky priest or Scobie. The frame of reference is sociological rather than literary-theological, and the social eye is always alert. Thus, the lapsed-Catholic student, Mark Underwood, looking for digs in the house of a motherly Irishwoman, Mrs Mallory, soon registers that he is in a devout Catholic household:

> The kitchen into which he was ushered confirmed his suspicions about Mrs Mallory's religious background: the evidence of the plastic holy water stoup askew on the wall, the withered holy Palm, stuck behind a picture of the Sacred Heart which resembled an illustration in a medical text-book, and the statue of St Patrick enthroned upon the dresser, was conclusive.

As one who grew up in something like the millieu described in *The Picturegoers* I find such descriptions disturbingly accurate. It has rarely been caught in English fiction, for the upper-middle-class converts who wrote Catholic novels had little contact with it, and the closest parallels are in Joyce's domestic interiors.

There are several interwoven stories in *The Picturegoers,* but the central strand concerns the growing love between Mark Underwood and Clare Mallory, who has not long left the novitiate in a convent. At first Mark is interested only in having a good time with Clare, but love develops between them, and then, under Clare's influence but also, to some extent, because of the natural goodness of the whole Mallory family, he returns to the Church. *The Picturegoers* preserves elements of the traditional Catholic novel. Mark is at Mass with Clare when his faith dramatically returns, and the intervention of grace is presented in a Greeneish simile: 'The priest stretched up, lifting the Host on high. Mark stared at it, and belief leapt in his mind like a child in the womb.' There are other stylistic traces of Greene; of a minor character it is said, 'he carried his failure before him like a monstrance.'

It looks for a time as if Mark and Clare are happily set on the road to Holy Matrimony and good Catholic family life. But God and the author have other plans: once Mark's faith returns it goes on developing in unexpected ways. Towards the end of the book he experiences an unmistabkable vocation to enter the priesthood, and Clare has to be given up; she bravely and unflinchingly lets him go. Grace has undoubtedly been at its inexorable and mysterious work; but the author has also, in D. H. Lawrence's words, been putting his thumb in the scale. The lesson is that marriage may be a high Christian state, but celibate priesthood is a higher one; such sacrificial instances were familiar in the Catholic novel, particularly its French versions.

Not that Lodge shows any Jansenist hostility to marriage in *The Picturegoers;* quite the opposite. Indeed, the inexperienced young author was inclined to sentimentalize and idealize it in the manner of a Catholic Truth Society pamphlet, and it is here, read in the light of Lodge's later novels, that *The Picturegoers* is most revealing. Mr Mallory is an English convert married to a Catholic Irishwoman, and they have had eight children. He likes looking at film stars and pretty girls in the street, and he still finds his auburn-haired wife attractive and, it is suggested, still makes love to her. At this point the text of *The Picturegoers* presents what recent criticism would identify as a significant absence, a lacuna, a *vide.* It seems that the couple are quite content with eight children and indeed have not had any more for several years. How have they arranged this—assuming that Mrs Mallory is still fertile—since contraception is firmly forbidden to Catholics? The text is silent.

This subject, from being an absence in *The Picturegoers,* becomes an obsessive presence in *The British Museum is Falling Down* and *How Far Can You Go?* The former describes a day in the life of Adam Appleby, a Catholic graduate student of English Literature, who already has three children and who, notwithstanding valiant endeavours to operate the system of temperature charts and calendars required by the safe period, is haunted by the likelihood that a fourth is on the way. *The British Museum is Falling Down* is a very funny novel, where the hero's anxiety is constantly offset by farcical events in and around the Reading

Room of the British Museum. With this book Lodge emerged as a gifted comic novelist; the early influence of Joyce and Greene was supplemented by that of Kingsley Amis, of whom he has written, 'I suppose that, as a Roman Catholic, I could scarcely be more distant from Amis's view of the eternal verities. And yet I constantly experience a strange community of feeling with him. . . .'[12]

The British Museum is Falling Down is a self-reflective novel, with taproots to Lodge's criticism. Adam Appleby is supposed to be writing a thesis on the language of English fiction; a year or so later Lodge published a book on that subject. One of his aims in this novel is to suggest that the contemporary novelist has an uphill struggle to achieve any kind of original expression, since so much has been done already by the masters of the recent past. To illustrate the point, the narrative of *The British Museum* keeps lapsing into witty parodies of the style of twentieth-century novelists, Graham Greene prominent among them:

> Holding the two dusty volumes limply in his hands, he remembered the oozing wall of the urinal in the school playground, the tough Middle English paper in Finals, the fly-speckled oleograph of the Sacred Heart in the Catholic doctor's waiting room, and Barbara crying on the unmade bed; and the will to resist any longer ebbed out of him like water out of a sink, leaving behind only a sour scum of defeat.

In its Catholic aspects *The British Museum* reflects the hopes aroused in the 1960s by the Vatican Council that there might be some relaxation of the ban on contraception, which restricted Catholics who wanted to limit their families to the complex and unreliable safe period method. Officially the ban was a matter of fundamental dogma and immutable—all sexual activity had to remain 'open to life'—but the topic had at least become discussable, and fresh arguments were presented against it: the traditional teaching was based on a narrowly biological view of sexuality, reinforced by scholastic philosophy and Roman legalism, and should be revised in the light of a more modern understanding of sexuality and human personality. Adam Appleby satirically expressed his exasperation by composing an entry for a Martian encyclopaedia compiled after life on earth was extinguished by atomic warfare:

> Roman Catholicism was, according to archaeological evidence, distributed fairly widely over the planet Earth in the 20th century. As far as the Western Hemisphere is concerned, it appears to have been characterised by a complex system of sexual taboos and rituals. Intercourse between married partners was restricted to certain limited periods determined by the calendar and the body-temperature of the female. Martian archaeologists have learned to identify the domiciles of Roman Catholics by the presence of large numbers of complicated graphs, calendars, small booklets full of figures, and quantities of broken thermometers, evidence of the great importance attached to this code. Some scholars have argued that it was merely a method of limiting the number of offspring; but as it has been conclusively proved that the Roman Catholics produced more children on average than any other section of the community, this seems untenable. Other doctrines of the Roman Catholics included a belief in a Divine Redeemer and in a life after death.

In Lodge's new novel the Catholic characters are older, sadder, wiser, and in some cases no longer Catholics by the time we reach the end of the book, which follows their progress from the early 1950s to the late 1970s. It is a middle-aged novel, genial in some aspects, bitter in others. The geniality shows itself in the frequent interventions of the author's witty Fieldingesque persona, who freely comments on the action and refers back, on occasion, to Lodge's earlier novels: it is a highly traditional way of foregrounding the text. The bitterness is apparent in the cold Voltairean irony with which familiar Catholic doctrines are discussed.

The novel opens, in February 1952, with a group of Catholic students of London University attending an early weekday mass in a gloomy church. There is Angela, pretty, blonde and very devout, reading French; and Dennis, a burly youth, reading Chemistry, not very devout, and only at the Mass because he is in love with Angela. (After a protracted, notionally chaste engagement lasting several years they will marry.)

Polly is a dark, pretty girl, already a bit of a raver, and destined to lose her faith and her virginity before long; she is reading English. So is Michael, a clever youth with a white face and dark, greasy hair, wearing what the author piquantly describes as a 'wanker's overcoat.' He is tormented by sexual temptations and a regular masturbator, haunted by women's breasts, even by the word 'cleavage' in popular newspapers. He will grow out of this in time, grow up, and have a happy marriage, though still retaining an intense, voyeuristic interest in sex in all its aspects. After graduating he writes a thesis on the novels of Graham Greene, and references to Greene's novels as they appear over the years provide a subtext relating Lodge's work to the admired master of the English Catholic novel.

Adrian is a formidably dull youth in a belted gabardine raincoat, carrying a large missal; he is reading Economics; he never really comes to life. Ruth, a plain girl with a strong personality, is reading Botany; she is to become a nun and have an unexpectedly interesting life later on. Miles, an elegant homosexual, is a recent convert, reading History; and Violet, is a pretty but plainly neurotic girl reading Classics; neither of them will achieve much happiness. Edward, serving Mass, is a medical student with a lugubrious expression, a dim though likeable figure.

The celebrant, Father Austin Brierley, is a young curate who acts as unofficial chaplain to the Catholic students. When the novel opens he is narrow-minded and priggish, but he is going to change a lot, as Catholicism changes during the 1960s and 1970s, and to have a lively though uncomfortable priestly career. He becomes more and more radical, discovering new modes of theology and biblical exegesis and moving into secular disciplines like sociology. By the end of the novel he has left the priesthood and married, though he remains 'a kind of Catholic'.

Lodge shows what happens to these young people and their spouses over the next twenty-five years, mostly in English professional-class milieux, but taking in an excursus to Southern California. Their lives embrace success and failure, happiness and, in the case of one couple, more than anyone's share of tragedy. The reader is kept steadily engaged, but rather more because of the author's skill in sustaining a narrative than because all the characters are intrinsically interesting. The women are more substantial and have more potentialities than the men, some of whom are never more alive than when we first see them as students. As a temperamentally comic novelist, even though writing serious fiction, Lodge is given to a sharp typological placing of his characters on their initial appearance. The process gets them firmly established, but it also, I think, limits them and their capability for convincing change and growth. *How Far Can*

You Go? is not a long novel, but even so it does not quite muster the fictional drive and energy to keep all the stories going at full pressure, and the narrative sags in places. But the book offers many novelistic satisfactions and the constant pleasure of recognition, as the sharp social eye registers innovations in society at large as well as in the sub-culture of the Catholics. Is this, for instance, the first time that an Open University Summer School, a bizarre mixture of intellectual intensity and sheer saturnalia, has been captured in fiction? *How Far Can You Go?* deserves the highest praise for observation, wit and intelligence.

Early in the book Lodge describes the Catholic world-picture that all his young people would have accepted. It took the form of a great snakes-and-ladders board with Salvation as the name of the game; at the top was Heaven, and at the bottom was Hell; prayers and sacraments and good deeds sent you scuttling up a ladder; sins sent you slithering down a snake. The rules were complicated, but anything you very much liked doing was almost certainly bad, or at least a moral danger. This was certainly the frame of reference of the old Catholic novel, with its perilous spiritual dramas and ever-present danger of Hell. Lodge's characters gradually come to abandon this world-picture, not by any conscious rethinking of doctrine but by a steady change in their sense of what seems credible. 'At some point in the 1960s', remarks the narrator, 'Hell disappeared. No one could say for certain when this happened. First it was there, then it wasn't.'

By then many of the married Catholics had had enough of the safe period and were using contraceptives; when in 1968 Pope Paul VI, against expectations, reaffirmed the traditional ban in the encyclical *Humanae Vitae,* there was an unprecedented storm of argument and protest in the Church; some progressive priests were disciplined, like Father Austin Brierley; and Catholic married couples quietly went on using contraceptives, in increasing numbers, rejecting Roman authority in what they saw as a matter of private conscience. Between pages 114 and 121 of his novel Lodge turns aside from the story to interpolate an essay on *Humanae Vitae* and its implications that is far more cogent than the theological discussions I have come across. This issue was perhaps the largest internal crisis faced by the Catholic Church since the Reformation; the fact that an immense number of Catholic lay people in the Western world decided to act like

Protestants and do, in good conscience, what they thought was right rather than what the Catholic world-picture required of them had incalculable implications and consequences, in attitudes to sexual behaviour, and to the nature of authority in the Church. The charming but reactionary Pole who now occupies the Throne of Peter—his arrival is signalled on the last page of Lodge's novel—evidently wants to get back to a more dogmatic and authoritarian mode of Catholicism, with all the old doctrines reaffirmed. But it is inconceivable that the clock can be put back to 1952 or thereabouts.

Lodge has described the recent changes in the Church—intellectual, liturgical, pastoral—with faultless precision. What is largely missing from his book, though, is a sense of what motivates the religious life. 'Why did we put it off so long?' his people ask one another, when they have decided to do the sensible thing and use contraceptives. Their conclusion, endorsed by the author, is that they were afraid of Hell. This fear was, without doubt, a common motive, particularly where sex was concerned. But I think it was also the case that many people positively wanted to do God's will, as it was presented to them by an infallible, teaching Church. Conservative Catholics would be entitled to ask Lodge's intelligent and articulate characters what they thought the Church was, if it was not an infallible teaching body. The answer they would probably get was that Catholicism was the highest form of Christianity, which was the highest form of world religion, but that they did not need to accept all the dogmatic apparatus that traditionally went with Catholic Christianity. Broadly speaking, this answer would satisfy me,, but there are a lot of people it would not, John Paul II among them.

Lodge's people are decent and likeable and one intimately understands and sympathizes with their struggles. But they are also *gens moyens sensuels* and, when all is said, a rather mediocre lot. The collapse of the Catholic world-picture lifted a great load of anxiety, but it seems to have left behind a shrunken world, where Catholics share most of the assumptions of a secular, hedonistic society, and religion seldom appears as a mode of transcendence or transformation. There are no great passions in it, either: people are more concerned with sex—getting enough of it, of a respectable quality—than with love. This is in marked contrast to the old Catholic novel where, as Conor Cruise O'Brien has shown, carnal passion and divine Passion could become dangerously confused.

Lodge has moved down from those dangerous peaks and that rarified air to the flat, populous plain where most of us live our daily lives. If we are Catholics we shall discover in this excellent novel what we were and what we have become, and non-Catholics should find the discovery interesting too. What we or our children shall be, what Catholicism in the West, if it survives, is likely to become, are questions that it poses but cannot answer.

NOTES

1. Graham Greene, 'Francois Mauriac' in *Collected Essays* (London, 1969; François Mauriac, 'Graham Greene' in Samuel Hynes (ed), *Graham Greene: A Collection of Critical Essays* (Englewood Cliffs, 1973).
2. Mrs Ward's novel lapsed into obscurity, but a reprint for which I have written an introduction is appearing from Tabb House.
3. *Collected Essays,* p.125.
4. There is a case for regarding Muriel Spark as a later practitioner of the Catholic novel. It has been well argued in an intelligent essay by Ruth Whittaker which is somewhat marred by a simplistic conception of Catholicism. See 'Angels dining at the Ritz: the faith and fiction of Muriel Spark' in Malcolm Bradbury and David Palmer (eds), *The Contemporary English Novel* (London, 1979).
5. *The Diaries of Evelyn Waugh* (London, 1976), p.779.
6. 'T he John Mortimer interview', *Sunday Times,* 16 March 1980.
7. 'David Lodge interviewed by Bernard Bergonzi', *Alta: University of Birmingham Review* (No.7, Winter 1968-9).
8. *Times Literary Supplement,* 1 September 1978.
9. Martin Green, *Yeats's Blessings on Von Hugel: Essays on Literature and Religion* (London, 1967), p.74.
10. *Collected Essays,* p.50. I have corrected a slight misquotation by Greene. These words of Eliot provide an epigraph for Anthony Burgess's *Tremor of Intent* (1966), which is a Catholic novel of sorts as well as a spy thriller.
11. Graham Greene, 'God and literature and so forth' (interview), *The Observer,* 16 March 1980.
12. David Lodge, *Language of Fiction* (London, 1966), p.249.

14

The Terry Eagleton story

Terry Eagleton's position as our top Marxist critic and literary theorist remains unchallenged. But in 1983 he reached the age of forty and thus joined what Péguy called *le parti des hommes de quarante ans,* membership of which is likely to complicate one's ideological stance. In that year, too, Eagleton published his tenth book, *Literary Theory: An Introduction*, which looks as if it will be his most popular and widely read. This seems a good occasion on which to look back over his intellectual career, which though limited in location—being entirely confined to Cambridge and Oxford—has been marked by rapid movements between the many mansions in the spacious house of Marxist criticism.

The title of Eagleton's first book. *The New Left Church* (1966), recalls that he grew up as a Lancashire Catholic, and that as a young man he was a leading member of a group of left-wing Catholics whose commitment to social justice led them to attempt a fusion of Marxism and Catholicism, and who disseminated their ideas in the journal *Slant*. What began as an attempt at intellectual and practical co-operation between Catholics and Marxists ended as virtual absorption by the latter; at least, several onetime members of the *Slant* group are no longer Catholics. *The New Left Church* ambitiously draws together literary criticism, Catholic theology and liturgy, and Marxist political analysis. It is a very 1960s book in its easy eclecticism, where all sorts of names are cheerfully thrown into the pot: Marx, Sartre, Heidegger, Wittgenstein, Leavis, Laing, Raymond Williams. But for all the political and philosophical name-chasing, Eagleton's frame of reference is clearly literary-critical, heavily indebted to Leavis and to Raymond Williams, who was his supervisor at Cambridge. *The New Left Church*, though an immature book, provides early examples of Eagleton's basic qualities of mind. From the beginning he has been a fast, volatile thinker who leaps rapidly from idea to idea, or position to to position, without any indication of difficulty or of the obdurate way in which the world resists one's mental processes. There is an obvious contrast here with Raymond Wiliams, whose writing conveys an almost physical sense of the difficulty of saying just what one wants to say. Williams struggles with thoughts, whereas Eagleton seems to slide over them.

Eagleton's early Catholic education at the De La Salle College, Pendleton, was an important formative factor. *The New Left Church* is the work of an orthodox Catholic, though it is noticeable that Christ is referred to much more often than God, and that Eagleton seems to regard Christ as in some sense a metaphor for humanity. More interesting, though, is his constant recourse to the analogical thinking characteristic of scholastic philosophy and traditional Catholic apologetics. Throughout his career Eagleton has been ready to regard analogies and parallels as having actual logical force. *The New Left Church* is pervaded with them, of which one sweeping example can suffice: 'What happens to money under capitalism is what happens to language in a symbolist poem, and to the eucharist in a ceremony like benediction.'[1] (What happens in all these cases is the process of reification.) It is common enough for French or Italian Marxist intellectuals to have had a Catholic education in youth. Eagleton offers the much rarer example of an Englishman who has followed the same path. He shows how the subtle scholastic distinctions of Catholic theology can be adapted to Marxist dialectic. Something more particularly distinctive of English Catholicism in its older forms—that is to say, those that were current in Eagleton's schooldays, before the new ecumenism introduced by the Second Vatican Council in the early sixties—is a matter of tone. Eagleton's public tone has always been brashly self-confident, frequently arrogant and jeeringly dismissive of those who take a different position from himself. Something very like this tone, aggressive, hard-hitting and yet basically defensive used to characterize the polemics of English Catholics; Hilaire Belloc was a notable exemplar. Both Catholics and neo-Marxists are likely to feel at one and the same time members of a small beleaguered minority in England and representatives of a major world of thought and commitment elsewhere, whether represented by the Catholicism of Latin Europe or by Continental Marxism.

Eagleton's first book of literary criticism proper was *Shakespeare and Society,* published in 1967. It is dedicated to Raymond Williams, whose influence is rather fulsomely acknowledged: 'My chief debt, however, is to Raymond Williams, to whom I offer this as an extension of his own explorations, and without whose friendship and influence the book would not have been written.' *Shakespeare and Society* is a systematic application to a group of Shakespeare's plays of the argument in Williams's earlier books about the need to overcome our habitual belief in a necessary opposition between 'individual' and society'. Eagleton's treatment is both moralistic and schematic; Martin Green has summed up his view of *Hamlet* as 'Hamlet exemplifies a life-pattern we should avoid' and has dryly observed that in his treatment of *Anthony and Cleopatra* Eagleton wants to turn Cleopatras into bigger and better Octavias.[2] *Shakespeare and Society* remains Eagleton's least interesting book.

It was followed in 1970 by another book of literary criticism, *Exiles and Emigres: Studies in Modern Literature*, and a short work of religious and philosophical speculation, *Body as Language*. The latter contains Eagleton's last overtly Catholic writing. It shows the same energetic eclecticism as *The New Left Church,* lining up Catholicism, Marxism and phenomenology, but is subtler and generally less brash than the earlier book. It was considerably influenced by Fr Herbert McCabe a left-wing Dominican theologian associated with the *Slant* group. Eagleton takes his taste for instant analogies to great lengths, notably in the chapter called 'Priesthood and Leninism', where he proposes an appropriate role-model for the Catholic priesthood in the Leninist ideal of a group of trained and dedicated revolutionaries who live among the people, sharing the privations of their daily lives, whilst leading and inspiring them in a revolutionary struggle. The idea that the local parish priest ought to see himself as a kind of guerilla leader or underground activist fighting the bourgeois world is piquant enough, but it raises the question of how far Eagleton wants such analogies to turn into actual identities. His thought often seems at the mercy of his intellectual models. One notes in passing his extremely starry-eyed view of the Leninist elites, who in practice were ready to undertake any kind of terror for the good of the revolutionary cause. But the idealization of Lenin, in contrast to the dethroned Stalin, was characteristic of the New Left of the sixties.

Body as Language points to a growing tension between Eagleton's Catholicism and his Marxism, which is emphasized rather than concealed by his ready recourse to ingenious analogies. He freely restates Christian concepts in Marxist language, as when he says of theology, in a dense burst of Lukacsian jargon: 'Its aim is nothing less than to become, at every changing historical moment, the "totality of totalities": the definitive totalization of the varied meanings of human history.' At some point after 1970 Eagleton appears to have abandoned Catholicism, though he has never publicly repudiated it. One can assume, though, that whereas a Catholic could have written *Exiles and Emigrés* and even *Myths of Power* (1975), the whole temper of *Criticism and Ideology* (1976) is irreconcilable with any form of religious commitment.

Lukács's concern with totalities and totalization pervades *Exiles and Emigrés*, though Lukács is not in fact mentioned in the book; the acknowledged influences are, again Raymond Williams, and Perry Anderson's well-known essay, 'Components of the national culture'.[3] Anderson argued that in the first half of the twentieth century the commanding heights of English intellectual culture had been taken over by Continental émigrés, usually Austrians or Poles of conservative ideological views, such as Malinowski, Popper, Wittgenstein, Namier and Gombrich. Eagleton adapts this approach to the literary situation: 'With the exception of D. H. Lawrence, the heights of modern English literature have been dominated by foreigners and émigrés: Conrad, James, Eliot, Pound, Yeats, Joyce.' And Lawrence, as a working-class Englishman, was scarcely less alien to the displaced hegemonic circles of the national culture. Their abdication is seen to indicate a deep-seated crisis and loss of nerve in English society in the early twentieth century: the Strange Death of Liberal England, in fact, completed by the First World War. *Exiles and Emigrés* can be recommended to students of modern literature for its value as provocation rather than as insight or understanding. Indeed, to try to see what is wrong with the book, what it leaves out and what it distorts, would not be a bad way of sharpening one's sense of the period. Eagleton's readings of modern English authors are brashly reductive, directed in all cases to probing for some significant trace of contradiction or ambiguity or ambivalence, which is homologous with the contradictions permeating the culture at large. Thus, Virginia Woolf sometimes satirizes and sometimes endorses English upper-class values; in Waugh there is a struggle between a sense of morality and a sense of style; Orwell shows an unresolved conflict 'between an impulse to lonely and defiant moral gesture and a sense of the collective decency of drably normative life'; Greene's Catholic orthodoxy is denied by a humanism which is itself affected by Catholic attitudes. It did not need the vogue of Deconstructionist criticism to tell us that conflict and ambiguity are features of many literary works that we admire, but Eagleton takes them as signs of fatal weakness, both ideological and personal. Now and then he goes beyond conflict-detection to a mode of vulgar-Marxism, as when he says of *Women in Love*, 'What is shown is the despairing vacuity of a particular group of bored middle-class intellectuals, hopelessly alienated from the concrete social realities they analyse at such length.' One does not have to be a Leavis to find this an absurdly inadequate account of a major modernist text.

After *Body as Language* and *Exiles and Emigrës* Eagleton brought out no more books for five years, but he made up for this longish abstention by publishing three books during 1975-6; *Myths of Power: A Marxist Study of the Brontës* (1975), *Marxism and Literary Criticism* (1976) and *Criticism and Idelogy* (1976). The Brontës book is one of Eagleton's best achievements in straightforward literary criticism. It makes one ask how far 'Marxist' readings of literature are necessarily dependent on the Marxist metaphysic of dialectic and class struggle and historical materialism. In this book Eagleton places the Brontës in a concrete historical context, as a group located between the gentry and the emergent industrial class of the West Yorkshire manufacturers. I find his approach often illuminating, and a useful corrective to the romantic individualism that dominates criticism of the Brontës. Eagleton develops this distinction with a free use of analogies and polarities: the opposition between old gentry and new bourgeoisie is paralleled by a succession of other oppositions located in the Brontë texts: 'past/future', 'imagination/society', 'fantasy/realism'. Eagleton uses them to look for some underlying grammar: 'The fundamental structure of Charlotte's novels is a triadic one: it is determined by a complex play of power-relations between a protagonist, a "romantic-radical" and an aristocratic conservative.'[4] The objections to this kind of analysis are familiar and are often made; that it is abstract and schematic and adds nothing to our appreciation of the unique literary work. To speak for myself I find the uncovering of such family resemblances more helpful than not, as opposed to the atomistic examination of one discrete text after another. But the only point I want to make now is that this is a critical debate which can be conducted without much overt or prolonged reference to ideology. To write the kind of criticism in *Myths of Power* one needs a good understanding of social history and a taste for analogies and homologies; one does not absolutely need to be a Marxist. Indeed, much of the criticism in this book is at bottom quite traditional, concerned with the interactions of character and theme, and the accent is as much Leavisite as Marxist. In so far as there is a conceptually Marxist element in *Myths of Power* it is derived from that heterodox Marxist, Lucien Goldmann. Eagleton takes from Goldmann the idea of 'categorial structure', which is described as 'a primary mediation between the novel and society, a crucial nexus between the fiction and history'. Goldmann's 'categorial structure' has many affinities with Raymond Williams's 'structure of feeling'. Eagleton points out that his 'admiration for Goldmann's work is laced with strong reservations'. However strong these reservations, there is no doubt that 'categorial structure' is a fundamental concept in *Myths of Power:* 'Text, author, ideology, social class, productive forces: these are the terms I shall seek to bring together, by the mediating concept of categorial structure.'

Marxism and Literary Criticism is a brief, lucid, dogmatic introduction, comprising four essays on major aspects of Marxist criticism, together with a fighting preface warning off academics who think that 'Marxist criticism' is just one more method to be ranged on the shelf alongside Freudian Criticism or myth criticism. (The vehemence with which Eagleton, who has spent his whole life as an academic, excoriates other academics is a notable feature of his writing). 'Marxist criticism', he claims, must be seen as part of Marxism, which is itself 'a scientific theory of human societies and of the practice of transforming them.' What Eagleton, or any other Marxist, means by 'scientific' in such canonical formulations is something I have often wanted to know and never been told. In this particular context Eagleton is insistent that 'Marxist criticism' is only for the truly committed. It is as if he wanted to put firmly behind him the awkward possibility raised in *Myths of Power* that one might write 'Marxist criticism' without actually being a Marxist. *Marxism and Literary Criticism* exemplifies one of Eagleton's strongest qualities, his capacity for the clear exposition of complex ideas. Inevitably the summary implies the author's attitude of acceptance or rejection, and there is a good deal of rejection in this book, notably of Lukács and Goldmann, to whom Eagleton had been indebted in his preceding books of criticism. Eagleton's impatience with Lukács is now evident. Many of Lukacs's intellectual and personal positions are, of course, vulnerable to attack, whether from a Marxist or 'bourgeois' position, given the contradictions between the trimmer and the dedicated intellectual. In Eagleton's book Lukács is criticized for being more Hegelian than Marxist, and condemned for his conservative literary tastes and for his bourgeois ideas about the nature of the aesthetic. With Brecht set up as an opposing figure, Lukács is found wanting on many counts. Eagleton is even more severe about Goldmann; he is denounced for holding a concept of social consciousness that is more Hegelian than Marxist and thus seeing too direct and undialectical a relation between social consciousness and literary text. In saying this, Eagleton is implicitly rejecting the approach he had employed with some effectiveness in *Myths of Power*. Other errors by Goldmann are summarized in the notes: 'an incorrect contrast between "world vision" and "ideology"; an elusiveness about the problem of aesthetic value; an unhistorical conception of "mental structures"; and a certain positivist strain in some of his working methods'.[5]

There are favourable references in *Marxism and Literary Criticism* to Louis Althusser and Althusser's disciple, Pierre Macherey. In *Criticism and Ideology*, the much more substantial book published in the same year, Eagleton emerges as a committed Althusserian, give or take a few reservations. The Althusserian moment in English Marxism might be described as a storm in a doll's teacup, given the small number of people, even on the left, who knew anything about it. Yet for a few years in the seventies the impact of Althusser generated much bitter debate among Marxist intellectuals. These arguments were described and documented from the hostile standpoint of a humanistic Marxism in *One-Dimensional Marxism: Althusser and the Politics of Culture* (1980), edited by Simon Clarke and others (the book is dedicated to Marcuse, to whom its title alludes). Whereas the New Left of the fifties and sixties had taken its bearings from the young humanistic Marx of the 1844 manuscripts—a particular inspiration to the would-be Catholic Marxists of the *Slant* group—the Althusserians dismissed all that out of hand. The essence of Marxism was said to be scientific not humanistic; at the centre of the revolutionary view of history was the class struggle. The Althusserian view of things was intensely pessimistic, since in modern 'bourgeois' society ideology pervades everything like an invisible poisonous gas, while all social institutions, and particularly education, are 'ideological state apparatuses' committed to keeping things the way they are. For a time this grim world-view attracted some Marxists working in political studies, sociology, philosophy, English and film studies. The Althusserian was the kind of macho intellectual who enjoys being a hard man, pessimistic and anti-humanistic. (The historical analogues of this state of mind are to be found not on the left, but in proto-fascists such as T. E. Hulme). Althusserianism was fiercely attacked by humanistic Marxists like Simon Clarke and his colleagues, and was already declining when the movement was given some kind of *coup de grace* by the tragic events of 1981, when Louis Althusser's mind finally gave way and he strangled his unfortunate wife. But it was in such company that Eagleton inserted himself in 1976 with the publication of *Criticism and Ideology*. Although he has by now implicitly or explicitly repudiated much of this book it remains the work which established his international reputation as that rare creature, an English Marxist intellectual. This role is one that Eagleton has consciously accepted for himself. In his next book, *Walter Benjamin or Towards a Revolutionary Criticism* (1981), he writes: 'Let us review some of the names of the major Marxist aestheticians of the century to date: Lukacs, Goldmann, Sartre, Caudwell, Adorno, Marcuse, Della Volpe, Macherey, Jameson, Eagleton.'[6] Eagleton's self-confidence in thus categorizing himself is nicely balanced by his modesty in placing himself at the end of the list.

The defiantly abstract and theoretical nature of *Criticism and*

Ideology is apparent in its chapter headings: 'Mutations of critical ideology', 'Categories for a materialist criticism', 'Towards a science of the text', 'Ideology and literary form', 'Marxism and aesthetic value'. The rebarbative note is, no doubt, a deliberate affront to the qualities associated with traditional literary criticism: humanism, empiricism, aestheticism. At the same time, there is a faint hint of parody about the book, as if Eagleton were not so much producing a stern, 'scientific' Althusserian treatise as a very accomplished imitation of one. This is particularly evidence in the second chapter, where he states: 'It is possible to set out in schematic form the major constituents of a Marxist theory of literature.' They prove to be six in number: General Mode of Production (GMP); Literary Mode of Production (LMP); General Ideology (GI); Authorial Ideology (AuI); Aesthetic Ideology (AI); Text. Having launched these symbols Eagleton proceeds to play Space Invaders with them for the remainder of the chapter: 'A double-articulation GMP/GI-GI/AI/LMP is, for example, possible, whereby a GI category when transformed by AI into an ideological component of an LMP, may then enter onto conflict with the GMP social relations it exists to reproduce.'[7] Once the game is under way, there is no reason why it should ever end. My difficulty is in telling just how serious Eagleton is in large parts of *Criticism and Ideology*. Assuming that he is indeed (or was at the time) wholly committed to the truth of what he writes, much of the book provides an extreme instance of his tendency, already evident in his early Catholic writings, to find in words, signs and concepts, not uncertain pointers to reality, but reality itself.

Not all of the book is so perversely expressed. In so far as there is an argument in it, coherently developed in words, it directs itself to the literary text as something placed midway between 'ideology' and 'science'. The critical enterprise is seen, following Macherey as tracing and opening up the gaps and absences in a text, so that it may symptomatically reveal the ideological forces which produced it and which it endeavours to conceal (in this kind of discourse texts not authors are the active elements). Eagleton does not wholly throw overboard his abilities as a literary critic, and the chapter called 'Ideology and literary form' contains a series of short essays on nineteenth and twentieth-century English writers. These symptomatic readings are uncompromising in method and terminology; yet Eagleton thows out sufficiently arresting or challenging remarks about his subjects to give one some new ideas about them. It is interesting to compare his tortuous but considered judgement of *Women in Love* with his simplistic dismissal of it in *Exiles and Emigrés*.

> That work's break to synchronic form, away from the diachronic rhythms of *The Rainbow*, produces an 'ideology of the text' marked by stasis and disillusionment; yet it is precisely in its fissuring of organic form, in its 'montage' techniques of symbolic juxtaposition, that the novel enforces a 'progressive' discontinuity with a realist lineage already put into profound question by *Jude the Obscure*.[8]

Notwithstanding the terminology—and the scattering of quotation marks may point to Eagleton's own unease with it—something relevant and suggestive emerges about Lawrence's novel.

In 1976 Eagleton undertook the repudiation of various critics who had previously influenced him, such as Lukács and Goldmann. In *Criticism and Ideology* he devotes twenty pages to a polite but pained exposure of the errors and inadequacies of his former mentor Raymond Williams, who had been a dominant presence in Eagleton's early books. The demolition begins with generous but ritual praise—Williams has produced 'the most suggestive and intricate body of socialist crticism in English history', for which there is no available English parallel, and which must be placed for comparative assessment alongside the work of Lukács, Benjamin or Goldmann (though in this phase of Eagleton's development invocation of Lukács or Goldmann seems back-handed praise). After this friendly opening gesture Eagleton warms to his task and demonstrates that Williams's work is marred by Romantic populism, idealist epistemology, organicist aesthetics and corporatist sociology. His development as a critic of the left has been gravely hampered by his theoretical thinness and intellectual provincialism. In his attachment to personal experience and the concrete empirical response he is still unhappily influenced by his Leavisite origins. Eagleton concludes by comparing Williams not only to Leavis but to Lukács; and this time the comparison is not meant to be honorific.

It is an understatement to say that *Criticism and Ideology* is a bold book. Unrelenting in its scorn of 'bourgeois' attitudes and beliefs, it is equally harsh about much of the cultural thinking of the left. It is not altogether surprising, therefore, that the severest treatment of the book that I have come across is not by a 'bourgeois' critic, but by another Marxist, Kiernan Ryan, in a review-article on Eagleton's three books of 1975-6 published in the West German Marxist review, *Gulliver*.[9] Though critical of the book on the Brontës, Ryan finds much to admire in it; but he is strong in his condemnation of *Marxism and Literary Criticism* and *Criticism and Ideology*. Ryan gives Eagleton credit for having energetically provoked debate about Marxist approaches to literature, then adds, 'But insofar as his work has at the same time moved increasingly towards the kind of anti-humanism and theoretical elitism so characteristic of Althusserian intellectuals it must also be strongly criticized as the dehumanized literary history of a dehumanized Marxism.' Ryan, writing as a Marxist humanist, is scandalized by Eagleton's attacks on Lukács and Williams and what he regards as the Althusserian technologizing of intellectual discussion. He concludes his account of *Marxism and Literary Criticism* with these words:

> The fully dehumanized, technologist approach to literature to which this book implicitly points is realized all too successfully in the thoroughly alienated, elitist theoreticism of Eagleton's latest book, the arid and opaque *Criticism and Ideology*. Its main virtue is as a warning of the cold dead end to which the Althusserian road invariably leads; theory, declutching from any meaningful sense of praxis, spins on furiously but vainly in a self-generating void.

Writing as a 'bourgeois' critic, I find Ryan's eloquent denunciation very much to the point; 'arid and opaque' is a fair description of *Criticism and Ideology*. Ryan is particularly telling in his comments on Eagleton's compulsive use of the word 'ideology': 'continually invoked but never clearly enough defined to be very meaningful, the term begins to sweat blood from all the duty it has to do.' However much Eagleton has now moved on from the positions in *Criticism and Ideology* his use of that word still deserves Ryan's criticism. 'Ideology' is a valuable concept in intellectual discourse, and not only for Marxists. But it is inevitably complex and ambiguous, as many Marxists have realized.

In *Marxism and Literature* Raymond Williams grapples with the term in his thoughtful, characteristically dense fashion, and offers three different definitions: (1) a system of beliefs characteristic of a class or group; (2) a system of illusory beliefs—false ideas or false consciousness—which can be contrasted with true or scientific knowledge; (3) the general process of the production of ideas and meanings. Eagleton's loose but compulsive use of the term tends to be restricted to Williams's second sense, and at weak points in an argument he reaches for it with the automatized gesture of a heavy smoker lighting up one more cigarette. Eagleton evidently sees ideology, as Eliot said of Pound's hell, as being for other people. The privileged Althusserian critic is assumed to wear a kind of gas-mask to protect him from the prevailing cloud of ideological contamination; or, to switch the metaphor, he keeps within a magic circle where he is safe from harm. As Eagleton puts it, 'criticism must break with its ideological prehistory, situating itself outside the space of the text on the alternative terrain of scientific knowledge.'[10] Ryan insists that the idea of such a safe terrain is illusory: 'the notion of a privileged "neutral" domain of scientific knowledge "beyond ideology" is a positivist fantasy.' The same passage from Eagleton has come under attack from a different quarter; Christopher Norris has shown how Eagleton is imprisoned by his visual and spatial metaphors.[11]

Perhaps in response to such attacks, Eagleton decided within a few years that the Althusserian territory he had moved into in *Criticism and Ideology* was no longer tenable and must be evacuated. The repudiations of 1976 were to be followed before long by self-repudiations. In 1979 Eagleton wrote in a symposium on E. P. Thompson's *The Poverty of Theory*:

> There is no doubt at all that Thompson's ferocious broadside against Althusserianism is an admirable intervention against those younger English Marxist intellectuals (including, I should add, myself) who some years ago managed the difficult dialectical trick of appropriating certain Althusserian concepts in blithe ignorance or disregard of their guilty political context. Whether the exposure of that repressed context means that every single Althusserian concept then topples neatly to the ground, as Thompson himself would certainly seem to believe, is perhaps a little more problematical. But the task of exposing and denoun-

> cing that context has been begun in England by Thompson, Simon Clarke and others, and the British Left are enduringly in their debt.[12]

The phrase in a parenthesis is as deft and economical an autocriticism as one can imagine.

Eagleton's new bearings emerged in 1981, with *Walter Benjamin or Towards a Revolutionary Criticism*, which contains elements of a muffled retraction: 'the book marks a development from my *Criticism and Ideology* . . . which was less overtly political and more conventionally academic in style and form.' Certainly *Walter Benjamin* seems much more the work of a human being; after the computerized dogmatism of its predecessor, it is personal, self-reflective and dialectical (the last concept meaning that contradictory propositions can both be true if one wants them to). It is also a more directly political book, considerably influenced by feminism and in particular by the political model offered by feminist criticism. I do not feel competent to discuss the book's central argument, which is that Walter Benjamin, far from being the marginalized Marxist intellectual and aesthetician of customary 'bourgeois' accounts, in fact shows the way for a truly revolutionary criticism. In Eagleton's new phase Althusser and Macherey, though not totally dismissed, are less favourably regarded than Benjamin and Brecht and Bakhtin. The book also contains partial rehabilitations of critics who had been roughly handled by Eagleton in the intellectual purges of 1976. Thus, he remarks, 'the current fashionable dismissal of Lukács in certain quarters as some latter-day Don Quixote who mistook the working-class for the World Spirit is over-ripe for interrogation.'[13] This, too, reads like an implicit autocriticism, though expressed in oddly Stalinist language: 'certain quarters . . . over-ripe for interrogation'. Five years before Eagleton had been talking about Lukács in roughly those terms. The new account of Williams, though without conceding too much in essentials, also contains an element of self-criticism:

> My own earlier work, while certainly critical of Althusserian theory at key points, remained theoretically limited by that problematic and culpably blind to its political implications.

> Though I would still for the most part defend its essential critique of the work of Williams, its own residual idealism and academicism compare unfavourably with Williams's bold efforts to shift attention from the analysis of an object called 'literature' to the social relations of cultural practice.[14]

Eagleton has recently taken the rehabilitation of Williams somewhat further by giving him half the dedication of *Literary Theory*, which is reasonably handsome, though still restrained compared with *Shakespeare and Society* where Williams had the dedication all to himself, together with very warm words of praise and admiration. But that was a long time ago.

In his next book, *The Rape of Clarissa*, Eagleton returned to more or less straightforward literary criticism. This is a generally excellent—and very readable—short study of Richardson, in which Marxism no longer holds the stage alone but is harnessed in a troika with psychoanalysis and feminism. Richardson is an author of both psychological and social-historical interest, being at the same time a kind of proto-feminist and a master-printer who moved into literary production. Eagleton's book is full of incidental insights and provocations, but what it essentially does is to offer new arguments for an old (and valid) case: that *Clarissa* is a great novel. Like the book on the Brontës, *The Rape of Clarissa*, despite its sophistication, presents a traditional approach; the reading of Richardson is basically in terms of characters and author-psychology. In so far as Marxism now coexists with, or is diluted with, psychoanalysis the book might well be a source of suspicion to ideological hard-liners. Marxists' traditional opposition to Freudian ideas has always struck me as quite justified, given their premises. In so far as *The Rape of Clarissa* does make use of a Marxist frame of references, it raises, as did *Myths of Power*, the question of how far its critical insights actually depend on Marxist presuppositions. Leszek Kolakowski observes in the third volume of his magisterial history of Marxism:

> One need not nowadays consider oneself or be considered a Marxist in order, for instance, to study the history of literature or painting in the light of the social conditions of a given period; and one may do so without believing that the whole of human history is the history of class conflict, or that different aspects of

> civilization have no history of their own because 'true' history is the history of technology and 'production relations', because the 'superstructure' grows out of the 'base', and so forth.[15]

Some people, of course, have a psychological compulsion not only to believe these things, but to believe they are a 'scientific' account of the way the world is.

Literary Theory: An Introduction, Eagleton's latest book to date, offers a remarkable combination of good and bad qualities. Like *The Rape of Clarissa* it is clearly and vigorously written, which is in itself a problemetical element; lucidity and ease of communication are regarded in some Marxist quarters as ideologically suspect, since they fit altogether too neatly and smoothly into the system of capitalist cultural dissemination. The case against the 'tyranny of lucidity' is made by the Marxist-structuralist-feminist Catherine Belsey in her book *Critical Practice* (1980) (itself, as it happens, a very clearly written work).

Some such assumption evidently underlay the many obscure passages of *Criticism and Ideology*. Moving publishers from New Left Books to the established but expanding firm of Basil Blackwell may have given Eagleton the sense of a different audience and made his tone correspondingly mellower. (The conspicuous readiness of capitalist publishers to bring out Marxist books is a feature of the present cultural scene that undermines Althusserian arguments about the way ideological apparatuses work.) At its best *Literary Theory* is an admirable example of *haute vulgarisation*. Eagleton, with his insatiable appetite for ideas, has read very widely in recent work in literary theory and shows an impressive capacity to summarize much abstruse and knotty material in a lucid, lively, sometimes slangy way.

The middle chapters of the book, 'Phenomenology, hermeneutics, reception theory', 'Structuralism and semiotics', 'Post-Structuralism', 'Psychoanalysis', can be recommended to the intelligent enquirer who wants to have some idea of the subjects of recent arguments and to know what, roughly, is now going on in literary studies. These chapters do not attempt to conceal their bias, and are full of coat-trailing remarks, jokes, and assorted raillery and jeers. On the whole, these things do not much disrupt a reasonably fair and straightforward exposition. In the opening and concluding sections of the book, however, Eagleton's tendentiousness becomes confused and misleading. The opening chapter, 'What is literature?' dwells at length on the problem of adequately defining literature. As a concept it is, of course, notoriously hard to pin down. Eagleton makes much of the fact that some kinds of writing—philosophy, historiography, religious discourse—can be treated as literature, even though they were written as something else. From this fact, and the indisputable further fact that all attempts at formal definition of literature are partial and inadequate, Eagleton tries to conclude that there is no such thing; or almost so. At the end of the Introduction he writes, 'What we have uncovered so far, then, is that literature does not exist in the sense that insects do.' Many things, it seems to me, do not exist 'in the sense that insects do', like love or justice or music or the labour theory of value or the Catholic Church. Yet we do not conclude that they do not exist. At the end of the book the insects have been dropped, and Eagleton writes, 'I began this book by arguing that literature does not exist.' Eagleton may have tried to argue that case, but he certainly hasn't established it. The real problems of defining literature are better met, I think, not by saying that there is no such thing, but by seeing it in terms of W. B. Gallie's discussion in *Philosophy and the Historical Understanding* of 'essentially contested concepts'. This approach might help one to cope with some perennial problems in literary debate, such as how far 'literature' is a wholly honorific term, as Leavisites would claim, or a wholly descriptive one as the Russian Formalists believed. Eagleton can only offer assertive obfuscation of this genuinely difficult question.

He puts up a stiff resistance to the idea of literature as specifically aesthetic discourse. This is partly, one imagines, a matter of individual psychology, but it is also a characteristic of the generation of neo-Marxists who have been affected by Althusserianism, like a number of contributors to the Methuen 'New Accents' series. The idea of art and the aesthetic—including the literary—is seen as so ideologically contaminated that every effort must be made to expunge it. There is nothing specifically Marxist about this purist extremism. Trotsky, in *Literature and Revolution*, advanced the rational and humane argument that art was indeed a reality, one of the great treasures of the human race which had been appropriated by the exploiting classes; after the Revolution it was to be made available to the whole of humanity. However much Eagleton has shifted from his Althusserian stance the approach to literature in *Literary Theory* is still symptomatic rather than aesthetic or affective (though there is an unexpected reference to 'pleasure' and 'enjoyment' on p.212). To have no aesthetic sense, or to have had one and deliberately extirpated it for a political end, is clearly a misfortune. But strange things can happen to a consciousness which is convinced that the class struggle lies at the heart of reality. The impression one gets from Eagleton's copious writings is of a sensibility that engages exclusively with words and ideas. He is widely read not only in literature and criticism, but also in theology and philosophy and politics; he has not, however, betrayed any interest in painting or music, architecture or landscape.

The conceptually incoherent introduction to *Literary Theory* is followed by a chapter called 'The rise of English', which surveys the nineteenth-century events leading to the establishment of 'English' as a major academic subject. This consideration of origins is worth undertaking, since it can help one to understand the much-discussed present crisis in English studies. Eagleton looks at the many strands that went to make up 'English'. There was the need to find a humane study that was available to more readers than Latin and Greek literature, particularly to women and to the increasingly better educated working class. Another strand was the cultural nationalism that emphasized the English heritage, closely entwining literature and history, and which left its great linguistic monument in the *Oxford English Dictionary*. Added to these was the moralistic search for a substitute for traditional religion which found its goal in literature; in this aspect of the subject there is a clear continuity from Arnold to the 'Newbolt Report' on the teaching of English in 1921, and then on to Leavis and *Scrutiny*. Eagleton covers all this ground rapidly and lucidly and much of the chapter is usefully informative. His overarching assumption, that the whole process was a capitalist conspiracy to keep the lower classes in line, is unconvincing enough to be ignored. There is, though, at least one place where Eagleton succumbs to the besetting danger for expositors in a hurry, of repeating other people's errors. He quotes a curious and significant phrase in defence of the proposed Honours School of English at Oxford. In the debate in Congregation on the proposed School, held on 5 December 1893, William Sanday, Professor of Theology, was reported as saying that he was in favour of English because of its usefulness to women and to what he called the second and third rate men who were to become schoolmasters. Eagleton quotes this phrase, which nicely encapsulates many assumptions, but places it sixteen years too early, attributing it not to Sanday but to an unnamed witness to the Royal Commission on Oxford and Cambridge in 1877. The source of the reference is correctly given in D. J. Palmer's *The Rise of English Studies*, but Eagleton does not take it from Palmer but from a contributor to *New Literary History* in 1982 who has carelessly misread Palmer.

In the concluding chapter Eagleton argues, quite sensibly, for a revival of the ancient discipline of rhetoric, so that any piece of writing, indeed, any semiotic system, can be analysed in order to see how it works and to what end. The value of rhetorical understanding has always been one of the unacknowledged bases of 'English' (along with the aesthetic and the cultural-nationalist) and there is nothing very new in the idea that the skills involved in the close reading of a literary text might well be directed at other kinds of text. As it happens, departments of rhetoric are well established in leading American universities. Eagleton makes good sense in what he advocates here, even if he is to some extent pushing at an open door.

Most of the chapter, though, is engaged in re-enacting and extending the confusions of the opening chapter: literature and literary theory don't really exist; nevertheless, for many purposes it is convenient to talk about them as if they do exist. Eagleton argues that the theories and approaches examined in the preceding chapters are really political, whatever they present themselves as, and more often than not political in unacceptable ways. Eagleton's argument takes a predictable turn here: to say that a literary theory is 'really' political sounds as if one is attributing an essential quality to it, whereas a simple tautology applies, in that everything is political for those who have decided to see everything as political. Foucault is an underlying presence in this final chapter; Eagleton regards literary discourse, like all discourse, as fundamentally about power. But Foucault's idea of how power operates, in so far as I understand it, seems to me closer to Hobbes than to Marx; everyone is trying to exercise power over everyone else, all the time. Malcolm Bradbury's Howard Kirk is perhaps a relevant figure to invoke in this context. As the chapter unfolds Eagleton unveils an Althusserian argument: 'Departments of literature in higher education, then, are part of the ideological apparatus of the modern capitalist state.' Eagleton adds that this particular apparatus does not work very efficiently, since literary study can inculcate quite other values than those of the dominant society (one of the traditional defences of 'English' as a source of value). To this extent the capitalist state is spending a lot of money for no very sure return. There is also the consideration that graduates in English are not at all well placed for getting good jobs in the power-holding ranks of society and thus reinforcing the dominant ideology. But Eagleton tends to be at a loss when his ideas impinge on current social and political realities. Having looked forward to the prospect that departments of literature as we know them might cease to exist he acknowledges that such an eventuality might well be in line with current official thinking; so, 'it is necessary to add that the first political priority for those who have doubts about the ideological implications of such departmental organizations is to defend them unconditionally against government assaults.'[16] Eagleton has got himself into a difficulty here, but it is an understandable one. The coincidence in time of doubts and debates about literary study with the Thatcherite combination of sado-monetarism and crass philistine populism may not be accidental; it may well be a sign of an underlying loss of nerve. Leavis, in his day, provided a powerful and compelling rationale for 'English', which is now pretty well exhausted; the fashionable derivatives from Formalism and structuralism offer an intense but narrow interest, directed at professionals rather than the broad readership envisaged in the early years of English as a discipline. Eagleton has focused on a real and urgent problem, though his own solution of a totally politicized criticism is not likely to appeal widely, either theoretically or practically.

For all his advocacy of the primacy of politics and his jeers at liberal-humanist compromises, Eagleton remains, deep down, a literary critic in a traditional mould, much influenced by the Leavisite atmosphere of Cambridge in the early 1960s. It shows in his language, as when he unfavourably compares what he calls the abstract democracy of the ballot box with 'specific, living and practical democracy'; it is interesting that this phrase slips in after much previous condemnation in Eagleton's writing of the empirical critic's opposition between the 'abstract' (bad) and the 'specific and living' (good); Eagleton treats this opposition as highly ideological and mystificatory, but it is still at the roots of his own thinking. Similarly, he has devoted much space and energy to attacking the 'organic' approach to literary texts, which finds ultimate value in unity and the reconciliation of opposites. If one regards the text as an analogue of society 'organic' readings will paper over the cracks which ought to reveal the naked class struggle. Nevertheless, Eagleton's own conception of a political criticism is inspired by a kind of moral organicism, which wants everything in society to relate to everything else, so that activities like reading literature can be directly connected to social struggles. It is, perhaps, a scandal, though not a new one, that some people should write poetry or read it or write about it or teach it, while other people are starving or homeless or in prison or undergoing torture. If one finds the scandal unbearable one can give up literature and devote oneself wholly to political activity or social reform; that is a possible and honourable course. But to insist on a quasi-organic yoking together of the cultural and the political is to distort both activities. Eagleton's likely rejoinder, that there is no difference between them, requires far more solid argument than he has ever found it necessary to produce. To say, as he has done on occasion, that everything is political, is to deny the term any differentiating force or real meaning: if everything is political then nothing is. In rejecting Eagleton's political organicism, I am included to take over his own Althusserian way of looking at texts and apply it to civilization itself, which is riven with gaps and fissures and contradictions, though they reveal not the ultimate fact of the class struggle, but the familiar spectacle of human villainy and folly. Eagleton quotes Walter Banjamin's famous dictim, 'There is no cultural document that is not at the same time a record of barbarism.' I am inclined to agree with this, assuming it is a proposition that asks to be agreed with; Auden expressed something similar in 'Musée des Beaux Arts'. But I cannot deduce any specific political programme from Benjamin's words, nor see them as a recommendation for tearing up cultural documents.

Leszek Kolakowski, who was toiling at the coal-face of Marxist thought when Eagleton was still absorbing Catholic apologetics at De La Salle College, has summarized the organicist appeal of Marxism: 'Marxism has been the greatest fantasy of our century. It was a dream offering the prospect of a society of perfect unity, in which all human aspirations would be fulfilled and all values reconciled.'[17] In addition to this fantasy, Marxism offers a system of scholastic complexity and rigour, which also provides opportunites for the dialectical play of mind. Such a system is obviously attractive to a voracious intellectual like Eagleton, who was previously trained in an earlier scholastic system and who thinks readily in models and categories and analogies. Yet, within the framework of a broad Marxist allegiance, Eagleton's development has been mercurial, rapidly reactive, and impelled by a series of partial self-repudiations. At the same time, his own uncertainties and shifts of position have never prevented him from dismissing, confidently and aloofly, the liberal-humanist critics whom he sees as caught up in soft-headed woolliness and confusion, in contrast to the 'scientific' rigour of Marxist thought (this, again, is a variant of traditional Catholic rhetoric). I must declare an interest here, having myself been thus categorized by Eagleton, and placed in the distinguished company of what he calls 'the Kermode/Lodge/Bergonzi/Bradbury establishment of liberal-empiricist aesthetics. . . .'[18]

Eagleton has stayed with Marxism longer than many of the people who were drawn to it in the sixties. In France a whole generation of intellectuals has abandoned Marxist allegiance, and compared with twenty years ago Marxism seems to have run out of conviction, even though no Western intellectual can disregard its influence. (Its current vogue among some Eng. Lit. academics seems to me strangely belated, and perhaps one more sign of the notorious insularity of the English.) In terms of practical politics, the suspicion has been growing that terror and repression, the secret police and the prison camp, may be inherent in the system itself rather than an easily dismissed Stalinist aberration. To say this is not to admit any allegiance to the New Right, many of whose positions look like an ideological mirror-image of Marxism. A proper scepticism about political claims has always seemed appropriate as an attitude for literary critics. How Eagleton will move on from this interesting historical and personal juncture is unpredictable. Despite himself, he has become a familiar English type, an Establishment radical; and, as I have suggested, his current combination of Marxism with psychoanalysis and feminism may lead him towards an intellectual eclecticism that he would once have found unacceptable. Eagleton is an important enough public figure, as critic and intellectual, to deserve discussion at some length; though how far his importance is symptomatic and how far it is intrinsic is a matter for very fine discrimination.

NOTES

1. *The New Left Church* (London, 1966), p.78.
2. Martin Green, 'British Marxists and American Freudians' in Bernard Bergonzi (ed.), *Innovations* (London, 1968), p.169.
3. In Alexander Cockburn and Robin Blackburn (eds), *Student Power* (Harmondsworth, 1969), pp.214-84.
4. *Myths of Power: A Marxist Study of the Brontës* (London, 1975), p.74.
5. *Marxism and Literary Criticism* (London, 1976), p.80n.
6. *Walter Benjamin or Towards a Revolutionary Criticism* (London, 1981), p.96.
7. *Criticism and Ideology* (London, 1976), p.61.
8. *ibid.*, pp.160-1.
9. *Gulliver*, Band 3, 1978, pp.222-9.
10. *Criticism and Ideology*, p.43.
11. Christopher Norris, *Deconstruction: Theory and Practice* (London, 1982), p.81.
12. *Literature and History*, vol. 5, 2, Autumn 1979, pp.141-2.
13. *Walter Benjamin*, p.89.
14. *ibid.*, p.97.
15. Leszek Kolakowski, *Main Currents of Marxism*, vol.III, *The Breakdown* (Oxford, 1978), p.524.
16. *Literary Theory*, p.213.
17. Kolakowski, *op. cit.*, p.523.
18. *Literature and History*, vol. 5, 2, Autumn 1979, p.232.

Index

Substantial discussions are indicated in bold type